PRAISE FOR
A Home on the Field

"The story of the ascent of the Jets would be dramatic enough, but Cuadros also explores the tensions that arise in a community suddenly swelling with Hispanic workers and their families. . . . *A Home on the Field* probably ought to be required reading for anybody who favors the construction of a wall along the country's southern border."
—*Boston Globe*

"A wonderful book. . . . It is exactly because of its small scale, exactly because we can get to know each of the characters involved, that the story Cuadros tells touches the heart and the emotions so intimately."
—*New York Sun*

"[H]is message ultimately is one of hope, as he relates how a team that was jeered during its first season became, through its championship run, a unifying force for the entire community."
—*Education Week*

"The team's rise to glory and a dream season are placed firmly within the context of the immigrant community's struggle for assimilation and the stark realities faced by the Latino youths who wear the team's uniforms."
—*Durham Herald-Sun*

"Ambitious . . . a complex book, and an invaluable resource as Americans debate immigration."
—*The News & Observer* (Raleigh, North Carolina)

Catharine Carter

About the Author

PAUL CUADROS's family moved to the United States from Peru in 1960. An award-winning investigative reporter, he has written for *Time* magazine and Salon.com, among others. In 1999, Cuadros won an Alicia Patterson Foundation fellowship to write about the impact of the large numbers of Latino poultry workers on rural towns in the South. He moved to Pittsboro, North Carolina, to conduct his research and stayed on to document the growing Latino community in the Southeast.

A
HOME
on the
FIELD

HARPER

NEW YORK · LONDON · TORONTO · SYDNEY

A

HOME

on the

FIELD

How One Championship Team

Inspires Hope for the

Revival of Small Town America

PAUL CUADROS

HARPER

A hardcover edition of this book was published in 2006 by Rayo, an imprint of HarperCollins Publishers.

HarperCollins books may be purchased for educational, business, or sales promotional use. For information please write: Special Markets Department, HarperCollins Publishers, 10 East 53rd Street, New York, NY 10022.

FIRST HARPER PAPERBACK PUBLISHED 2007.

Designed by Stephanie Huntwork

Library of Congress Cataloging-in-Publication Data has been applied for.

ISBN: 978-0-06-112027-5
ISBN-10: 0-06-112027-8

ISBN: 978-0-06-112028-2 (pbk.)
ISBN-10: 0-06-112028-6 (pbk.)

08 09 10 11 DIX/RRD 10 9 8 7 6 5 4 3 2

For my father, Alberto, who taught me how to play the game,
and for my brother, Alberto, who taught me to win at life.

INTRODUCTION

For the past fifteen years, the country has been experiencing a silent migration of Mexicans and other Latin Americans who have been crossing the border and migrating to the interior portion of the United States. Only now, however, has the country become aware of this migration and its impact on our society. This migration has since caused a tumultuous debate about immigration and what the country will do with the more than 12 million unauthorized immigrants in the country. But the origins of this issue can be found in the very free-trade policies of the United States that have compelled poor peasant farmers in Mexico and Central America to migrate north in an attempt to feed their families.

In the 1990s, the U.S. passed the North American Free Trade Agreement with the idea that free trade between the U.S., Canada, and Mexico would help the economies of all participating countries. The agreement ended up being a disaster for the Mexican farmer. It allowed heavily subsidized U.S. corn and other agribusiness products to be dumped into Mexico. Millions of Mexican farmers could no longer compete against these artificially lower prices and many were forced to leave their farms for the central cities like Mexico City. Not being able to find work in urban communities, they migrated north into the U.S. where they found jobs in the meatpacking and poultry-processing industries.

The food processing industry was undergoing a transformation in how it raised, slaughtered, and processed food to the American consumer. Processing companies were integrating vertically, encompassing all aspects of the business including supplying animals to farmers or growers, providing the feed and medicine needed to keep the animals alive and healthy, and slaughtering and processing the animals to prepare them directly for sale to supermarkets and restaurants. Gone forever were the days of the local butcher that prepared your meat for consumption. Companies needed a compliant and pliable labor force that could endure the grueling conditions of plants and that wouldn't complain of conditions, wages, or want to unionize. They found their labor force in the Latin American worker and began recruiting Latino workers along the border and in Mexico. Some companies even provided transportation and promised housing if they came to the Midwest or Southeast to work in their plants. In addition, they offered incentives to workers to bring their family members from their local villages to also work. Because turnover in the meatpacking and poultry-processing industry can be high, there was always a need for new workers once the old workers either moved on to other jobs or were too injured to continue working on the killing floor.

The food processing industry served as a gateway industry for many Latino workers as they began migrating into such states as North Carolina. But after enduring the work at a chicken plant many workers sought out new jobs and many found them in such other industries as landscaping, textiles, furniture manufacturing, and construction. The construction industry was experiencing a boom in the South building new housing developments, roads, and office buildings. States like North Carolina were beginning to develop and attract new businesses and people to the area.

In 1996, Latino workers began to bring their families. The migration of Latinos was no longer a temporary phenomenon. Schools began to see an increase in their Latino student population that continues to grow to this day. Longtime residents began to realize that this migration was going to be permanent—Latinos were going to be settling in their communities.

Small rural communities like Siler City, North Carolina were at a crossroads when the Latino migration began. In the early 1990s, the town was suffering through several major plant closings in the textile and furniture manufacturing industries, losing a thousand jobs in a town of only five thousand people. Without sustainable jobs, many young people began to leave Siler City. The town was growing older and its vitality was flowing into other larger cities. In 1990, the median age for Siler City was 37 years, according to the U.S. Census. The town was aging out.

The migration of Latino workers and their families has been like a shot in the arm to Siler City. It has restored and spurred growth and development in a town that was dying. By 2000, the influx of Latinos had dramatically lowered the median age to 31 years. The increase in population and buying power has also translated into new business growth and opportunity.

But adjusting to the migration has not been easy for Latinos and for longtime residents. Culture clashes were frequent and continue to cause friction. One of the areas where the two groups confronted each other was in how they played.

Like many rural communities, baseball and football were the top sports. Schools and parks are designed around these two American bastions of play. A small town's identity can be bound up in how well its high school football team does on Friday nights. Saturday afternoons were reserved for Little League and softball games at the park.

Latinos wanted to play soccer. They passionately love the sport. But there were no places to play soccer in Siler City. Makeshift fields were created to accomodate the Latino workers who wanted to let off some steam after a hard shift at the chicken plant. The children of these workers were growing up playing in their back-yards, in the streets, and at the parks. It was inevitable that in addition to the other culture clashes between Latinos and longtime residents there would come a time when these struggles would be taken to the high school football field itself.

This story is told over three seasons of soccer at Jordan-Matthews High School and encompasses many of the issues faced by Siler City. The stories contained within the three seasons did happen and the events have been like a whirlwind. I set out to report on the Latino Diaspora to the Southeast and not to write a book about soccer or coach a team. But along the way, I met a great group of kids with a dream that soon became my dream. The book features some of the most courageous young people I know. Many of these kids have faced terrible hardship and now face an unknown future because of their immigration status. The names of the players and others have been changed or nicknames have been used to protect their identities. I hope one day this story can be told with their true names and they can at last emerge from the shadows to claim their true identities and accomplishments.

Congress is currently debating immigration issues and what to do with the some 12 million unauthorized immigrants in the country. Siler City has a lot to teach America about how to handle this situation. I hope one day in the not-too-distant future when the historians begin to write about the Great Latino Migration to America they will consider this story of how a town and a team came together and found a way to share.

First
Season

1

The boys were on time for a change. There was no such thing as "Latino time" during the state high school playoffs, that customary half-hour tardiness in which they showed up one by one, drifting onto the field still in their street clothes. They arrived tonight dressed to play in their white home jerseys, royal-blue shorts, and white socks pulled up over their knees to keep their legs warm from the cold November night. They went right away to the bag of soccer balls on the sideline, took one, and ran out onto the field like colts bolting over an open plain, kicking and jumping in the crisp autumn air. They immediately started taking shots on goal, warming up our goalkeeper, "Fish," for the game.

I went out to meet them—handing out pinnies, warm-up vests in bright yellow—to divide them into two teams so they could go through our normal warm-up drill before a game. "*¡Eh! ¡El juego de posesión! ¡Ahorita!*" I yelled at them, blowing my whistle. "Hey! The possession game! Now!" The boys quickly split off into two teams and started playing keep-away with the ball, possessing it with the pass, two-touch only, moving it from one side of the field to the other on the ground, passing it around from one player to another as fast as they could.

Across the field, the Hendersonville Bearcats were performing their own warm-up drills. They had traveled more than five hours on their school bus from the Appalachian Mountains to Siler City, North Carolina, a small poultry-processing town in the middle of the state. They were vastly different from my team. Their soldier-like warm-ups included jogging together in a straight line across the field, kicking their legs up high, and touching their toes with the tips of their fingers to stretch their leg muscles. My stomach tightened when I saw their size and height. They were the opposite of the Jets. These were tall, big, beefy white mountain boys who played a physical game known for its long-ball style; they kicked the ball up the field and sprinted after it, outmuscling the opposition and shooting on goal.

"Mira, Cuadros, son grandes," said Perico, one of our forwards who barely stood more than five feet tall and whose name means little bird. "Look, Cuadros, they're huge."

I looked at him as I put my hand on his shoulder and laughed. "It doesn't matter, they're always bigger than you, right?" Perico's face lit up and he smiled, nodding. I wasn't even much taller than he was. We were Latinos and we had learned to play a different style of game against bigger teams—excellent ball control, tricky moves, and possessing the ball on the ground. We focused on being quicker, making short passes, moving the ball around, and attacking at high speed. It had won us the conference championship for the first time and we were about to put our style to the test against a team that had crushed us during our first season.

Two years ago, we had traveled the five hours to Hendersonville in the second round of the play-offs only to be bruised and beaten by the Bearcats. We were an excellent team, loaded with talent in every position, but the Bearcats played aggressively, physically, knocking our guys down and battering them. We were too one-dimensional that first year. The soccer program at Jordan-Matthews was new and I had not had the time to train them out of their bad habits, refine their game, and help them learn how to play more as a team. We could not possess the ball then. After we lost to Hendersonville 1–0, it had taken me two years to break bad habits, bad thinking, and put in place a new system, a new style, one that did not rely on one player who could be shut down, but on an entire team of players who could step up and win games.

I wanted them to win this game very much: not only to move the team to the quarterfinals of the play-offs and put us one step closer to the finals, but also as a way of putting that horrible night behind us. As a coach, you have to keep a lot of your feelings inside and only carefully, strategically, let them out. But deep inside, against a team that beat us badly, and where the atmosphere was so poisonous against our boys, I felt it personally. Soccer is not like other sports. It is passionate. It is volatile. It is emotional.

Unlike so many sports in the United States, the clock doesn't stop in soccer. There are no time-outs, no commercial breaks, and no strategic stoppages where the coach can affect the game. Soccer is a players' game. The players play on despite fouls, penalty kicks, missed shots, vicious slide tackles, elbows to the face, unseen hand balls, fights, arguments with refs, and screaming fans and coaches. The players have to figure out for themselves how to come through all those emotions to win.

The best teams can do it with grace and skill and they are a sight to behold. The worst teams do it through thuggery. Latinos are passionate, and that's why we love soccer so much. The game is always played in our throats whether you are a player, coach, or fan. Americans cannot understand how two countries could go to war after a soccer match, as happened in 1969 between Honduras and El Salvador. Latinos ask: How can you not?

The game was about to begin, and I gathered the team together for one last talk. I wanted them to feel the weight of the moment, to know that we were capable of rising to the occasion.

"Well, boys, here we are again." I needed to inspire them, fire them up, get them ready to go out to the field pumped up and ready to start the game. The best pep talks made the moment personal in some way. You have to connect with the players, reach into their hearts, their guts, their pride, and switch something on in them so they can believe in themselves. I spent hours thinking how to do it before a game, but when it came down to it, I had to feel it in me first before I could get them to feel it, too. If I didn't believe it, feel it, they weren't going to.

"Some of you remember this team from the play-offs two years ago." Several of the boys nodded. There was Fish, our goalkeeper, who got his nickname shortly after he emigrated to the United States from Mexico; his middle school teacher asked him what his favorite food was and unfortunately the only word he knew in English was *fish*.

Next to him was Indio, our main central midfielder, an extremely talented player and excellent student who had crossed the U.S. and Mexican border by himself when he was only eleven years old. To his left stood Bomba, a tall quiet kid from El Salvador. And in the middle was "Lechero", our lanky, sinewy sweeper, whom everyone called "the Milkman" because he had walked into school wearing an old T-shirt with a popular Mexican milk label on the front. They had all been there three years ago against Hendersonville and they had all suffered through the indignities of that night from the slashing slide tackles of the players and the shouts from their fans. I looked into their young brown faces and saw an intensity that belied their years. They knew what this game meant. I didn't need to tell them that. Tonight was about payback, putting a foe behind you and moving on to bigger things.

"A lot of you remember this team and what they did to us—what they said about us. I want you to remember all those feelings now. I want you to remember them now because things have changed. *You* have changed." I paused and looked each one in the eyes. I held them there for a moment. "This is not the same team they beat three years ago. This team is stronger. This is not the team that lost by one goal. This team can score *lots* of goals." The boys smiled and nodded. "This team is a different team. This team is a bigger team. This team has grown. This team is a championship team. This team is made of fire and iron!" And with that I held up the steel chain I had in my hand and shook it. I had started bringing a chain to the games for the boys to see and hold as a symbol of our unity. The boys hollered and jumped up and down, grabbing a piece of the chain from my hands. We had come together in a circle, everyone held together by the chain. They rocked back and forth gripping the chain, testing its strength, testing themselves.

Eduardo, or "Edi," our left midfielder, started the chant. "Who are we?" The *chavos* responded together, "Los Jets!" Again, "Who are we?" "Los Jets!" "Who are we?" "Los Jets!" And then, in unison they cried in English, "One, two, three—let's go, Jets!" and took the field under the big lights.

So much had changed from that first season when I had started the team with little more than equipment that I had borrowed, begged, or stolen. For the past fifteen years, Latino families from Mexico and Central America had been migrating to little towns like Siler City in search of jobs and a better, quieter life than that of the big cities. They had been met with fear, distrust, and dread. There was nothing worse than being a stranger in a small Southern town where everyone, black or white, knew your history and your family's history. What made things even harder was that the newcomers didn't speak English. As I watched these young Latino men take the field that nobody in town wanted them to play on, I couldn't help but think how close we had come to never reaching this point.

2

The Carolina sky was laid out before me like a billowing bedsheet for a brief moment, before drifting down to cover the length of my windshield. It was an uninterrupted, solid expanse of nursery baby blue with no clouds to be seen and the bright sun cut through it with little mercy, making everything underneath appear in stark contrast with sharp edges.

I had been driving for five hours from Washington, D.C.—where I had lived and worked as a reporter—in my small white Saturn loaded with furniture, clothes, and other items I would need after I found a place to live in Siler City. When I passed Chapel Hill, still heading south, I knew I had left the last remnant of urban, or at least suburban, living behind. I was heading into the country now, and as the road opened up before me with nothing but silver power lines and skinny brown pine trees, I thought; What have I gotten myself into?

For the past ten years, I had been living in big cities across America. I lived a year in Los Angeles, which was about all I could stand, spent eight years in Chicago, where I came into my own as a journalist and writer, and had just completed three years in Washington working for the Center for Public Integrity. It hadn't dawned on me until I passed Chapel Hill, but for the past decade I had been steadily moving to smaller and smaller communities in the United States, and now I was heading toward Siler City, a little rural town with a population of about seven thousand. I was leaving it all behind, the fancy restaurants, the movie theaters, bars, dance clubs, and an important policy-driven job. I was on my own, with the exception of an idea that I was onto something very important.

It was 1999, and I had just won an Alicia Patterson Foundation fellowship to write about the silent migration that was occurring in the rural South as Latino poultry-processing workers moved to little towns like Siler City to work in the chicken plants. The year before, while working on a book about Congress and campaign financing, I had written a chapter on worker safety. One of the areas that caught my interest the most was the food-processing industry. The staggering numbers of injuries and deaths that befell processing workers made it one of the most dangerous jobs in the country.

In 1991, twenty-five workers were killed and fifty-six others injured when hydraulic fluid from a conveyor belt sprayed over a gas-fired chicken fryer at the Imperial Food Products Company's chicken plant in Hamlet, North Carolina. The exit doors had been chained shut and workers were found trying to claw their way out. The plant had no fire alarm or sprinkler system. In 1997, Solomon Velásquez, a teenage sanitation worker who had not been properly trained, was killed in an industrial meat blender at the Lundy Packing Company in Clinton, North Carolina. Former Republican senator Lauch Faircloth had at one time owned more than $1 million in Lundy stock. Injuries and illnesses in the poultry-processing industry appear to have fallen from 1999 to 2003 in North Carolina from 15 cases per 100 workers to 9.4 cases in a work population of about 20,000, according to the North Carolina Department of Labor's survey of injuries by industry. But the reporting of injuries was seriously flawed, as companies did not have to report injuries to the department for analysis or investigation unless three or more workers were hospitalized. A dozen workers could be hurt, but if none were hospitalized, the state would never know about it.

In researching that chapter, I began to notice something odd—

many of the workers in the Midwest packing plants and Southern poultry plants were Latino. I had spent five years reporting on issues of race and poverty at the acclaimed *Chicago Reporter,* a feisty investigative journal that dispassionately dissected those hot-button issues in a city divided by race and class. I created a database of all meatpacking and poultry-processing plants in several states, listing their addresses and zip codes. I then added U.S. Census Bureau data on population change, including increases in Hispanic populations within those towns that had either a meatpacking plant or poultry plant, and found that there had been a steady increase in the number of Latinos since 1990.

I strongly suspected that life was being transformed in these hamlets in untold ways as Latinos moved in to work at the plants and that the food-processing industry was fueling a migration unlike any the country had ever seen before. That's because turnover at a meatpacking or chicken plant can be as high as 100 percent per year. These plants literally chewed up and spat workers out. To this day, many workers at many plants are routinely subjected to grueling, unsafe working conditions, injuries and illnesses, and fatalities. Many of the Latinos who were coming to work in the plants in the Midwest and South were undocumented, which meant that companies could fire and discipline them in any way they wanted—they were a highly pliable labor force and would bend to the will of their bosses. They were also some of the most hardworking and tolerant employees the industry had ever seen, and would endure all kinds of appalling conditions.

At about the same time—during the 1980s and 1990s—American consumption of chicken products began to skyrocket and the poultry producers took advantage of the change in the American diet. Beef was on the way out as heart-conscious consumers switched to poultry as a leaner alternative. These plants were like engines, requiring a constant and steady supply of new workers to replace those they had lost. This meant that Latino workers would always be in demand in these towns and that new workers were always on their way.

It also meant that unlike other agricultural businesses, which were dependent on a seasonal harvest, the meatpacking and poultry-processing industries worked year-round, six days a week, in three shifts. Workers would need to stay put and plant roots. This would transform the very character of rural America. The big cities have always had immigrants who spoke a different language, literally and metaphorically. But towns like Omaha, Nebraska; Greeley, Colorado; Siler City, North Carolina; and Gainesville, Georgia, had never had to deal with these issues.

By 1990, the U.S. Census Bureau confirmed my intuition about a migration occurring in the South. It found that North Carolina had a faster-growing Hispanic population than any other state in the country, an increase of almost 400 percent in ten years.

I decided to write about emerging Latino communities in the rural South. How would Latinos be welcomed in such communities that were still struggling with their own race and class issues? What kind of Latinos would emerge as the children grew up and how would they see themselves?

Highway 15-501 led south from Chapel Hill to Pittsboro, a small town of about two thousand and the country seat of Chatham County. The road went right into town, passing a two-block strip of quaint antiques stores, a soda fountain shop, and a hardware store, right up to the bronze statute of a Confederate soldier that stood in front of the Chatham County courthouse. OUR CONFEDERATE HEROES was written underneath in fading gray letters.

I went around the courthouse and took Highway 64 west to Siler City. I didn't have much time. I wanted to find a place to live quickly. I felt it was important to commit to the area and not parachute in as an outsider, report, and fly out never to be seen again. I wanted the townsfolk to trust me and I wanted to be held accountable for what I wrote.

Siler City is only fifteen miles west of Pittsboro. I had chosen Siler City because it had two poultry-processing plants within the town limits. Pittsboro had one. There were three plants and some three hundred chicken growers or farmers in Chatham County. Chicken was the largest industry in the county and the largest employer.

Highway 64 West stretches between Pittsboro and Siler City like a thin gray ribbon draped over gently rolling hills. The state was just completing an expansion of 64 into four lanes, an infrastructure improvement intended to facilitate commerce. All over North Carolina and the South, there was an unprecedented development of roads and highways, and residential and commercial growth. A lot of the men working along the highway expansions were Latinos, many of them undocumented. They were the cheap muscle for the South's modernization.

The first thing that struck me as I drove to Siler City was the smell along the highway. It was the pungent odor of boiled chicken. I rolled up my windows but the smell continued to leach into the car. I knew this was the country and that one should be prepared for nature, but this was nature on a giant scale.

Along 64 there were several long rectangular low buildings with enormous fans whirling on one end like propellers and royal-blue tarps flapping over the sides like sails. They were chicken barns and each held about fifty thousand chickens in various stages of development. The fans were used to keep them cool and the tarps were used to keep the light low. Inside, young chickens flocked and moved along the litter-covered floor like rolling waves. When they got bigger they could hardly move at all. In between flocks, when the barns were empty, the grower would remove the waste litter and compost it, creating an incredible odor.

When the chickens were fully grown, crews would be brought in from the processing plant to catch them and load them into cages onto trucks for slaughtering. The crews were Latino and they would scoop up the chickens and place them in cages. A worker could catch up to eight chickens in each hand, two between each finger. After a time catching chickens, a worker's hands would begin to suffer terrible pain. They'd freeze up and the worker would have to move on to some other job.

The trucks would then lumber down 64 toward Siler City with

the white chickens hunkered down in their cages awaiting their fate. The highway was dusted with white feathers—it looked like a light snow flurry had just passed. Above, black turkey vultures circled the sky waiting for the traffic to clear before swinging down and feasting on a dead chicken that had gotten through one of the cages.

The birth of Siler City comes from the same iron river that gave life to so many other small towns across America—the railroad. The town sprang up after a railroad depot was created between Sanford to the south and Greensboro to the north in 1884. The railroad encouraged the growth of general merchandise and agriculture businesses, and within a few short years, the little town had several tobacco stores, three livery stables, three hotels, a sawmill, and a cotton gin. By 1890, the town had 254 people. The town came to be known as the largest shipping point in Chatham County—if not the state—for rabbits. Over the decades, the town grew and after World War II major industries settled in Siler City—including the textile industry and the poultry industry. By the end of the century, poultry had become *the* industry in town and in the county.

But, like so many other towns across the South, Siler City lost commerce as the textile industry began to face stiffer competition from foreign countries. And private businesses shifted from downtown to franchise operations along the highway. North Chatham Avenue, once a thriving main part of downtown, deteriorated, as if the heart of the downtown community had been cut out and transplanted along the median of the highway.

I didn't know where I was going, I was just driving around and getting a feel for the community where I would be living for at least a year. It was off of North Chatham Avenue that I spotted something called the "Vínculo Hispano," or the Hispanic Liaison. It was an agency designed to help the migrant community in Siler City and its existence caught me completely by surprise. I had not expected to see anything like it despite the migration. I had expected to find no services for Latinos in the rural South, but I was wrong. In the near future I would learn how special Siler City was, in so many different ways, good and bad, than I had imagined.

I parked the car and went into the storefront. I immediately encountered a young woman with fair skin and raven hair pulled tightly back in a bun. She had intensely focused dark eyes behind thin glasses and was scurrying around. Her name was Ilana Dubester and she was the executive director and founder of the little agency. She was alone.

"Hello, can I help you?" she said in a soft accent I couldn't quite place. It wasn't a typical Latino accent. I introduced myself and asked about the Liaison. Ilana told me what the Liaison did, how it helped Latinos adjust to life in Siler City by providing translation services to understand how to enroll their kids in school, health care information, and other services. I told her what I did and why I was moving to the area.

"A reporter?" She gave me a skeptical look but said that I had a kind face. Ilana was originally from Brazil and had traveled the world and the country before buying land and building a house in Chatham County. When she noticed the increasing number of Latinos moving to Siler City, she founded the nonprofit organization in 1995. All across the state, similar communities were struggling with the same migration issues, but Siler City was unique in having such an organization. But it hadn't been easy. When she opened the Liaison many thought she wanted to unionize the workers. *Union* was a four-letter word in the South. That was not the job of the Liaison and over time the town and the industry have come to grudgingly accept it and work with it.

I didn't have much time to really get into the all the issues with Ilana, as I really wanted to find a place to live.

"Oh, you won't find a place here," she said, moving some boxes. Ilana was sharp and no-nonsense. She didn't suffer fools lightly and she got to the point quickly. "Housing is one of our issues here. Go to Pittsboro and find something there."

She wished me luck in perfect Spanish and I made a mental note to myself to come back and talk with her more about the migration and how the town was adjusting. I got back in the car, cut my sightseeing trip through Siler City short, and headed back on Highway 64 to Pittsboro.

Ilana had told me to go to an antique clothing store. I found the store, which was on the main strip in Pittsboro just off the circle where the courthouse rested. Pam Smith was a tiny woman with wavy salt-and-pepper hair and wide bright eyes that took you in and warmed you up like comfort food. She spoke with a low, lazy drawl that wove thick ribbons around you. But I was in a hurry to find a place to live and finalize my move from Washington. She told me that her husband was just completing the renovation of a one-bedroom little house. "I think Snuffy's finished with it, but why don't you drive out there and see for yourself," Pam said with a wide smile and a tilt of her head. Her eyes twinkled as if she were letting me in on a joke. I paused for a moment and thought, Did she say "Snuffy"? She shooed me out the door.

I pulled up onto a dirt driveway that led to the side of a small white house with two red brick columns in front of wooden steps that led onto a porch with a small swing. The house had a green tin roof that sloped sharply. In front there was a magnolia tree with big white blossoms and thick shiny dark green leaves that looked like they were made of plastic.

I knocked and asked if anyone was in. A slim man appeared in dusty jeans and a brown shirt. He had red hair and a red beard and wore thin gold wire glasses with a large straw hat. "Can I help ya?" he asked. I asked if he was Snuffy and when he said he was I explained I was looking for a place to live. He said he and his helper, José, were still finishing up the place to rent but that it would be done in a week. Snuffy invited me in to show me the place.

José was on the floor caulking and I said hello to him in Spanish. He was startled but pleased and said, *"Buenas tardes."* Off the living room was the bedroom, which was painted a light purple. Snuffy explained that the last tenant had selected that color and it stayed.

I asked Snuffy how much a month and he thought about it for a moment and said, "Well, five-hundred and fifty dollars." I wondered if that was the city-slicker rate but told him I would take it anyway. He seemed surprised that I would make such a quick decision. I asked him if it was possible for me to leave some things today. He was caught off guard. "I have some of my belongings in the back of

my car, could I just drop them off now?" He gave me a wide-eyed
look and I know he must have been thinking I was nuts. People just
didn't move that fast in Pittsboro. "Sure, why not." I got a few boxes
out and José helped me move some furniture into the bedroom. I
told Snuffy I would be back in a week to move in but I needed to
get back to Washington today.

As I climbed into my white Saturn I noticed my Doc Martens
were covered in thick red clay. It had rained the night before. Snuffy
noticed the mud and said, "You'll never get that mud off your shoes."
I looked at them. "That's okay." I smiled and shut the door.

3

Enrique took the pair of needle-nose pliers and twisted the loose threads of chicken wire together on the side of the large wooden cage. He was tinkering with the wire, making sure it was secure, and fixing the hinges on the door. He had constructed the cage himself from old discarded window frames and other scraps of wood. Inside the cage, a large brown-and-red rooster stood silently, not paying Enrique any attention. He was a proud bird with blue streaks in his feathers that gave him a shiny, waxy look. His eyes were as black as tuxedo buttons. "I'm going to breed them and then sell them," Enrique explained to me in a soft Mexican-American accent, pronouncing every syllable. "Yeah, you can make good money," he said, smiling, dreaming of his new business.

Enrique was thirteen years old, the oldest of five children in a fatherless family that included two brothers, two sisters, and his mother. He was strongly built, with a solid frame and round shoulders that were just beginning to fill out. He had small, sleepy eyes that disappeared when he laughed and his dark hair was clipped short—making his ears stick out. On the back of his head, cut into the stubbly black hair, was a spiral scar from a roundworm that was surgically removed when he lived in Mexico City.

"We got to get going," I said, glad that I had built in some extra "Latino time" to get to our soccer tournament.

"Paul, it don't take long for me to get ready," he said, laughing at my nervous-hen attitude.

It had been almost a year since I moved to Chatham County. I had first met Enrique and his family when I accompanied Gloria Sanchez, the Chatham County basic-needs coordinator and school social worker on her rounds. I had helped her carry several kerosene-heating units to poor families, including Enrique's. The family had just moved to Siler City and lived in a single room in a house. The room had no heat and Gloria had scraped together some money to buy the kerosene units. I had shown Enrique how to fill it up with kerosene safely and start the pilot light to ignite it. The unit kicked out quite a bit of heat but it lasted only about five hours before running out of kerosene. Dolores, Enrique's mother, used the heater sparingly because of the cost of the kerosene. The family mostly huddled together at night for warmth on their mattresses.

I had started coaching a soccer team of ten-year-old white kids from Pittsboro through the Chatham Soccer League, a volunteer organization. I had been bored living in my little house in Pittsboro and found it hard to make new friends in the country. We had a lot of fun, but as I began to report on Siler City and meet more and more Latino families, I realized that these kids didn't have an organized outlet for the sport they loved. There were no private leagues for the Latino kids who played in their backyards. They didn't get bright colorful uniforms, coaching, or games with referees.

I decided to bring these two worlds together on a special "challenge" team that was a step above recreational soccer. Recreational soccer was designed for kids who had never played the game before. Challenge soccer was for the intermediate players with greater skills. I wanted the parents from both groups to get to know one another.

In my months of living in North Carolina, I had come to realize how segregated the communities were. Latinos stuck to themselves either because of the language barrier or because of fear. Longtime residents didn't trust the newcomers because they couldn't speak to them. I thought: If I could get them on a team, they would at least come to know one another.

I also wanted to prove that Latino kids could play ball. Soccer in North Carolina's Triangle area, between Raleigh, Chapel Hill, and Durham, is huge. There are giant private leagues that provided good coaches, organized games on manicured fields, with shiny uniforms and referees. But these leagues had very few Latino boys or girls because of their cost.

American soccer thrives in the club leagues. That's where prominent coaches search and find talented players and enroll them in traveling private teams, or select them for the Olympic Development Program, or the U.S. national teams, or for college programs. Soccer has become a country-club sport in the United States, played in suburbia, and it limits access from other parts of society. If you were not on a prominent club team, your chances for an athletic scholarship at a university were slim. Parents paid thousands of dollars for their kids to participate at that level. This is one of the main problems with the sport in America today—the unwillingness to open the game to other economic strata. I believed that the Latino kids with their street soccer skills could compete against these teams, opening up the game to more players.

I had dropped by Enrique's house to pick him and his brother Edi up to take them to a tournament for our private team. I had driven from Pittsboro to the outskirts of Siler City in the country to a new house the family had found. They had moved twice since coming to Siler City and had found cheap rent at this house. There were two trailers next to it in sort of a makeshift park; Dolores shared the house with another family, who lived upstairs and helped pay the rent.

We met up with several other families, both Latino and white, and drove two hours south to Fayetteville, where the tournament was being held. We had entered into the Mid-State Soccer Challenge Tournament for boys, fifteen years old and under. The tournament featured more than sixty private club teams from throughout the state. We were the only team to have any Latino players. Edi had been a star from the start, scoring three goals in two games. We won the first two games and secured a spot in the finals.

Dolores was only fifteen years old when she got married in Mexico to an older man in order to get out of her mother's house. She was in love and she thought she was mature enough to handle it. The couple moved to Chicago, where they had relatives. Dolores gave birth to her five children there.

The family lived in Pilsen, a Mexican immigrant neighborhood located on Chicago's South Side. Pilsen was often the first home for many Mexican immigrants to arrive in Chicago before they moved on to the Little Village, or La Villita, on Twenty-sixth Street on the West Side. All over Pilsen there were beautiful murals depicting the rich cultural history of Latinos.

In the 1980s, Pilsen was very much a poor immigrant community, but by the 1990s, it was slowly being gentrified by artists, actors, and the University of Illinois at Chicago, which had a campus close by and wanted to expand, but it maintained its deep Mexican roots. When I lived and worked as a reporter in Chicago in the early 1990s, I often drove the mile south to Pilsen from Little Italy, where I lived, to do my laundry, go to church, and have lunch. I sought out Pilsen to connect to my own roots, to feel that unique beat that thrives in a Latino neighborhood, and hear and read Spanish. I felt comfortable and tied to the people of Pilsen. The people I saw on the sidewalks looked like me and I would cruise the streets of the neighborhood shooting rolls of film and feeling a part of the community.

I had grown up in Ann Arbor, Michigan, where there were few Latinos. It had been hard growing up in a predominantly white city, I never felt like I fit in anywhere. And while Pilsen wasn't my home, I felt that I belonged in a way.

By 1996, Enrique and his family had moved to Cicero, a suburb of Chicago on the West Side that was becoming predominantly Latino. The family was now fatherless. Dolores and her husband had separated while she had been pregnant with her fifth and last child.

I have often told the family that we were destined to meet since I had lived so close to them in Pilsen and had reported on the migration of Latinos from traditional inner-city neighborhoods like Pilsen and the Little Village to western suburbs like Cicero and Berwyn. I had written several stories for the *Chicago Reporter* on how the suburbs were desperately trying to curb the migration by passing occupancy ordinances and other housing laws. They were enforcing laws that had been on the books for decades but never acted on before.

Cicero had passed an occupancy inspection ordinance that brought the real estate market to a dead halt. Latinos had been buying up housing in Cicero before the ordinance was enacted, but afterward, a city inspector would have to evaluate whether a family had too many members to buy the house. In the end, none of these measures really worked and the suburbs have since become predominantly Latino. The family lived with Dolores's sister in the basement in what was known as a mother-in-law unit, the same sort the town had tried to ban with their occupancy ordinances. The children were enrolled in the local school and settled into a normal life.

Along with the migration of Latinos from traditional Chicago neighborhoods came street gangs and violence. The largest of these gangs were the Latin Kings, but there were other smaller ones as well, the Playboys, the Foxes, and the Spanish Cobras. Latino gangs in Latino neighborhoods fought and killed one another for turf or pride. African-American gangs like the Gangster Disciples or the Vice Lords controlled most of the drug trade and didn't have the petty fights and shoot-outs that the Latino gangs were known for.

One crisp fall day that made the air clear and bright, Enrique and Edi were walking home from their school. Edi was twelve and had developed a reputation around the neighborhood for being athletic and for having a quick temper. Enrique was the opposite; at thirteen, he was quiet, pensive, with more patience.

The boys had attracted the attention of a local gang called the Foxes, whose members were looking to recruit them. Several older high-school-age boys would follow them home, taunting, coaxing them, trying to convince the boys to join, but they were afraid and refused. They told no one what was happening to them. When the older boys couldn't convince them they began to menace them, running after and threatening them, and eventually even throwing rocks and bricks at the two young boys.

On the way home that fall day, they suddenly found themselves surrounded by a group of older boys who had jumped out of an alley. They had hidden in wait for the boys to pass before springing out on them. The Foxes ignored Enrique and crowded around Edi, cutting him off. They were particularly interested in Edi because they knew he would make an excellent recruit. Edi was fearless and quick to respond.

"They punched my brother," Enrique said, remembering the way it started. "Edi's a nice guy, but he's the kind of guy that if you punch him, he has to punch back."

The Foxes wanted to provoke a response out of Edi. Edi stared back at the boy who'd hit him with growing anger. "Okay, you did it because you wanted to do it; now, I want to punch you." And with that, Edi struck the older boy in the face.

The blow was a signal for the other boys to jump in and attack Edi. They knocked him to the ground and began kicking him. Enrique stood there, afraid at first, not knowing what to do. But seeing his brother being beaten was too much—he jumped into the fray and struck one of the Foxes.

"They didn't know he was my brother. I tried to get in to try and stop them, but they grabbed me by the hand and they just, like, this guy came in kicking me all over."

Enrique went down and fell next to his brother. The two boys lay there, taking blow after blow until the Foxes tired. Enrique looked up from the street and saw people looking at them from the windows of their homes. No one came out to help them. No one called the police. They were all afraid to get involved.

The Foxes left the brothers bloodied and battered on the street. A small crowd finally came out to see if they were still alive. They huddled around the boys. Dolores had begun to worry when the boys hadn't come home, and she went looking for them. She came upon the crowd. "When she went to see what's up, I think that was the worst time of her life, she started to cry," Enrique said. The boys were taken to the hospital, where they stayed for weeks recovering from their injuries. Enrique had several broken ribs and Edi had his arm broken. "We couldn't eat anything because we were kicked in the stomach, the ribs, everywhere. We just drank water."

Over the next two months, Enrique asked his mother to go to the school and pick up his and Edi's schoolwork. The boys were afraid of being left behind in their studies. "I could still write and read," he said. "But I couldn't stand up." The boys managed to keep up with their schoolwork even as they recovered. When they were released from the hospital they believed their ordeal was over, but in fact, it was just beginning.

The boys returned to school and were not bothered again. They walked safely to and from school without any problems. A month went by, and just when they started to feel safe and comfortable again, the Foxes started following them home again. They were scared and helpless.

On the way to school one morning, Enrique and Edi came across a dead boy hanging from a basketball court net. He had been shot. Enrique recognized the boy as one of the Foxes who had jumped them. He later learned that the gang member had been killed in retaliation for the beating that he and Edi had taken from the Foxes. The Latin Kings, Chicago's largest and oldest Latino gang, had sent a message to the fledgling Foxes. The boys had been living in Kings territory and were under the protection of the Kings. They felt the Foxes had infringed on their turf by the attack and attempt to re-cruit out from under them.

It was enough for Dolores. She sold their Chevy and moved her children to North Carolina to escape the violence. She had relatives in rural North Carolina and felt this was the only way to protect her family. The gang recruitment was not going to stop. Whether it was the Foxes or the Kings, the boys would be pushed into joining a gang sooner or later just to protect themselves. She and the children arrived first in Burlington and then moved to Siler City, where she found work in one of the poultry plants.

For Enrique, Siler City was like a dream. It was a small town with not much to do, but he liked that. After the violence of Chicago, he took to the country immediately. "I saw it like a beautiful place, like a nice place," he said. "It was nothing like Illinois, it was just like— beautiful. You could run out really late at night, outside, and not hear anything. Nobody would look at you and try to chase you or steal your things."

Since 1990, hundreds of thousands of Latinos have moved to the Southeast, many of them fleeing the violence of cities like Chicago and Los Angeles. They followed the advice of family members who told stories of quiet little towns where there was lots of work, far away from the *pandillas,* the gangs that were choking the life out of the Latino communities in the big cities. The flow of Latinos to the South had two sources, like two rivers coming together into one body of water. The first were Chicanos, like Enrique's family, who were turning their backs on the troubles of the inner city. The second were Latinos escaping poverty and despair from their home countries. These two streams flowed into Siler City and began to change the town in small and profound ways.

Enrique and Anthony—an American boy on the challenge team—crept up behind me and dumped the five-gallon cooler of water on top of me—an American coaching custom. The players and their families all laughed, the flashes flickering. We had won the tournament, 4–0, with Edi scoring three of the goals. He led the team now on a victory lap around the field—something we had never done before. The white kids joined them.

Dripping wet, I watched them circle the field close together in a group, jogging side by side; I couldn't help but wonder what would happen to them after this day. This was the end of the season. The white boys from Pittsboro would probably never see the Latino boys from Siler City again. They would go on to try out for their soccer team at Northwood High School in Pittsboro and hope to make junior varsity. The Latino boys didn't have that option.

All of them were extremely talented players and would have stellar careers in high school and perhaps college. Winning the tournament had proven that these kids could compete. But Jordan-Matthews High School didn't have a soccer team. Latino athletes at JM ran cross-country or tried out for track. Many didn't try out for teams at all, and few participated in the other clubs or programs offered by the school. They just didn't feel welcome. Siler City was a football town, it was not a soccer town, and many wanted to keep it that way. Soccer was seen by the longtime residents as yet another imposition on the traditional Southern way of life. Latinos had already "taken over" parts of the local park with their game. For some, a line had been drawn around the football field at JM. There would be no soccer there. But the thought that excellent players like Edi, Indio, and his brother Perico would never get a chance to shine for their school and community filled me with anger at the very moment I was feeling elated for their achievement that day. Enrique would soon be entering the ninth grade and would miss playing.

The Latino boys *wanted* to play. It was all they ever did. But they were relegated to the dusty dirt fields of the Siler City parks to play where no one would see their talent or cheer their goals. Even though JM was becoming predominantly Latino as more migrant kids moved through the school system, the thought of players in shorts on the football field under the big lights was too much for some. But for me, it was impossible to think, to believe, there would be no soccer program at the school. They deserved the chance to play.

4

Lenin had grown up in Siler City. His was one of the first Latino families to move to the little poultry-processing town in the early 1990s before the migration picked up speed. The family had driven over two days from Texas, and when they reached Siler City, they found themselves homeless. No one would rent to a Latino family. They slept in their car for two weeks until someone finally rented them a little house. Lenin's father soon found work at one of the chicken plants and Lenin settled into his new life.

As one of the first Latino children at the elementary school, Lenin assimilated quickly and learned perfect English. He was a short kid with a round shaved head and a devilish smile capable of disarming any teacher or authority figure.

For three years Lenin waged a campaign to establish a soccer program at Jordan-Matthews High School. He had started his freshman year gathering names of kids interested in playing and trying out for a team. He got all the Latino boys' names on a list and some of his white friends, too.

Lenin took his petitions and list of players to Mr. Hamilton, the principal. He turned in lists with twenty-one names on it, more than enough to field a team at a small school like JM, which only had about six hundred kids.

"But, Mr. Hamilton, he would always shoot it down," Lenin said. "Mr. Hamilton asked me where we would play and I told him 'the football field,' and he gave me this little grin, like 'no way.' He didn't want it there and that was all. You know that school, at JM they love their football."

It was true. Siler City was a football town. Thousands of residents would turn out every Friday night to watch the Jets. It didn't matter if they hadn't won a conference championship in years, it was just what you did on a Friday night in Siler City. It's where kids could hang out, and parents could get together to talk and socialize. There wasn't really anything else to do but go to the game. There was no theater, no movies, no downtown to speak of, no shops to walk along, no mall, and no video arcade.

Unlike those in some other small Southern towns, Siler City residents were not fanatic about winning. And I think that spoke well about the people in Siler City. They had some perspective about the game. Maybe it was because the town was so small; it was difficult to have hard feelings or be too pushy when people rubbed up against one another so much.

But like any small town, it did have its big-time supporters, traditionalists who remembered better days and games and who wanted to keep things the way they were. They were the keepers of the football faith. They had played the game here and remembered the way it was and they wanted to preserve that for their own kids. It was football on Friday nights, with raffle sales, hot dogs, T-shirt sales, and the game on the local radio. Everything and everyone had a place in Siler City—even at the football field on Friday nights.

The field itself was surrounded by a four-lane concrete track. On the south side, right behind the brick school building, were the home stands and the press box. The metal bleachers were divided into three sections. On the west end, students sat with the teachers and coaches. The middle section had a mixture of parents, teachers, and students. The third and last section was where the black parents and fans sat. The segregation was noticeable from the moment you entered into the stadium. There was some mixing in the middle section, but the third section seemed almost exclusively reserved for black parents and their fans.

When I asked Reverend Barry Gray of the First Missionary Baptist Church about it, he said, leaning against the chain-link fence in front of the stands, "That's the way it's always been." The most integrated part of the stadium was the football team itself. There were, however, no Latino players on the team.

Like many towns in the former Jim Crow South, Siler City had been a segregated community. The local grocery store across from the public library had been an all-white store. The Sidewalk Café downtown once upon a time had a "white" entrance and a "colored" entrance. African-Americans who endured the days of Jim Crow in Siler City were left with a lingering bitterness that they feel to this day. There were still places blacks couldn't or wouldn't go into because they knew they were not welcome. And it wasn't too long ago when the city finally removed the "NE" designation from streets to demark the "Negro" sections of town.

Jordan-Matthews High School had been an all-white school. It took more than ten years after the Supreme Court's landmark ruling in *Brown v. Board of Education* to end school segregation at JM. And when it did end in 1968, there was an uprising by the new black students.

On the front of the main building, painted in dark blue, was the figure of a ghost with white eyes that loomed over the entire school. Jordan-Matthews's mascot was the Blue Phantoms and the black students had a great deal of trouble accepting what they saw as a thinly veiled allusion. The ghost had hovered over Siler City for too long.

"The African-American people felt like that represented the emblem of the Ku Klux Klan," Reverend Gray said. He remembers times during the football games when the mascot would come out onto the field in a sheet to the cheering crowds. This was too much for the African-American community in Siler City to tolerate. If they were going to go to school at JM the ghost had to go—

they fought the school administration and the town to have it changed. Many people fought back. They didn't want to give up their traditional mascot. But black students wouldn't retreat. "They rioted until they changed the name from the Phantoms to the Jets," Gray said.

And so JM became home to the now innocuous-sounding Jets and the town had to give up the ghost—literally. The blue ghost on the front of the school was painted over by the word *Jets*. But for JM's black students, the fight left bitter feelings. Gray felt there were hard feelings on the part of the teachers toward integration. "I'll never forget a white teacher putting me out of the class simply because she said I was 'staring her down,'" he remembered. "I thought that was a clear case of racism to the bone. Didn't say a word to this lady." Gray went on to play football at JM and became an excellent athlete. The football team was the one place where integration happened quickly. And even though the fans couldn't quite come together in the stands, they were all united in cheering for their local heroes.

By his senior year, Lenin had completely given up. Each year Mr. Hamilton turned him down and after every year, as he neared graduation, his resolve grew weaker. I knew what he was going through. My brothers, Al and Sergio, had experienced an almost identical frustration. Ann Arbor Pioneer had a soccer club that practiced and played games but soccer was not an official varsity sport. Most of the kids who played in the club were immigrant kids, foreign kids whose parents were teaching at the University of Michigan. By the time I reached high school, soccer had become an official varsity sport, but my brothers had been one year too late. I became determined to find a way for Lenin to play.

I quickly learned that there was no interest in forming a program at JM and that there was an active interest against the idea itself. It would not be just a matter of solving problems but of breaking through a fixed mind-set.

Mr. Hamilton, the principal, was a man in his sixties. He sat behind a large desk and listened quietly as I listed the reasons why a soccer team would be beneficial to Jordan-Matthews.

But before I could get too far, he interrupted me and began a litany of excuses as to why there could be no team. At the top of his list was the fact there just wasn't that much interest from the student body to sustain a program. He told me he had conducted several surveys and the number of names weren't sufficient to create a program. He told me that you had to have at least twenty-two kids participate.

I had learned from being a reporter that when someone starts talking it's best to let them talk as much as they want, take notes, and then come back to certain points. He explained that he had been the athletic director at another high school that had soccer and that it was an expensive addition. He told me that he didn't disagree with the idea that a program was needed at JM but that the time wasn't right.

"The problem that we have with our Hispanic kids is they really do not understand being eligible to play the sport," he said. He then explained the eligibility requirements according to the state. "When we looked at the Hispanic population that was interested in participating in soccer, we couldn't get enough of them that were eligible to play because of grades but especially because of attendance."

Hamilton didn't stop there. He had more reasons why the idea of starting a soccer team wasn't viable. There was the cost of the uniforms, the goals, and the balls, because the Athletic Boosters Club wouldn't pay for those. There was also no way for the sport to produce revenue. There were only two revenue-producing sports at the school, football and basketball. The other sports—tennis, golf, cross-country, baseball, softball, and track—all ran in the red. I sat quietly and listened.

The more Hamilton offered me excuses and obstacles to the program, the angrier I became, because they were clearly designed to discourage me. But I knew a Herculean effort would not be required to start the program. You just needed the will to do it. Then Hamilton hit me with the real reason why soccer couldn't and wouldn't come to JM.

"And you can't play at night because there are no lights at the park," he said. He explained that he had *already* worked out a deal where the school could use Bray Park as the field location *if* soccer came to JM. But the real message was clear. The soccer program would not play on the football field.

Bray Park was the central park in town and it was mostly a baseball park, with several fields, a tennis court, and a swimming pool. But it also had an open field where Latinos played soccer on the weekends in their La Liga games, the private Latino soccer league. La Liga was composed of men who worked at the chicken plants all week and then played hard-hitting soccer on the weekends. The field was in terrible shape. It was slanted, and you literally ran down hill toward one goal. The grass had been stripped long ago and it was mostly dirt now, there were no bathroom facilities close by, no lights, and no stands for fans.

This was the place where Hamilton had decided the high school team would play. It was incredible to even consider that a school would allow one of its own teams to play off campus, let alone in such conditions.

Hamilton went a step further to make his point perfectly clear. "And you can't play on the football field because it's not a regulation soccer field," he told me. This was too much. He had been hinting that the football field was off-limits and that he had a plan *in case* soccer did come to JM. Now he came out and said it. There would be no soccer on the football field. The fact that hundreds of high schools across North Carolina play on their own football fields meant little to Hamilton.

Schools adjusted to the constraints of their fields. Some schools pushed the limits, usually getting more length than width in their soccer fields, but teams just dealt with it. Not having a regulation soccer field didn't stop the sport from being played in other high schools; why should it do so at JM? In fact, the only place in the state where there were "regulation" soccer fields were at the big universities like UNC or North Carolina State University.

I didn't bring any of this up. I had come to propose a team to

Hamilton and to discuss why it would be a positive thing for the school, especially as its population was changing. I wanted to listen to what he had to say first, openly, honestly, and then deal with the problems as they came up. I wasn't there to argue or to plead. I was there to learn and to begin the work to overcome.

I wrote down all the things that would need to be done. I would need to petition parents and students to find out their true interest. I would need to educate parents about the importance of grades and attendance in order to participate on the team. I wrote down that the team would somehow need to be self-sustaining and generate its own revenue. The team could play and practice at Bray Park but there was no school location for a field and no interest in using the football field.

I left Hamilton's office with two feelings—determination to see this through, and anger that Hamilton had just focused on only the obstacles facing the Latino students at JM in trying out for a soccer team. In our conversation, I had not mentioned that the team would be created *for* Latino students or that they would be the ones who would play. This was never my intention. I saw the team at JM as being like my club team, a mix of students who wanted to play. In fact, I had gone out of my way to be general because I felt the campaign to bring soccer to JM would be stronger if it weren't focused on only one ethnic group. Hamilton himself had brought up the ethnicity of the kids who wanted to play soccer. He had made the inference that soccer was primarily for the Latino kids.

What became clear during my conversation with Hamilton was that soccer would come at the expense of the football program, and because of that, there could be no soccer at JM.

That summer, on a hot July day, Rick Givens was hanging out at the Siler City Police Station when one of the officers approached him about a problem. Givens, the chief of the Chatham County Commissioners at the time, took a minute to listen to the officer.

The officer told Givens of the problems the police department was having with undocumented workers driving without licenses, leaving the scene of accidents, and not showing up when summoned to court. But the law enforcement officials weren't the only ones who were now complaining of the newcomers. Health care officials were worried about overcrowded clinics and patients without health insurance, and the schools were becoming overcrowded with kids who spoke little or no English.

The town was expending resources to deal with the labor force the poultry industry was actively recruiting. It was subsidizing the poultry industry, making up for inadequate and costly health plans that workers didn't choose, and an increase in the number of students. And workers couldn't get driver's licenses without showing a Social Security number. But that didn't stop them from driving to the chicken plants each shift.

Givens, a short, wiry man with a reddish complexion, was a retired airline pilot and a Vietnam veteran. He came up with the idea to send the INS a letter asking for greater enforcement in Chatham County. He convinced the other county commissioners the letter would be a good idea. He wrote it and sent it. "More and more of our resources are being siphoned off from other pressing needs so that we can provide assistance to immigrants who have little or no possessions," the letter stated. "Many of these new needy, we believe, are undocumented or have fraudulent paperwork. We need your help in getting those folk properly documented or routed back to their homes."

Givens, like so many local government officials across America, saw the problem as a matter of black and white. If the workers were illegal, get them legal or get them home.

Word of the letter quickly filled Latino families with fear and dread—many were afraid to leave their homes because *la migra,* or INS, was coming to deport them. The poultry plants were upset because workers were afraid to show up. Latinos began expecting knocks on their doors in the middle of the night from *la migra.*

La migra didn't come—they didn't have enough manpower to enforce immigration law in every poultry town in the South. But the letter had other consequences. Givens had fired the first shot. Now others decided to take up the cause. Bashing Latinos had become legitimized in the eyes of Siler City residents. Discriminatory acts against Latinos increased dramatically. People were now asked to present IDs when they bought food, while others were threatened with deportation at traffic stops. People became openly hostile toward the newcomers. Siler City had lost its patience. Longtime residents began meeting at night in one another's homes to discuss the problem and what was to be done. At the top of the list was what was happening at the schools, and parents were not happy.

Siler City Elementary is a small school located in a wooded area on the outskirts of town near Highway 64. Ten years ago, it was a new school with shiny white floors and clean classrooms with dedicated teachers. The children who went to the school were a mixture of white and black, the majority being white. But in 1995, the makeup of the school began to change. A new group of children began to enroll at Siler City Elementary that no one had dealt with before. Prior to that year, many of the Latino migrants who had come to town to work in the chicken plants were solitary men. But sometime around 1995, people in town began to notice that whole families were now coming to Siler City and they had lots of children.

The population of Latino children at the elementary school skyrocketed to more than 40 percent in just five years—catching the staff, county school administrators, and other parents off guard. The rapid influx of children who spoke limited or no English sent educators scurrying for a way to teach this new group. By 1998, 9 percent of the student body in Chatham County was "Limited English Proficient" with almost all these children concentrated in Siler City and most at the elementary school. At the time, North Carolina did not provide any funds to local school systems to help teach these new kids or help them find qualified English As a Second Language teachers. Communities like Chatham County footed the bill until 1999, when the state finally recognized the need to help out.

From 1990 to 2000, Hispanic students accounted for 15 percent of growth in student enrollment in North Carolina. From 2000 to 2005, Hispanic enrollment growth had increased to 57 percent, according to a study by the Kenan Institute of Private Enterprise at UNC–Chapel Hill.

Siler City Elementary had gone from a predominantly white school with a black population to a growing-majority Latino school with a white and black minority, and many people didn't like it. White parents pulled their children from the school, complaining that teachers were spending too much time teaching children who couldn't speak English. They went to the school board asking for transfers to other predominantly white schools in the county. Teachers at Siler City Elementary began leaving too. Some black parents wanted to pull their children from the school but couldn't afford to drive them to other schools the way white parents could. A new kind of white flight developed around Latino children and began to devastate the school.

Rumors circulated that the quality of education at the school was dropping, that Latino kids didn't even know how to go to the bathroom, that their parents hadn't paid the taxes to build the school and so the children shouldn't be allowed to attend. White parents who wanted their children to attend Siler City Elementary were furious at the other white parents who were fleeing under the transfer policy. Some held that the more white children fled, the more it spurred the white flight. They wanted to stop it before all the white children were gone from the school.

Finally, in September of 1999, the school board called a special meeting at Siler City Elementary to discuss the transfer policy.

On the night of the meeting, the Siler City Elementary gymnasium was packed with parents and teachers. The parents sat in separate groups on folding chairs in front of a long table where the county school board members sat. To the side of the members a microphone was set up for people to speak directly to the board. White and black parents sat together and Latino parents sat among themselves off to the side. Latino parents sat in silence, and although the meeting was supposed to be about the transfer policy, they knew it was really about them and their children. The atmosphere was tense but there was also a giddy excitement that things were finally going to be said that needed to be said.

T. C. Yarborough, a detective with the sheriff's office, spoke up first. He was a tall man with a large mustache who had a little girl attending Siler City Elementary. He was worried that the white flight from the school was putting tremendous pressure on the remaining white parents who wanted to stick it out. He wanted the transfer policy to be stopped and he wanted the other white parents to stop fleeing.

"If you have a child at this school, next year bring that child back to this school," he told the crowd. He vowed that he would not transfer his little girl from the school and that the board needed to review the transfer policy and stop the white flight.

But as teachers and parents took the microphone, everyone latched onto the language barrier as the single reason why parents were transferring their children out of the school. The issues of race and ethnicity were covered for the moment and the focus was on how non-English-speaking children were taking up the teachers time. Donna Jones got to the point. "A couple of years ago the class my son was in, he cried every morning, he did not want to go to school because he was so bored because his teacher spends all her time helping kids who cannot communicate with her and that's not right," she said. Other white parents complained that their children's education was being shortchanged.

Kay Staley told the audience that her granddaughter had been only one of two white children in her classroom. "These two little girls were devastated and scared to death because no one spoke their language." The issue was not one of race and she was not prejudiced, but something had to be done about the language issue. She said that Siler City Elementary had once been a great school, "Now it's suffering and it's because of the problem with Hispanics. The one suffering the most now is the minority, and this is where they were raised, they're American citizens. Let us make a stand for them.

Are we going to stand back and see that our children have to be taken out of this school and be put into another school in order for them to get their education? Let's don't stand and watch. Let's stand up for our children and grandchildren," she said to applause.

And then she offered her solution, which has been the South's solution to all problems when it comes to race. "Maybe they need their alternative schools until they learn English and then we'd be glad to have them come to this school system, it's not our place to have to do that. We paid for this school. It's from our taxes, not from the Hispanics," she finished, to more applause and cheers.

Staley was not alone. Annette Jordan, an African-American parent of a little girl who attended the school, was also concerned. "I don't have a problem with the Mexicans or the whites or nobody, but I do have a problem when my daughter comes home from school and says the teacher didn't have time to teach me or show me how to do my homework because she had to take up all her time to teach those Mexicans because they don't understand," she said. She admitted that if she had her way she would have pulled her daughter out of the school, but her husband would not let her.

The meeting was devolving into a gripe session about Latinos. The room took on the atmosphere of a sporting event, where groups cheered and supported their side as each person took the microphone and vented his or her feelings about Latinos. But even as white parents lashed out at Latinos, others stepped up and defended the school and the Latino community and the idea that people could live together despite being different.

Heidi Green, a new teacher at the school, brought up the idea that a diverse school was an excellent experience for anyone's child because the country was becoming more diverse. "Ladies and gentlemen, I'm sorry to tell you this, but whether you like it or not, I'm not trying to be mean or anything, but we're being integrated, the U.S. is the melting pot of the world and we have to face this," she said.

Doris Marsh, a longtime African-American teacher at the school, struck out at the crowd. "I'm going to leave you with two questions: If all the black children were leaving this school, would we be having this meeting? If all the Hispanic children were leaving this school, would we be having this meeting? I don't think so. If there are white parents who are taking their children out of our school, they're taking them because they want to—then so be it."

Sam Gregor, the pastor of Siler City Methodist Church, blamed the problem on fear. "I don't care if my blond, blue-eyed daughter is the only white child in her class," he said to murmurs from the crowd. "As a Christian pastor, if you pull your child out of here, shame on you. My child is growing up in a home where she is taught that she is to love folks regardless of the language they speak."

Latino parents sat in silence not really understanding what was being said about them specifically but knowing that all the negative energy was being directed at them. But there was little they could do because no had bothered to provide a translator for them to respond to the ugly words that were being said about them and their children. One Latina parent, Virginia Tabor, stood up and took the microphone. "I know there's a language barrier, but that doesn't mean my little girl is retarded, or that she's a slow learner," she said to applause.

"The issue here is segregation and discrimination," David Gonzalez told the crowd to cheers. He lashed out at the idea that Latinos in Siler City did not pay taxes and therefore did not have the right to send their children to go to school or have them receive other services. The idea that Latinos do not pay taxes was an idea that was deeply ingrained in the minds of longtime Siler City residents.

The meeting was contentious and raucous and the white parents finally got a chance to express their feelings. They were abandoning their institutions in favor of places like the new charter school where their children would not be in the minority. They felt they had no choice. Their own prejudice and fear were pushing them out of their own town and they were mad. The white power structure in town was being challenged by the fast migration. Its members didn't know how to handle it. They needed the Latino workers to man the chicken plants and keep their economy going, but they didn't necessarily want the people or their children to live with them and share resources.

In my travels and reporting on Latinos migrating to the rural South, I discovered that each town deals with the migration in stages similar to the five stages of grief. First there may be denial, where communities ignore the growing presence of Latino workers in their town. The next stage is anger. The third stage is bargaining, and sometimes people would say that as soon as the economy took a downturn the Latinos would leave. The fourth is depression. I remember often hearing white people sigh mournfully about the Latinos who had moved to Siler City. One white woman, at her family farm auction, took my hand and said, "Oh, can you believe what those Mexicans are doing to Siler City?" She rolled her eyes heavenward and tipped her head back in disbelief at Siler City's misfortune. The last stage, of course, is acceptance, and in 1999, Siler City was nowhere near accepting the Latino population. Siler City was angry.

The townspeople were frustrated and angry that their way of life and the way it had been organized for hundreds of years was changing and that they needed to change with it. After the school board meeting, I knew that creating a soccer program at JM would be a monumental task.

5

Rick Givens grew up in the flatlands of western Kentucky, where folks dug coal out of the ground and were generally poor. His father had it better than most, working as a railroad switchman, and the family owned a mom-and-pop general store where Givens helped out. Givens said he didn't grow up poor but rather in "meager circumstances" and he remembered many times when his father would hunt through the family couch searching for a few coins to buy a cup of coffee.

As an air-force pilot, Givens had been through plenty of scrapes and tough spots, but it was nothing like the flak he was getting for conceiving the letter to the INS. He received complaints from Latino advocates, politicians, and the business community, which didn't want to lose its cheap labor force. He was portrayed in the media as a bigot, which he resented.

Like many Southerners, Givens dismissed the idea of race being a factor in any of his decisions. White Southerners had decided that the end of Jim Crow had also been the end of racism. They took it personally when they were accused of being bigots or racists—especially by outsiders. But race in America is an extremely complicated issue, intertwined with class and history, and it runs across the surface of many different issues like topsoil. African-Americans in the South had not moved beyond the subject of racism because they still lived it in the class structure in many towns like Siler City. Whites deeply resented being labeled racist. But what they didn't want to confront was that the economic and social structure of their communities favored them, to the disadvantage of others.

This, of course, was not a regional phenomenon. The North was equally troubled. The series of stories I wrote about Latinos in 1994, like Enrique and his family, moving to the western suburbs of Chicago and encountering terrible housing discrimination by local government, was much worse than anything I had seen yet in Siler City or North Carolina.

But the letter and school board meeting scared Latinos. Everyone seemed to be turning against them. They didn't understand why. Big business had invited them to come and work—in many cases, it had transported them, provided them housing, and given them jobs that others in Siler City didn't want. This is something that anti-immigrant advocates refused to admit. Many workers, whether undocumented or documented, had been *invited* by America's most influential and best representative—Corporate America. It was business that decided that it needed a more pliable and cheaper labor force, and it went out and got it despite, or encouraged by, Washington's lack of official immigration policy.

Givens and several other officials from Chatham County were invited for a weeklong trip to Mexico sponsored by the University of North Carolina's Center for International Understanding. Givens had been to Mexico before, but, like many Americans, had just visited the tourist areas. This trip would be very different.

When Givens and the group arrived in Mexico, they were taken to Puebla, a town located east of the capital. Givens was brought to a school where children attended classes underneath canvas tents in the open air. He had never seen such poverty before. "They didn't even have any books," he said. Most of the children didn't go to school beyond the sixth grade, which was true for many parts of Mexico.

It was at this school that Givens met a teenage student with a deformed leg. This young man would limp for miles on crutches just to attend the school. He stood up and read an essay to the delegates about how much his education meant to him. Givens remembered the hardships of growing up in Kentucky and was deeply moved. He pledged to give the student the money necessary to finish his schooling.

Givens was beginning to understand that the forces causing the migration of Latinos to North Carolina were far more powerful than he had realized. He had seen the conditions and had met mothers whose husbands and sons had made the perilous trip across the border and were living alone somewhere in the United States, sending what money they could to keep their families going. He had been present at the home of one family when they received a call from a poultry plant in North Carolina asking for its help in finding more workers. "They were calling looking for more workers, right there, that was from a poultry company," he said.

Givens realized the problem was beyond the scope of his letter. "I said then, why even bother, if the federal government can't control their own rules, this county doesn't have the time or resources," he said when he came back.

I still say illegal is illegal but I found out it wasn't just a simple black-and-white issue," he said. "I was wrong and I am man enough to admit it." He resolved to help the community assimilate and become more a part of the greater Siler City community.

The first thing Givens did upon his return was to help pay for the teenage student's education. He then met with North Carolina representatives to get Chatham County more funding for ESL education. And the county commissioners, led by Givens, approved $129,000 to create the Newcomer's Program, the county's first specialized program for ESL students.

The trip had produced some positive results instead of just punitive ones. But not everyone in Siler City saw it the way that Givens did. Many saw the county officials—Givens in particular—as traitors to their cause of getting rid of the Latinos in town.

It was a crisp February 2000 night and I was home developing photographs when the phone rang. I left several prints soaking in water and went to the living room to answer it. It was late, after 11 p.m., and I still had about an hour before I could quit printing. I had taken a set of photographs of hog-processing workers in Tarheel, a small town about an hour and half south of Pittsboro in hog country.

It was Ilana Dubester and she sounded agitated. "You will not believe it. *Pinche puta madres.* They're holding a rally," she said, puffing hard on a cigarette.

At first I thought *la migra* had finally come and were rounding up people. "Who's holding a rally?"

"The *pinche* KKK," she spat out. "They are holding an anti-immigrant rally in front of city hall in two weeks."

I had to admit that after the INS letter and the school board meeting, a rally at some point seemed logical. I had covered other rallies by the Klan and other hate groups in Chicago and in Michigan. This was going to be a disaster.

"And guess who's the main speaker?" Ilana said, taking another long drag.

"I have no idea."

She let out the smoke. "David Duke."

On the edge of town, nestled between the split of two roads like the flesh between your thumb and forefinger, was a small white service station. It was owned by Richard Vanderford, a tall man in his fifties with a salt-and-pepper beard. It was rumored that Vanderford had been a member of the Ku Klux Klan many years ago but now was a member of the National Alliance, a racist hate group headquartered in Reston, Virginia. On January 24, 2000, he decided to do something about the Mexican problem. He went down to city hall and requested a permit to conduct a rally in order "to protest the uncheck [sic] immigration of large numbers of un-assimilable [sic] non-American workers into Chatham County and Siler City. An influx which is putting an unburdenable [sic] strain on the indigenous residents here, our traditions, our institutions, and our infrastructure." Two years before, Vanderford fought the Division of Motor Vehicles to provide him vanity license plates that read ARYAN. He won.

The rally initially was supposed to be a local event for local folks to voice their opinions about the growing number of Latinos, but it quickly grew into something else. Vanderford invited the local director of the Raleigh chapter of the National Alliance to be a featured speaker. Then he hit on the idea of inviting David Duke, the former grand dragon of the KKK in Louisiana and U.S. Senate candidate. When Duke accepted, the rally morphed from a small event into a national incident, attracting spectators, the media, and supporters and detractors from all over the state.

Ilana and the Vínculo wanted Latinos to stay home and not provoke a confrontation. Juan, a local poultry-processing worker, had been meeting with other workers to discuss the situation and decide how they should react. Some wanted to fight the *encapuchados* (hooded ones), while others wanted to stay in their homes. They decided to listen to the Vínculo and stay home.

The rally was scheduled for February 19, a Saturday, and as the day approached you could feel the town tighten with tension. Everyone began to take sides.

African-Americans in Siler City seemed to have decided to sit this one out. They had been through this kind of thing before and felt this was not their fight. But as the day of the rally approached, and David Duke's arrival drew near, they had a change of heart. African-American pastors began to rally their congregations in support of Latinos and in denunciation of the rally. They reasoned that if it were still possible for Klan supporters to hold an open rally after all the previous suffering, there was no guarantee they were any safer than before. But it was more than self-interest at work in their support for Latinos. The specter of the rally had opened their eyes to the plight of Latinos in Siler City and they saw that their situations were not so different.

The Reverend Brian Thompson of Union Grove AME Zion

Church was adamant that his congregation take a stand against a "Klan rally without the hoods. And not a violent stand but a stand to say that we're not only here for the Hispanic community, for the black community, for the white community, we're tired of *all* the blatant acts of racism," he said.

In Siler City, African-American pastors met frequently with white pastors, but they had found it hard to connect with the Latino churches. They reached out to Latino pastors at the Latino Baptist church, the Latino Methodist church, and the evangelical churches—but couldn't seem to connect with St. Julia's Catholic Parish, which boasted the largest congregation of Latinos in the county.

Latino children went to school in fear and trepidation as the day approached. They couldn't understand why people were so against them. Their families worked hard and supported themselves, they went to school, why did people hate them so much? What had they done?

The schools ignored what was happening.

"There's so many times when they don't feel like anyone at the schools really care," said Willa Mae Thompson, who worked for the county migrant education program and is African-American. She had gotten to know the community very well.

"You have two or three counselors at the schools and nobody pulled them aside to say, well, this is going to happen and we want you to know we are not a part of this and we're here for you," she said.

Many white residents didn't support the rally and disliked the reputation Siler City was getting because of David Duke. "I don't want anything to do with them," Joyce Gibson told a newspaper. "I don't want them in my town."

St. Julia's Catholic Parish had always been cut off from Siler City. Many of the Protestant churches saw the little Catholic church as an oddity. It had been a small church with few members who kept mostly to themselves; that changed dramatically with the migration. The little church grew threefold in a short time and Father Daniel Quakenbush was performing more masses in Spanish than English.

Now, the night before the rally, the little church was once again packed with people from every community in Siler City, white, black, and brown; they had come together to pray and ask God to help them through their town's most difficult time. I went inside where Father Dan was leading the people in prayer. I saw Margaret Pollard, a county commissioner who is African-American, seated on the edge of a pew. Her family had been living in the area for hundreds of years. Margaret was a kind person, in her sixties, with graying hair and a reputation for making time to listen to folks. Sometimes she would sit with her cousin Wilbur, who sold the vegetables he grew on his farm on an empty lot in Pittsboro. She'd be there frequently, in her customary big straw hat, convincing people to buy pumpkins or whatever else Wilbur was featuring that day.

She was usually smiling, but tonight Margaret looked grim. I asked her whether the letter, which she had signed and helped Givens send to the INS, had precipitated the rally. She looked up at me, her forehead creased in thought. She said she hoped that the letter had not been the catalyst for this event. She hoped instead that the letter had been the trigger for her trip to Mexico with Givens, a means of coming to an understanding for everyone.

"Sometimes bad relationships start at the beginning of good relationships," she told me. I knelt down next to her so she wouldn't have to look up at me. "So long as there is no talking there is no chance of resolution. When the conversations begin, even though they may begin in conflict, it is out of conflict that we get a sense of those things that unite us and see our common issues, our humanity, our common needs."

I've often thought of Margaret's words. There is no doubt that conflict brings into sharp relief those things we keep hidden beneath the surface. Even my struggle to create a soccer team at JM was born of conflict—between the dreams of the Latino students and the traditionalists in the administration. I hoped that what had begun as a bad relationship would end in a good one.

I pushed my way through in the aisle and joined the congregation in song.

> My country's skies are bluer than the ocean,
> And sunlit beams on cloverleaf and pine;
> But other lands have sunlight, too, and clover,
> And skies are everywhere as blue as mine.
> O hear my song, thou God of all nations,
> A song of peace for their land and mine.

Highway 64 stretched out before me—forlorn and empty. It was late morning and the sky was the color of a dirty washcloth that had just been used to wipe a table. It had rained earlier in the morning, leaving a dampness in the air that made it feel colder than usual. I drove on toward Siler City and the rally. I was dressed in jeans and an Eisenhower jacket that I liked to use in my reporting because of its pockets. On the seat next to me was my camera, loaded with black-and-white film. Color film seemed inappropriate today. On the radio, Los Lobos played a Tejano tune.

Siler City was abandoned. The McDonald's drive-through, normally humming with the sound of idling engines from the breakfast patrons, didn't have a single car in line. Raleigh Street was empty and the houses appeared as though they had their backs to the road—like they didn't want to see what was going to happen.

City hall stood like a temple in the middle of Second Avenue along the main downtown thoroughfare. It was a short, three-story structure and the main courtroom was on the top floor. The stone walls were light gray with white trim and there was a small balcony on the third floor where police officers stood between two square white columns surveying the street. Barricades had been placed on the side of the building and a driveway cut through to keep the media from entering the main area where the speakers would be addressing the crowd on the front steps. The rally's main supporters would be allowed to gather on the front lawn. Other people were relegated to the street down the sloping hill. It was enough of a buffer to provide protection for the supporters.

People began arriving in trickles at first and then suddenly there was a commotion behind city hall—it appeared that Vanderford, his supporters, the National Alliance people, and David Duke had arrived.

I stationed myself on the driveway reserved for the media and began shooting pictures. A group of about forty hard-core supporters appeared and stood in front of the building. There was an older man with a Confederate-flag jacket and hat, some skinheads, naturally, a young couple dressed in black, and others who looked like farmers and regular rural folk. Many carried signs that read LA RAZA GO HOME; THIS IS OUR LAND!; REPORT ILLEGALS; POLLUTION OF OUR POPULATION IS STUPID, and RECALL THE TRAITOR RICK GIVENS. One woman carried a homemade sign that read IF NC LEADERS WANT TO HELP MEXICANS HELP THEM IN MEXICO NOT HERE WE NEED NEW LEADERS. And my favorite, the word FULL inside an outline of the United States.

As I snapped pictures, I noticed, crouched near the ground of the concrete drive, another reporter. She had light wiry hair that stood out like summer straw against her maroon turtleneck and was pointing a black microphone at the supporters. I said hello and she smiled back a broad flashing smile that cut through the grayness of the day. She had pointed but delicate features drawn around large eyes and a slim but shapely figure. I asked the usual reporter question: "Who are you with?" It was always nice to know who was working a job with you.

"Public radio," she said, looking up at me.

"What do you think of this?"

"How come they're not over at the chicken plant?"

It was a good question. The reason was obvious. They could hold their rally in front of city hall, but if they tried to hold it in front of the Gold Kist or Townsends plants, the companies would have hustled them off quickly.

"What's your name?"

"Leda," she said, and then she looked down at her recorder and stretched her arm out to record more sound.

Richard Vanderford stepped up to the microphone that had been set up on the steps. He wore a dark shirt with white stripes, the kind you can get at a JCPenney, a light jacket, and a baseball cap with a picture of a truck and the words ALBRIGHT DIESEL. Vanderfold had a light beard and small piercing eyes like a terrier's—good for hunting under the ground. He asked the crowd that had gathered above and below on the street, now numbering in the hundreds, to pledge allegiance to the flag and everyone did. I thought Americans would pledge allegiance no matter who led it.

David Duke was tall and slim and he wore a blue suit. He had Hollywood good looks, wavy silver-and-blond hair, straight white teeth, and dimples that crinkled when he smiled—which he did often. He had the polish of a politician and an ease when speaking to a crowd. He was treated like royalty by the organizers of the rally—well protected, catered to, and pampered. He was the show.

Duke went immediately for the jugular. "What you have to understand is that this massive immigration in this country is changing the face of this community, is changing the face of America, and it will transform America into something alien to the principles and the values of the founding fathers of this country," he bellowed. "You will be eventually outnumbered and outvoted in your own land."

He touched on several points, including the role the poultry industry was playing in the migration. "What's going on in this country is a few companies are hiring illegal aliens and not American citizens because they can save a few bucks. I guess they need someone to pluck the chickens, but it's not just chickens that are getting plucked in Chatham County, because the people that are being plucked are the taxpayers and the hard working people of these communities that have to pay the bills."

He lashed out at the industry for "selling your birthright for a few dollars." And he called on African-Americans in the crowd to join him in opposing what was happening to their town. He said they had just as much at stake if not more.

Then he went on to attack Rick Givens personally. "Now here's a guy who got elected on the idea that he was going to defend you from the illegal alien invasion in this area. Then he went on an all-expense-paid vacation to Mexico and he's changed his tune hasn't he?"

Duke's complaints sounded eerily similar to the complaints in the INS letter and those voiced at the school board meeting. They echoed the same thoughts and sentiments found in the cable news shows about "broken borders" and "invasions." But somehow, because they were said by the leader of a racist hate group, the words were different from those used by the media pundits or the Minutemen. The rhetoric was the same, but the hate within the words was laid bare by the indentity of the speaker.

D uke spoke for more than an hour—lashing out at the poultry industry, Givens, Latinos, and imploring blacks to join his cause. He closed by invoking the Alamo; the bravery of the Texans who stood up against the Mexican assault on the mission, and how they won their country from Santa Anna's troops. "Your battle here is America's battle."

Many in the crowd cheered. More than three hundred people had attended the rally—including supporters and detractors, students from UNC, outsiders white and black, and a few Latinos.

The curious African-Americans who came out to watch couldn't believe this was happening again in their own town. They were sickened by the very notion that they should join with a former grand dragon of the KKK. Many white folks from Siler City deliberately did not come out to support the rally. They were not going to stand with Duke and the Klan. That most Latinos stayed away too was a testament to the organizing skills of Ilana and the other advocates. There was no confrontation today. But many in the crowd got a chance to express themselves and let out their feelings.

Dwight Jordan—a supporter—was angry. "I'm mad because there ain't no Greyhound buses here to load them up and send them back where they came from, every goddamn one of them," he told me. "Been living here forty-one damn years. I drive a truck." Jordan laid the blame for the troubles on the poultry industry. "Instead of trying to negotiate a decent wage with people that work there, they want it done cheaper," he said.

"We come here, and we appreciate the hospitality that we find, and how do we appreciate it?" asked Julio Perez, who worked for a local Spanish-speaking radio station. "We work hard and make the companies we work for happy to have us." He pointed out that it was the Latinos who were creating the booming economy in Siler City.

A middle-aged couple stood up with the main supporters in front of city hall. They had a daughter attending Bonlee Elementary School, a predominantly white school. They were afraid that Latinos would soon be coming to their school too. "I'm not angry at the people that are coming up and trying to better themselves," the mother said. "I'm angry at the ones they're letting come in and not have to pay a dime and they're taking jobs and they're taking education from my daughter."

The rally ended without incident. The only real outburst came from students from UNC who had arrived to protest the appearance of Duke, but no one paid them much attention. The crowd began to disperse and Duke came over to the barricade where the press had been positioned. I asked him what he thought was the cause of this situation.

"I think that greed has a lot to do with this problem because people are trying to make a few more bucks and not pay a decent wage and they know they can pay a lower wage," he said in a rather statesmanlike way. He sounded like a labor organizer. "And what happens is this community ends up paying the bills for it in higher health care costs, higher education costs, and it's really not quite fair."

"If that's the case, then why wasn't the rally held at the poultry plants?"

He chuckled and tilted his head back. "The air smells sweeter here," he said flippantly. "Maybe we'll head there next."

But that's not where Duke headed next. He was hungry. It was hard work spouting vitriol for two hours, and he and Vanderford went to the Golden Corral restaurant on Highway 64 outside of town. A source had informed me they were going to have lunch there, so I went over ahead of them, hoping to get a chance to interview Duke more thoroughly. I took a seat near the back and waited for them to arrive. There were already some skinheads and other minions seated hunched over their tables. They looked over my way and one of them said, "What are you looking at?"

Duke and Vanderford and a group of others walked into the restaurant. Duke stood out in that crowd. He was the tallest, the best-dressed, and the best-looking, though there wasn't much competition given the good ol' boys, skinheads, and rednecks that accompanied him. The tension in the place was palpable and the waitresses looked at one another nervously. I tried to get over to Duke to continue our interview but he was too well protected. I decided to sit and watch. Maybe a chance would open up if he went to the bathroom.

Duke had spent two hours bashing the poultry industry and the workers and then strangely drifted to other topics that had lost the crowd's interest. When I watched him after the rally signing his new book, it was clear that he was little more than an opportunist. This was a chance for him to sell a few books and pocket some cash. He wasn't interested in Siler City. It was just another carnival stop for him.

I was about to leave and give up on getting anything further from Duke when I saw him get up from his chair with a plate in his hand. I thought this might be my chance to talk to him, but for some reason I held back. I saw Duke go to the buffet and, aluminum tongs in hand, select several pieces of fried chicken and put them on his white plate. He was a good Southern boy after all, and he loved his fried chicken.

As he walked back to his table, I lowered my head. I didn't have to see any more. Duke had said it all with what he put on his plate. He had said it all for everyone in America who views the migration and Latinos the way he does. They didn't want the workers or their families living in their towns but they sure wanted their chicken. And that was all that mattered. America spoke with its stomach and it wanted its tomatoes picked, its cucumbers gathered, its oranges harvested, its blueberries busheled, its hamburger ground, its pork processed, its Thanksgiving Day turkeys slaughtered, its Christmas trees cut, and its chicken butchered, and it didn't much care how that was done as long as the people who brought its food were kept invisible and cheap.

Duke had spent two hours bashing the very workers who had brought him his fried chicken. He didn't even realize the full extent of his hypocrisy. None of them did when it came down to it. Not Lou Dobbs, Bill O'Reilly, Representative Tom Tancredo, or any other anti-immigrant proponents. If they were sincere about reducing illegal immigration, they could take a stand and refuse to buy these products. They could stop eating fried chicken, bacon, hamburgers, steaks, lettuce, turkey, hot dogs, tomatoes, grapes, wine; and stop purchasing other products like furniture and textiles; and deny themselves services like landscaping and construction. But I suspect that, like Duke, most would simply help themselves to a nice plate of chicken.

I left feeling depressed and weighed down by the self-righteous duplicity I had just witnessed. All my life I have dreamed the American Dream and worked hard to achieve my share of it. But I have never been embraced as a true American. I cannot recount the number of times people have asked me whether I speak English or if I am a citizen. I love this country but it's an unrequited love. I think that many Latinos, especially the newer generations, feel this way toward America. We love it, but America can be capricious with her affection, leaving us like jilted lovers, world-weary, but perennially hopeful.

I didn't think I could feel more down, but I learned later that sometime the night after the peace prayer, St. Julia's had been vandalized. Someone had punctured the tires of two cars in the parking lot and destroyed the lighted church sign in front. The police conducted an investigation but no one was caught or held accountable for the attack.

Two months later, outside the First Missionary Baptist Church in downtown Siler City, a group of people gathered to hold a response rally to David Duke. It was led by the Reverend Barry Gray, the Reverend Brian Thompson, white and Latino pastors, and Father Daniel Quackenbush. They marched to city hall and spoke about healing and peace. Only forty people attended.

6

Maria Hitt had spent several weeks during the summer of 2001 compiling a survey of what Jordan-Matthews High School students wanted from their community. Hitt worked for the county health department and she devoted much of her time to educating the Latino community about the dangers of sexually transmitted diseases. Earlier in the year, I had helped her and the department conduct a massive syphilis intervention in Siler City's Latino community.

The county had sent health care workers and translators door-to-door focusing in on the trailer parks where Latinos mostly lived. We knocked on doors in Snipes Trailer Park, a notoriously dilapidated facility. The trailers were coming apart, the floorboards were decaying, the walls had holes, there was no heat in the winter and no air-conditioning in the summer, and sometimes not even electricity. A white owner who wanted to provide housing to African-Americans had originally created the park. He placed it in the Lincoln Heights area of Siler City, the traditional black neighborhood in town. But he sold the place to John Snipes, an African-American who later rented the park to the growing Latino community.

Snipes was a neglected facility, and, as such, it attracted crime, drug dealing, and prostitution—both from the Latino community and the white community. Non-Latina prostitutes hooked on crack cocaine frequented the park to service the men who resided there and collect enough money to buy a twenty-dollar rock. They would knock on the doors of the trailers and turn out the entire trailer for a couple of bucks each. Sometimes they were so desperate they would take the change in a man's pocket.

The department suspected that the prostitutes had exposed the men to syphilis. But that turned out not to be the case, for some reason that couldn't be explained. They found little infection among Latino men they tested.

Hitt presented her findings of the student survey at a community forum that included several stakeholders, people from the community, including John Phillips, the newly appointed athletic director at JM. John was in his early forties and had grown up in Bennett, a small rural town just south of Siler City. He was an extremely intelligent man who taught social science at the school and often hid his intellectual abilities. He was the school basketball coach and had won a state championship several years ago. A confirmed bachelor for years, John had recently married a Latina woman and had a child. In his own way, Phillips challenged the old guard through his intellect, his ability to see two sides to a story, and through his marriage.

At the top of the list for the Latino students at JM was the need for a school soccer team. This was real proof, provided by a disinterested party who had found a need and desire for a team. But even with this data, the school would not budge.

I was angry. It all seemed so ridiculous. Why was a soccer team such a difficult idea to swallow at JM? Soon I began to hear rumors that the longtime football coach at the school, a man revered in the community, was opposed to a soccer program at JM. It seemed as though soccer threatened the old guard at the school, perhaps in the same way as the growing number of Latinos in town threatened the community.

But the situation changed over the summer. The school principal, Mr. Hamilton, retired and David Moody was hired to replace him. Moody had been the principal of a large school outside the county, which had a soccer team. That was good news; a team would not be an entirely new concept to him. I learned that Moody had been a football player himself and had a son who played ball for North Carolina State University. But I was still optimistic that a new perspective was needed and Moody would at least bring that.

David Moody was a large man. He stood over six feet tall and was solidly built. He was losing his light blond hair on top and he had a middle-age gut, but he cut a commanding presence. At times he seemed more drill sergeant than principal, but he was reasonable and would listen to a good argument. Moody quickly took control of the school. Where Hamilton seemed to let things go, Moody tightened the daily operations of the school right away. He had a vision of how JM should be managed, and he began implementing his plans the moment he slid in his nameplate.

I thought that Moody deserved a chance to start the process of debating a soccer team from scratch and I approached him openly about it. He said he would listen and we arranged a time to talk more.

In the interim, I started gathering other members of the Siler City community to help me secure sponsorship. One of the first people I tapped was Kathy Cockman, a parent and member of the JM Boosters Club. Cockman had been advocating for a soccer team for years. She helped me get in touch with the Optimist Club, which pledged to buy the goals. I then got promises from the local McDonald's for soccer balls, and uniforms from Dennis de St. Albans, a local businessman who had played in college. But we still needed a coach. I had always felt that a teacher would be the most appropriate person, and Cockman got me in touch with Chad Morgan, a physical education teacher at Chatham Middle School who had also started coaching soccer there. Morgan had coached in private club leagues in South Carolina and had experience. He was the perfect choice to head up the team when it was eventually created.

When I finally had a chance to talk with Moody over the summer, he quickly made it clear that creating a team would be problematic. He began by telling me that he had talked to folks about the team when it had come up before, but those plans had also fizzled out because there wasn't enough interest on the part of the students. He then gave me the same excuses that Hamilton had outlined—the lack of field space, the start-up costs, the lack of a practice field, the question of a playing field, and the grades and attendance of the Latino students that would render many of them ineligible to play.

"If they want to play, we'll give them the opportunity to play, but I didn't find that the need or interest justified us putting three thousand dollars out there," he said.

Listening to Moody, I suspected he had discussed the proposal with the football coach and come back with the same conclusion as Hamilton. But whereas Hamilton had been completely closed to the idea, Moody at least humored me and recommended that I compile yet another list of interested students.

Together with Cockman, Morgan, and a parent at Silk Hope Middle School (a feeder school for JM), I put together another list. But I made the mistake of including names of some kids who were attending Chatham Central High School. Some white parents at Silk Hope had been transferring their kids out of the JM district to Chatham Central, a predominantly white school located in the very rural, lower east part of the county. The transfers were blatant cases of white flight and the school board allowed them.

The list that I gave Moody had names of kids who had transferred to Chatham Central and might be interested in attending JM if soccer was a sport. There were only four names from Chatham Central out of a total of nineteen, but it allowed Moody the traction to jump on it as a reason for rejecting the list.

"That's illegal and that's recruiting and we're not going to recruit." He laid into me in his best sergeant voice.

Moody was right, of course, the team needed to come from JM and not from the school the white students had fled to. I realized I had inadvertently set the cause back. I would have to start all over again. I had been trying to develop some rapport with Moody, trying to figure him out and the best way to approach him. But I had stumbled; I was unaware of all the politics I would need to master. We couldn't afford any more mistakes.

I went back to the kids. I met with Enrique and Indio and we strategized about the list. I wrote down names and telephone numbers of kids who attended JM or were going to attend the next year so that Moody and Phillips could call the kids to ask if they were interested. I even offered to help translate during those calls, but Moody said that Phillips's wife spoke Spanish and they wouldn't need me. I waited to see while the administration checked on the new list.

But by the time school started we were still nowhere. That's when I learned that no one had called Enrique or Indio to ask whether they would be interested in a team. I checked with some of the other kids on the list and they hadn't gotten a call either. This was too much for me. I had tried to comply with the conditions that the school had set in order to start the team. Each time they had turned me away. The lists themselves had become an impediment to determining serious interest in the sport. The real problem was one of commitment. The school needed to commit to the kids first before the kids could commit to the team. If you build it, they will come, right? Well, the powers at JM felt they needed to come *before* they built it.

I talked with Moody again about the lists. He explained that over the summer, Phillips had had limited success in contacting the kids on the list—most likely because many Chatham Latinos didn't or couldn't keep their phones current. I should have predicted it, but Moody did offer a ray of hope. He said that there had been interest on the part of a number of girls who wanted to play soccer and that perhaps starting a girls' team now could lead to a boys' team in the future.

"We thought that with the sampling of phone calls that we made that we had much more interest in females playing than males," Moody told me to my surprise. None of my lists had any girls' names on it. My campaign had been focused on the boys. And then

Moody revealed the real reason why the school was suddenly interested in a girls' team. "To be honest about it, I got to look at Title IX, and it turns out I can't have a bunch of male sports and not have anything for the females."

I learned that the women's cross-country team at JM had folded the year before due to lack of interest. This left the sports program short one women's team, and adding a male team like soccer would present Title IX problems. Title IX was the Supreme Court ruling that public schools needed to have a balanced sports program for men and women. A women's soccer team would do two things; first it would solve the school's Title IX issue, and second, it would not threaten the football program.

I had no idea what level of interest there was at the school for a women's soccer team. I suspected that having a men's team contingent on a women's team was yet another obstacle. My experiences with Hamilton and the school had left me feeling distrustful.

I'd had enough. It was time for a different tactic, new allies, and real power to move the situation forward.

During the INS letter fiasco and the David Duke rally, I had gotten to know Gary Phillips, the new chief county commissioner. Phillips was a liberal Democrat in a blue-dog Democratic county—he was a supporter of many progressive issues like conservation and slow growth. He was a tall man with a wide chest and he sported a handlebar mustache that was a throwback to the eighteenth century. He was relatively young, in his late forties; he had grown up in western North Carolina and had good Southern credentials. That was important in local politics. It was nearly impossible to get elected unless you had been born in the county. He knew how Southerners thought, how the good ol' boy network was set up, and how best to use it.

I had been a big-city reporter for more than ten years and had covered everything from city and state to federal politics. I knew how things got done at the local level and I had learned many tricks from covering the Chicago political beat. In Chicago, real power was found only in the backroom dealings of aldermen or the mayor. If you needed something and you were a businessman in Chicago, you went to your alderman for a favor. He would ask for a favor in return, and if he got you what you wanted everyone was happy. It worked.

I needed a way or a person to cut through the obstacles at the school. I honestly believed that Moody was open to the idea but that he needed some way to explain it to the old guard who didn't want to budge.

So I talked to Gary Phillips about the problem. He just shook his head. He was appalled at how hard it was proving to be to put a high school soccer team together. Phillips was in. He would talk to Larry Mabe, the superintendent. He would ask for a favor. "He owes me," Phillips said. "I stuck by him during the latest school budget and he pretty much got what he wanted."

In September 2001, Phillips met with Mabe at the county school administration offices and they hammered out a deal. Mabe picked up the phone and dialed the number for Jordan-Matthews High School. He spoke to Moody. "Do everything you can to support soccer at JM. Do nothing to obstruct the formation of a soccer team at JM. This has nothing to do with football and we'll find the money to support the sport." Mabe then hung up and promised Phillips as long as there were kids interested in playing, he would see it through. And with that one phone call, JM finally got a soccer team. All the excuses, the lack of interest, the lack of a practice field or a place to play, the cost of the equipment, the eligibility excuses, the numerous lists—everything fell away and the program was given a green light.

The change in attitude had immediate and dramatic results. Moody was on board and he advocated for the team with his full authority. We set up a meeting between Moody, myself, Gary Phillips, Lex Alvord—a member of the Chatham Soccer League—and a parent. The meeting was direct, but the message was clear—there would be a soccer program at JM. "I stand at the same place I stood in the summer," Moody told us. "I want a viable program."

But Moody also wanted some concessions. He wanted to try a

women's team first. He would not allow a team to be formed this current year even though some of the boys were informally playing *cascaritas* or pickup games with a visiting international teacher from Chile named Ricardo. He wanted a teacher at the school to be the head coach, a requirement not imposed on other sports at the school like tennis and softball. We decided that Ricardo would be the coach and I would help out. Chad had been cut out. Ricardo loved the game but had never coached before and had no experience with American high school athletics.

The team would be set for next fall. As the meeting ended, Moody came over to me and in his best gruff commanding voice said he wanted me to commit to help. I looked at him. "I know I started this mess, and I know I have been a pain, but I will give you my word I won't walk away now. I will do everything I can to help out. That's a promise."

When I made that promise to Moody I knew I was getting myself into a situation that had the potential to get out of hand. I never wanted to coach a high school team. It was a lot of work and a big-time commitment. But I had pushed this through and I couldn't just walk away. Moody was right. I needed to make a commitment as much as the school needed to, a commitment as strong as the boys' desire to play. I felt the weight of that promise but it was a good feeling. It gave me purpose and provided me direction. No matter what would happen in the next few months or even years, I would be there for the *chavos,* for the boys.

Moody, Lex, and I went outside the school to check out the football field. Lex impressed upon Moody that many schools played on the football field. I suspected he wouldn't commit to allowing soccer on the football field until he had talked to the football coaches. I passed the fight to Moody, who would now have to wage the real battle to push the program through. He would have to take on the longtime coaches. But I had provided him the best ammunition possible. Moody could always say that orders for this new program were coming directly from the superintendent's office. I knew, politically speaking, that this would make it much easier.

As we stood on the football field discussing how we could play soccer there, Moody turned to me and said. "Paul, I know you think I am the enemy here, but I am not. I always wanted to have a soccer team here, but I want more than a team. I want a real program."

"I know you're not the enemy," I told him. "You've just got to understand we were blocked for a long time and I know the kids want to play."

We laughed. It was a nervous laugh, the kind between adversaries who now found themselves allies. We were just starting to communicate. Moody said he wanted me to support the Boosters Club and get them on board with the program. The air had cleared between us and I felt elated. The boys were finally going to play for their school. They would wear the school's colors and finally become Jets.

I t was a cold September afternoon as I walked onto the soccer field at Bray Park. A dozen Latino boys from JM were ready to begin the *cascarita* game with Ricardo. The field at the park had been so worn by the soccer games played by the Latino men from the chicken plants that it was little more than dirt and dust. The goals were pockmarked with rust and the nets had gaping holes in them. The field itself was slanted; you literally ran downhill. It had been a ridiculous idea that a high school team could play in this park.

I said hello to Ricardo and we shook hands. Slung over my back was a bag of old soccer balls that I had collected over the years coaching my club team. They were pretty beaten up and some had lost that familiar hexagonal cover, exposing the fuzzy peach skin of the balls. They would have to do. Ricardo had been playing *cascarita* with them after school for the past month. And while some of the boys loved the *cascarita,* it was not a real game against a real opponent. They were eager to take on a real team.

"Is it true that we're going to have a team next year?" asked Rogelio, a tall sad-faced boy with droopy eyelids and large ears.

"Yes, it's true," I told him.

The boys looked at one another with a passing flash of wonder. It was coming. They could feel it. They could feel it in their feet as they took the balls from the bag and started taking shots on the rusty goals. I took out my whistle and started the *cascarita*.

7

It was a hot August afternoon when we started the first day of practice in heat that bent the air, drained the water from your body, and weakened your legs. But the kids who showed up that first day of the new Jordan-Matthews soccer team didn't seem to mind. They were excited, thrilled, and happy that this day had finally arrived. There were more than thirty boys—all Latino except for two—on that first day. Any doubts about the interest level for the sport at the school were burned away in the brilliant rays of the Carolina sun.

We had gathered together on the baseball field and the boys sat cross-legged in front of the visitors' dugout. They represented all the grades and ages at the school and were dressed in worn shorts, torn T-shirts, and dusty mud-caked black cleats. They sat together and waited for Ricardo and me to officially open the practice and explain the rules and outline the upcoming season. They joked with one another, hit one another on the arm, cut farts and laughed about who did it, and called one another *guey,* pronounced "way," which meant guy or dude. *"Eh, guey." "No, guey." "Tú guey." "Órale guey."*

Across the field, beyond first base, sat the longtime baseball coach in the home team's dugout, his arms folded across his chest, his eyes fixed on us. Coach had reacted angrily when Moody told him that the soccer boys would be practicing on his pristine outfield during the off-season. Moody explained to Coach that everyone had to share facilities.

But Coach felt less than charitable about a team of boys tearing up his beloved outfield even if it was during the off-season. He treated his baseball grounds like a garden—showering it with love and affection. It was a field waiting for the boys of summer and not for the *chavos* of the fall. Now he sat there watching us like a scarecrow with a flock of crows in his field.

Many longtime residents in Siler City had been asking over the past several years how it had come to this. Now folks at the high school were asking it. Change had finally come to JM. There would be brown boys running on the fields. There would be brown boys who would be Jets.

Ricardo and I gathered the boys together in a semicircle to explain what was going to be expected of them during the season. Matt, a graduate student from UNC's school of public health who had been a goalkeeper at Dartmouth College, was also lending a hand.

"Let's talk about eligibility," I said.

We then explained the eligibility requirements and some of the boys dropped their heads. I knew we would lose several of them after today because of poor grades or lack of attendance. The state high school rules required student athletes to have passed three of four classes from the previous semester before they were eligible to play. All ninth graders were automatically eligible because they had not been in high school the year before. Students also had to have attended 85 percent of the required school days from the previous year. This usually translated into missing no more than fourteen days of school without an excuse. Some of the boys would be ineligible simply because they had missed too many days of school.

Chatham County Latino families frequently didn't understand how missing school could have serious consequences. Families would keep their kids home from school for birthdays, or take them to court to help with translation, or to work. Many students often missed their first class or perpetually arrived late because they had to take care of a younger brother or sister. Latinos didn't use day care, they used family.

"If you did not pass three of four classes you cannot play," Ricardo told the group. We asked the group who among them did not qualify and some raised their hands. They could stay today but they could not come tomorrow.

After the talk, we got up, formed a circle, and began stretching for the practice. Following the stretch, the boys were required to run four times around the entire baseball park to warm up.

"Why, Cuadros? And what about the *cascarita?*"

I told them that there was to be no *cascarita*. They needed to practice. We had two weeks to prepare for the opening game and there would be no time for play. This was to be a team, not some pickup game. I wanted to firmly establish this fact in their minds, to set the tone, to make sure they knew this was not going to be La Liga.

We were going to do some sprints and some plyometric exercises, drills that would strengthen their legs and prepare them for the games. The boys had no idea how intense high school soccer could be. Many had played *cascaritas* in Indio's backyard; some were even playing in La Liga. But none of those experiences could touch the high school game for intensity and emotion. It was a whole other level.

We had the boys stand in two lines. They were going to do straight forty-yard sprints to us. After several sprints, they were going to sprint with their hands in front of them, lifting their thighs high enough to slap their hands. Then they were going to hold their arms and hands behind them and sprint-kick their heels high enough to slap their hands on their backsides. We would do these exercises over and over again and then move on to some basic defensive drills.

The first pair to line up were Lobo and a kid everyone called Borracho, because he had gotten drunk on Coronas at a party. Lobo was a strong, sensitive kid with a solid muscular frame and was easily one of the fittest kids on the field. He was a sophomore but should have been a junior. A lot of the immigrants were behind a grade or so because of their limited English proficiency.

Enrique lined up against Oso, a senior and the tallest and biggest kid on the field. Oso had spent the previous year playing for Chatham Central before learning that JM was going to have a soccer team. He transferred back to JM to play. His family was from Honduras and he was a bright kid—ambitious, mature, with a plan to become a dentist one day. He stood about six four and was a bit overweight. He had soft curly dark hair and his skin was coffee-bean black.

The guys had taken to calling Enrique La Mosca, or "the Fly," because of the black athletic glasses he wore when he played. They were an old pair of mine that I had used in high school when I played. Enrique had borrowed them.

Edi lined up next to Loco, a frolicking and intense freshman I had coached on my mixed club team for the past year. Loco had quickness and speed. He could burn people on the field with his fast footwork and dashing runs. But he could never sit still. He was always juggling a ball, kicking it, shooting it, during our talks. I could be telling Loco something and he would be juggling a ball and saying, "Watcha, Cuadros, watcha," and then send the ball flying twenty yards toward the goal. Great, but we were talking about *possessing* the ball.

Pee Wee and Caballo lined up next. Pee Wee was originally from L.A., a skateboarder who had played soccer at his school. His family had moved to Siler City to get away from the gangs and all the violence. His father was Puerto Rican and his mother El Salvadoran. Pee Wee was one of the most assimilated players on the team. He was into rap, had black friends and Latino friends, and could easily cross the line between the various groups at the school. He was also a talented midfielder, a player who could control the ball on the dribble, penetrate, and set up plays.

Caballo was a stud. He was eighteen but only a sophomore. The players called him "Horse" for a couple of reasons. He ran incredibly fast, was quick on the turn, and had a grace about him when he played that was visibly equine. They also called him Horse because his face was long and flat and his eyes were wide and thin. He could make streaking runs with the ball at his feet and then finish the run by shooting on goal, beating the keeper. He was a thoroughbred, a racehorse with a soccer ball.

Indio and Fish stood together, jostling each other at the line before I blew the whistle to let them run. Indio had crossed the border by himself when he was just eleven years old. A freshman, and determined to win, he fought hard during every game and would never get used to losing at *anything*. He wanted to win all the time. It made him a great younger player, perhaps the one with the most potential for doing something with his game beyond high school.

Fish had skills far above most of the players who showed up that day. He was an extremely talented goalkeeper even though he was just a sophomore. Fish had started playing with his younger brother, Guero, in the makeshift field Indio's father had built next to the cemetery in the family's backyard. Indio and his younger brother, Perico, would take on Fish and Guero and play all day long and well into the night. But during those *cascaritas,* Fish would find himself in the goal, perennially stopping the shots of the other kids. He loved being in the spotlight and making fantastic saves. He learned to throw his body in the air and swat flying balls away with one hand. He had the agility of a cat and refused to panic when someone was charging at him. With Fish, we would be a contending team immediately.

Next up were La Pepa and Fidel, both freshmen and inseparable. They hung out together every day, wasting time and playing ball. Pepa was tall and thin and his name meant "cucumber" in Spanish. He had played on one of my club teams and was eager, had some talent, but was not focused and lacked discipline. Fidel was the same but unfortunately lacked obvious talent on the field. The kids took to calling him El Robot because he swung his arms from side to side when he ran instead of pumping them up and down.

Bringing up the rear were Bomba and Lechero. Bomba was a quiet kid, originally from El Salvador, whose family had emigrated to escape the horrors of civil war. He was a freshman and a solid player. Lechero was a sophomore. He played tough defense and wouldn't let anyone get past him. He had a slight build, was skinny, but was also sinewy and strong.

We put the boys through the warm-up drills and then switched to drills that would show us what they could do when it came to one-on-one defense. I set up two lanes, one for Ricardo to monitor and the other for me. The boys lined up on either end of the lanes with one player having the ball. The exercise started when the kid with the ball passed it to the other player at the end of the lane. That player would then attack and try to dribble the ball across the other player's line, trying to get around him. It was a good exercise to see how well someone attacked offensively and how well someone defended. When the boys went through it a couple of times, I stopped them and explained what they needed to do to prevent attackers from beating them on the dribble.

"Okay, there are four defensive points you need to learn," I started. "First, you have to close the space between you and the person with the ball. Pressure him. That means sprinting to them, don't wait for them to come to you. Second, don't overcommit on the attack. Don't just jump in and allow him to beat you. Third, attack him on an angle and try to get him to go down the lane, show him the outside, and use the sideline as another defender. Fourth, be patient. Stay with him and delay him so that your teammates can come and help you out."

When we had gone through that exercise and the guys had gotten the principles down, we changed the exercise to include two defenders against one attacker. The principles were the same except the role of the second defender was to provide cover for the first defender at an angle in case he got beat.

The guys tried the drill, but every time they did it they went back to their old *cascarita* habit of everyone jumping in, committing early, and attacking. They never supported one another. The ball drew them in like a magnet. They needed to learn discipline, to play a role, and have confidence while playing the game the right way.

Lechero had not supported his defensive partner, Pee Wee, and had gone in when Pee Wee had on Caballo. Because Lechero came in with Pee Wee, it made it easy for Caballo to beat them both at the same time with a swift move.

"Lechero, *mira*. Look. You have to support Pee Wee. If he gets beat, you are the last defender. If you go in with him, you both get beat and there is no one back. You have to be patient, stay back, not too far, at an angle, and if Caballo beats Pee Wee, then you go in, pressure him, don't commit, push him toward a side, and wait to steal the ball."

"Cuadros, and if he beats me, what then?" he asked, not convinced of the strategy.

"*Pues,* Pee Wee has to get back and support you, and if he gets beat you have to run back to support him. You have to have support always."

They tried it again, and this time Caballo again beat Pee Wee, but Lechero hung back, waiting, and when Caballo went around Pee Wee, Lechero closed the gap, quickly applied pressure on Caballo, and took the ball away along the sideline. When the guys had seen that the system worked against Caballo, they began to buy into and apply it.

We then switched the exercise to include two attackers and two defenders but the principles were the same. After working on defensive drills and teaching them the fundamentals of defensive play, we changed the exercise to include taking some shots. The practice had to be fun for them.

We had about a half hour left of practice and we opened it up for the *cascarita*. The boys split into two teams, with one side wearing yellow pinnies, or scrimmage vests, that I had brought. Ricardo and I each sided with a team to play with the boys. But even as I ran and played with them, making my own moves on them and running to receive the ball, I also watched to see who could play the game. Many times you had players who could have great practices, but when it came time to play, they were no good.

The boys would have kept on playing all night if we had let

them, but Ricardo and I had to get home. Indio and Lechero needed a ride, they lived on the same road and so they piled into my car with their book bags and clothes. As we drove, I asked the guys how they thought it went. Indio was used to my practices; he knew what to expect and had been schooled in the principles of defense. But it was all new to Lechero.

"It was good, Cuadros," Lechero said. "It should have been harder. We need to run more." Lechero was one of seven children in his family. He had dark chocolate-colored skin with a triangular-shaped face, large eyes, and a broad nose. You could see the indigenous features in him.

"What about the principles of defense?" I asked.

He smiled at me. He had learned something about soccer today, probably the first time he had actually been taught something strategic about the game. *"Sí, estaba bien,"* he said, and smiled. I could see Indio smiling in the back in the rearview mirror.

The second day of practice saw only sixteen players arrive. Several had not been eligible to play on the team and had dropped out. Others had found the first practice too hard, too uncomfortably hot in the sun, and stayed home. Others didn't like the regimental form of practice and only wanted to play *cascarita*. Many couldn't come because they worked after school.

Work was very important to these kids. Most had jobs or were looking for them. Work defined who they were. If you had a job you were somebody, you were not lazy. For these Latino families, work was so important it took a backseat to almost everything in the family. It didn't matter what kind of work you were doing as long as you were working and making money. Some Latino kids had no choice, they had to find a job to help pay the bills at home. Latino families expected their children to help pay for the household expenses once they got older. Many families rationalized that if their children were in Mexico and were sixteen, they would already have been done with school and out there working. Some took jobs in home construction, fast-food restaurants, garages, whatever could be found. Some even worked at the chicken plant on second shift at night, using false IDs because they were under eighteen.

The work issue was a definite impediment to the team. Some could not make it because of their jobs. I asked them to shift their schedules for the season and many did. Others could not or would not. The bottom-line requirement was that they needed to be at practice at least three days during the week.

After two weeks of hard practices that focused on teamwork, Ricardo and I ended practice without the usual *cascarita* the boys loved so much. We gathered them together in a circle and talked about the next week. We were starting the season in earnest that week with a home game against our county conference rivals, Chatham Central.

Now I left Ricardo with the boys, went to my car, and brought back two large boxes. I dumped them down in the middle of the boys. It was time. The boys needed to play in uniforms and I had ordered some at a discount with the Chatham Soccer League, of which I was a board member. A local businessman paid for them.

When I opened the box, it was like the ground had transmitted an electrical shock to the boys' feet. They jumped up and crowded around. I shoved them away and told them that seniors would get the chance to pick first, followed by juniors, sophomores, and freshmen last. The *chavos* grumbled, but it seemed the only fair way to hand them out. We called the seniors to the box first and the boys stepped up and picked out a uniform. There were two sets of uniforms, for home and away games, and the numbers needed to match. The home uniforms were white with royal-blue sleeves and gold piping. The shorts were royal blue and the socks white with blue stripes. The away uniforms were royal-blue jerseys with gold piping, gold shorts, and blue socks. On the chest of each of the uniforms was the word JETS. The boys immediately put on their jerseys, laughing and touching the silky fabric. It was the first time they had ever worn JETS on their chests. They were giddy with joy.

"Está chido, Cuadros," Loco said when he got his jerseys. "It's cool, Cuadros."

Hearing Loco say that and watching the boys don their jerseys made me think of all the effort it had taken to reach this day. It was the first time that Latino boys at JM finally felt like a part of their school, like they belonged, and that they had a chance to bring honor to their school and community. They were no longer on the sidelines watching teams compete as Jets. They were now Jets themselves and they were eager and excited about their first game.

It was only Oso, a senior, who recognized the significance of the moment and the work that had gone into it. He came up to me, towering over me in his white jersey, and softly said, *"Gracias, Cuadros."* He wrapped his big arms around me. Oso had the maturity to see what an important moment this was at the school. Last year he was playing for Chatham Central because they had started a soccer program the year before and he wanted to play. He had transferred specifically to play on their team but had always wanted to play for JM. When he heard we were going to have a team, he rescinded his transfer and came back to be a Jet. He wore the jersey now with dignified pride.

As the boys pulled the white-and-blue jerseys over their heads, I gathered them together. I tried to say something to capture the moment.

"You are the first," I started. "Remember that you are getting the chance that many other Latinos at this school wanted but never got. You are the ones who are making history today. You are the first *Latino* Jets."

The boys stopped for a moment and turned to me.

"There were some who never wanted to see this day but here it is. There were some who didn't want you to wear those colors, but here you are in blue and white. There were some who didn't believe you could make the grades, or stay in school, or behave as a team. But here you are. Now you have to prove to everybody that you can win because that's what they want to see, that's what you know you can do. Win. Now we'll see if you have the will. The *ganas*."

"*Sí, Cuadros, sí,*" they said. "*Yamos a echarle ganas.* We're going to try hard."

I thought about that word—*ganas*—for a moment and all that it meant. The word not only asked the speaker to try to give everything from his heart, but it asked what his heart was really made of. And that remained to be seen.

The following week we started the first game of our conference season. We were in the Yadkin Valley Conference, which consisted of nine teams scattered over three counties in the middle of the state. Many of the schools in the conference were located out in the country, tucked away in fields, or on the outskirts of small towns dominated by a single industry or two.

Our first game would be against our county rivals, the Chatham Central Bears. They were located in a little community called Bear Creek in the lower west corner of the county and were known as the rural school. Kids at Chatham Central saw the kids at JM as being from the big city, with big-city problems and troubles. I marveled at their perspective. Remember, Siler City had a population of only seven thousand.

There was a lot that had to be done to prepare for our first home game. The goals had been set up and were ready. The Optimist Club had donated them at a cost of more than $2,000, a generous gift to the formation of the team. They were regulation size, eight feet tall by twenty-four feet wide, white with square posts. The nets were also white. I had borrowed corner flags from the Chatham Soccer League because I hadn't found anyone to donate them yet. The program was up and running without any start-up costs absorbed by the school. I had handed the administrators the program ready-made and I knew the Boosters Club appreciated that. The Boosters supported most of the teams at the school through concession stands at the football and basketball games. I hadn't gone to them that first year asking for a lot of things. Instead, I had gone into the community to find donors and supporters for the program.

But before we could actually play at home, the football field needed to be lined for a soccer game. The high school rules called for a color other than white, which was used by the football team. I used blue paint supplied by the school. I borrowed a field paint machine from the soccer league and went out to the field the day before our game to line it.

It was a beautiful Sunday afternoon as I walked onto the field to lay down the lines. The deep green Bermuda grass was spongy to the touch. The football program had not lined the field yet and the entire field was bare, a green carpet. The soccer parameters would be longer and wider than the football field. We had made it as large as we could fit inside the track. While we had good length, the width was narrow. This was not uncommon for schools that employed their football field as their soccer field. The state rules allowed for it. I chuckled at the thought of JM's ex-principal Hamilton telling me that we couldn't play here because it wasn't a regulation-size field.

The field had a tall crown in the center to help drain it when it rained. Many football fields were designed this way to help rainwater flow to the sidelines and keep the center from becoming too soggy. If you stood on one corner of the field you had trouble seeing to the other corner across the crown. I wondered how this would affect passing and realized it was something we would have to get used to.

I took my shoes and socks off to begin lining the field. The blue paint from the can would get on my shoes, so I went barefoot. The grass felt cool on my feet, soft and rubbery. I started in the corner and went down the back end line where the goal would be placed following the string I had laid down. With the back line done, I moved on to the large penalty box, which was the most important part of a soccer field. It extended eighteen yards from the back line.

I enjoyed marking the field. It was relaxing work and allowed me to concentrate on the upcoming game, let my mind wander. My thoughts ran down the field, following the lines I left behind, and I stopped the machine at about the fifty-yard line. I looked over my work and wondered what those blue lines really meant for us. I was tracing over Siler City's traditional lines. The blue lines were new and different. Some of them were inside the football field and some would stick out beyond it. We all had our own ideas about what was in bounds and what was out-of-bounds. Siler City was adjusting to new boundaries.

It took me four hours to paint the field. When I finally finished, my fingertips were royal blue from the paint. I left the field marked and ready for our first game.

The next day I learned that some people had been shocked and confused when they noticed the blue lines on the football field. They didn't understand what they were for and complained that someone had messed up the field.

The game against Chatham Central started tentatively as the Jets got used to their positions and playing together in a real game, for the first time. Fish was in goal. On defense we had Bomba, the freshman from El Salvador on the left wing, and Dominic, a German exchange student Moody had brought to practice. Dominic was built like an engine block. He intimidated attackers with his size and speed. Oso took center and we hoped that with his height he would be able to block any balls sent over the midfielders' heads. Edi played sweeper, and with his speed and fearlessness we knew he could cut down any attack that slipped through the defensive line. In the midfield was Chuy, a lanky senior who was bright but always getting into trouble. On right wing was Chuy's brother Loco with his frenetic energy. Anchoring us in the middle and controlling the game was Pee Wee. Up front on the attack were Lobo, Indio, the talented freshman in the middle, and Caballo on right wing.

Chatham Central came into JM confident that they could handle the fledgling team. We were greenhorns after all. The boys were excited and eager to play. When it was time to start the game, we huddled together and started our cheer. We began it in our stomachs, a low growl that rose up through our lungs into our throats until at last we let it burst forth. "One, two, three, let's go, Jets!"

The game was on. Almost from the first whistle of the game, the

Jets took control of the ball and never it let it go. Within a few short minutes, Caballo had scored the first goal for the Jets and put Chatham Central down 1–0. By halftime, he had scored three goals and the Jets' rout was on. With a commanding lead, Ricardo and I emptied the bench and let everyone get a chance to play.

When the referee blew the final whistle, the game ended with the Jets posting their first-ever win, 5–0. I thought that if all the games were going to be this easy we would win the conference championship. It had been a great night. The team had won its first conference game in dramatic fashion and sent a signal that we were going to be contenders for the title.

The next morning I got a call from Moody. I was surprised he was calling me at my office.

"Paul, we got a problem," he said. My thoughts raced wildly as I wondered what had happened. I knew he was referring to the game, but what could it be to warrant a call from Moody?

"Okay." I waited for Moody to tell me what had happened.

"Did you play a student named Juan?" His voice was extra gruff now and accusatory. I didn't know if we had or not. Juan was on the team. He was an older kid, should have been a senior, but was a sophomore. He was known to be a troublemaker. I would have to check my notes to see if he had played or not. I didn't want to answer if I didn't know the actual truth.

"He's on the team, but I would have to check my notes if he played last night."

"Well, if he played we might have to forfeit last night's game," Moody said with all the weight of a hammer hitting me between the shoulder blades. "He's ineligible."

Ineligible? I thought. How could that be? We had asked the kids. I realized then that we had trusted them too much. We had won our first game. The local newspaper had been there and taken pictures. Now we would have to take it all back and be disgraced. My mind was on fire. I could just hear the people who had stood in the way of the soccer team chortling, "See, those Hispanics . . ." Juan's ineligibility would not only erase the win and negate the positive signals we were trying to send to the conference, it also put the program in jeopardy. We would not be known as winners now but as cheaters, a team that needed to win with ringers, a team without honor. I remembered the story about the Baby Bronx Bombers, the Little League team of Hispanic kids that had won a championship only to be stripped of their title when it was revealed that their star pitcher had lied about his age. I told Moody that I would have to check with Ricardo and verify if Juan had played or not.

I immediately contacted Ricardo, figuring Moody had already talked to him. Moody was looking for verification not information. After reaching Ricardo and going over our notes, we found that Juan, while on the team, had not shown up to play that night and had instead gone to work. The very thing that we had asked the kids to try to avoid had saved us. Ricardo and I breathed a sigh of relief.

Moody came down hard on us and demanded that we check all the names on our roster for eligibility and show him the list before games. He had put his reputation and the school's on the line and he wanted to make sure there were no more slipups. I came into the school's offices and met with John Phillips and we went over each kids' grades and attendance. Moody was satisfied but still angry. He didn't like sloppiness and I didn't blame him. The program was in the spotlight too much for rookie mistakes.

That afternoon at practice Ricardo and I took Juan aside and asked him about his eligibility and he lied right to our faces, saying he was eligible. Ricardo and I just looked at each other. A kid like Juan felt isolated and alienated. He wanted to be a part of something and had tried out. But his dishonesty had almost killed the team and I let him know it.

"Hey, Juan, don't you see what you've done?" I lit into him. "You've placed the entire team in danger. We might have had to forfeit the game. It would have been a disgrace. We asked you guys to be straight with us and you weren't. Why? *¿Por qué, hombre?*"

He looked at me from the corners of his eyes and then looked back down to the practice field. "I just wanted to play," he said. His response caught me off guard. It was such a natural reaction. The kids just wanted to play. What kid didn't? He didn't care about eligibility rules, they didn't mean anything to him. In Mexico the schools didn't have teams. There were no uniforms or rules. You just played. But the boys were not in Mexico.

So much of their lives had already been spent getting around rules, being informal, bending the law. Many of them owed their presence in North Carolina to deceit. Their parents worked with *chuecos,* fake documents they paid handsomely for, sometimes just to get a job at the chicken plant. They lived in two different worlds with two different identities. I had met workers who had wept because all their achievements at work, their employee-of-the-month awards, their recognition for a job well done, medals, and plaques, were all in someone else's name. Sometimes they didn't know who they really were. When one identity no longer was useful they would save enough money to buy a new one and work under that new identity. If they were resourceful enough they would pay $3,000 for a really good *chueco,* not just a made-up name and Social Security number, but a real identity that someone had sold them, one that would last for years. But in the end, most of the fake names were discovered. There were some people I had met and known for years under one name only to suddenly to be asked to call them by their real name when they were found out.

And though this was the world the kids had grown up in, we had to tell Juan that he was off the team. Amazingly, he asked if there was anything that I could do to help him stay on the team. I told him it was impossible.

I needed them all to learn that there was a right way to do things and a wrong way. I wanted the team to live in an environment that was honest and up-front. The team was here to help its members in more ways that just winning games. The boys needed to know there was one place where things were absolute. They knew instantly where they stood on the team. They were either eligible or not. No in between. They had to make the grades and stay in school or they couldn't play. There would be no compromises, no deals, no informality about these rules. They needed to learn that the things they wanted in life came at a price. There would be no *chuecos* on this team.

8

Outside the bus window, the country rolled past rows of green-and-brown tobacco fields, the leaves popping out of the earth like open hands reaching for the sun. Acres of Golden Leaf blurred past us. It was the peak of the growing season and the heavy floppy leaves would soon be harvested and hung to dry in rickety wooden sheds that dotted the country. African-Americans had once been the primary labor force for tobacco, but over the past several decades they'd been replaced by Mexican migrant labor. Some of the fathers and mothers of the boys on the bus had once worked in the chest-high fields of leaves.

They endured hot days and long hours and suffered from the effects of pesticides and green tobacco sickness, a debilitating illness that left workers nauseated and dizzy. Workers contracted the illness from working in the fields early in the morning when the big leaves were wet and the nicotine in the water mixed with the sweat of the worker, collecting in the worker's clothes. The mixture entered the bloodstream through the skin and the worker got sick. In 2000, Wake Forest University's school of medicine, department of public health sciences, conducted a survey of 144 Hispanic migrant farmworkers and green tobacco sickness. They found that 41 percent reported having contracted the illness at least once during the summer. Most had taken no precautions against the wet leaves. The long-term effects are still unknown.

The South Stanly High School football stadium was built like so many other stadiums at small 1A schools. The main home cheering section was made of concrete, with a concession stand up top and a press box for the local paper and radio station. Painted in bright bold red and gray was the school's mascot: the Rebels. The school's mascot was the scarlet-and-gray-uniformed Confederate soldiers of the Civil War.

During that bloody war, Stanly County had sent six companies to fight for the rebel cause, in all more than seven hundred boys. They were among the brave men who made the Pickett-Pettigrew Charge at Gettysburg, where an estimated 54 percent of the 12,500 Southerners were killed or wounded.

It seemed Norwood, where the school was located, was still taking a rebel stand. Only now the young men wore the scarlet and gray for their school. In 2005, South Stanly changed its mascot from the Rebels to the Rebel Bulls.

The first half of the game against the Rebels went well. We dominated them on the field, scoring three goals by halftime. When the boys came over to the sideline at the half they complained that white players had been taunting them, saying things like "Stupid Mexicans," or "Go back to Mexico," and the usual "Bunch of wetbacks."

Enrique was visibly angry at the name-calling. I had already encountered it on my club team. "You are going to face this in life," I said, looking at them moving around the circle. Many of them were as angry as Enrique. Others were on the verge of tears. "I know what it is like. But you can't let it stop you."

I told them there were things they could do to fight back. "They call you a name. Score a goal. They say something bad. Score a goal. Do not hit them. That's what they want. They want to provoke you."

The boys went back onto the field and ignored the name-calling. We won the game easily, 5–1 tallying twenty one shots on goal. The defense pulled together and shut them out in the second half.

But this would not be the only time we would face harsh language. The situation got even worse when we traveled to South Davidson and faced the Wildcats. There, not only were the players mean and nasty, but their fans were too. They yelled terrible things from the stands to the players on the field. "Go back to Mexico!" and "We're going to call the INS!" and my personal favorite, "Hey, give that kid a green card, not a yellow card." It was one thing for the boys to pour it on against a nasty team; they could control that. They could do something about that on the field. It was another thing to hear it from parents and students. We beat them, 5–0, the first time we played them. And beat them 9–0 the second time.

The first half of the season had been a tremendous success. We stood with an impressive 9–1 record, losing only to the top team in the conference, the Albemarle Bulldogs. They had dominated the conference for the past five years, not losing a single game during that run.

But we started out the second half of the season in a slump. It took a last-minute goal from Oso, our giant defender who had once attended Chatham Central, to beat the Bears. Oso had scored from almost midfield, sending a hard low shot that squirted by everyone to find the back of the net. The next three games saw equally close scores against teams that we should have trounced. We held a team meeting to discuss what needed to be done in the second round of games to continue our winning streak.

It worked. After the team meeting, we returned to old form, beating South Stanly, 5–2, and West Davidson, 6–2. But we let Albemarle slip away. They beat us, 2–0. We had put up a good fight, but their organization crushed us. Despite the loss, we were second in the conference and the school was impressed that the program was proving to be so successful in its first year.

And so we entered into the last game of the season against East Montgomery with a record of 13–2, having lost only twice to one good team. The game against East Montgomery was going to be hard fought. We had just barely beaten them at home, 2–1, in the first half of the season. They were a tough, fast, skilled team. And like us, they were predominantly Latino. They were our mirror image in many ways, but in other ways they were very different.

There were a total of four teams in our conference that were predominantly Latino, including the Jets. We composed what I called the "chicken-bone circuit." These schools were all located in poultry-processing towns and had all seen the same migration influx as Siler City.

East Montgomery was located in Biscoe, a small town located only five miles from Candor, which is home to Perdue Farms and Mountaire Farms. Robbins, home to North Moore High School, the high school of former North Carolina senator John Edwards, also had a Perdue processing plant. The fourth school was Thomasville, known for Thomasville Furniture Industries and other manufacturing companies. Many Latinos had found work in furniture manufacturing and textiles.

These four teams were all relatively new, but the Jets were the newest addition to the conference. We brought a faster-paced game, a pressing attack, passion, and excitement. Our fans shouted out things like *"¡Muy bien, muchachos, muy bien!"* or "Very good, boys, very good!" Fans brought horns and drums and other noisemakers to games, as they would have done in their home countries. But we were different from the other three teams. While the other Latino teams had been around a little longer, they had not made a dent in the conference. And they faded quickly in the play-offs.

I could see that many of these teams were still playing the *cascarita*, and employing the style of game found in the lower divisions of La Liga. They were not organized well, the players were selfish, and they lacked real team unity and discipline. They had a tendency to throw cheap fouls, slide tackles from behind, elbows whipped high, and played all up through the middle. The boys on my club team had started this way. But over time and with training, we had worked our way out of this destructive and predictable style.

We were trying to do something different at JM. We wanted the boys to play together as a team. And while Ricardo and I didn't have a lot of time to train them, we were the best organized of the predominantly Latino teams.

East Montgomery had good players, including one central midfielder named Bocho, who was fast, strong, and talented. We had beaten them in overtime when Caballo got loose down the right wing and went in to hit the game-winning shot and goal. But it had been a hard-fought, even match that could have gone either way. Now we were going to play them at their stadium in the last regular match of the season.

Enrique and Edi's mother, Dolores, often waited a few weeks before driving to one of the laundromats in Siler City and washing all of her laundry at once. The laundromats were the meeting places for Latinas in town. None of the families owned their own washers or dryers, so they relied almost exclusively on the coin-operated machines. Sometimes, to save money, Dolores would wash the clothes at the laundromat, squeeze the extra water out of them, wringing each shirt or pair of pants out with her strong hands, then pack them trunk of her car and hang them out to dry back at the house. She had round forearms that were solid muscle. Her two daughters would be brought along to help her and they would complain, rightfully so, that the boys often got off the hook when it came to the housework.

Dolores was a Mexican woman, and even though it wasn't fair, she treated the girls differently from the boys. But she always told them, "I love you all the same. You are all like the five fingers on my hand. I could not love one finger more than the other." One morning, she went to the laundromat with a light load. Enrique and Edi had played two nights before and she wanted them to have clean uniforms for tonight's final regular game of the season. She planned to follow the bus with the girls and watch the team play.

She was pulling a second load of clothes from the backseat of the gold Chevy Impala that day when she felt the heavy, round, and cold edges of smooth metal jab into her left temple just below her black hair. She knew instantly what was resting against her skin. It was like a yellow jacket landing on your face. She instinctively tried to turn her head to see the direction it was coming from, but the barrel of the gun rammed against her head and then forced her eyes to turn to the backseat of the Chevy.

Her thoughts flew immediately to her children. Who would take care of them? A voice told her to give the man with the gun her money. She reached into her pocket and pulled out a plastic bag of coins she had brought for the washing machines. She heard the coins jangle as the man took them. Then the man reached into the front and pulled the car stereo out. Enrique had bought it with money he'd earned working late nights at a Pizza Hut. Around her, the traffic along Highway 64 continued to buzz past. Nobody noticed that Dolores was being robbed. She now saw that the man was black, in his thirties, and was wearing a blue shirt. He put the gun back to her head and Dolores looked at the backseat floor, saying, "Okay, okay, iz all okay," in her best English. All she heard was "Shut up" and the man fled behind the laundromat and disappeared. Dolores stood there for a moment shaking and then got in the car and drove home. At a stoplight she burst into tears, shaking her head, asking God why bad things always seemed to happen to her.

When Latinos had begun to move to the Southeast, they quickly found themselves the target of robberies, home invasions, and other crimes. The word spread fast that Latinos didn't use banks, they couldn't open accounts because they didn't have the right papers, and many didn't even know how banks operated. Instead, they relied on check-cashing stores, gas stations, grocery stores, and other places to cash their paychecks. Many were robbed on the way home. Others had their doors kicked in and their trailers or apartments ransacked by thugs looking for a stash. They knew these Latinos saved all their money in cash.

In Durham, a gang of thugs terrorized an apartment complex, breaking down doors, raping women, and stealing the life savings of the Latino families who lived there. It got so bad, local Latino advocates created a credit union for workers and their families to safely deposit their money. The ringleader of the gang was eventually caught and convicted. But a few years later, he was released on appeal because the prosecution could no longer find the witnesses who had previously testified against him.

On the day she was robbed, there was nothing Dolores could do. The man would never be caught. She didn't care. What left her shaking, exhausted, was the thought that her children could be left alone. There was no one who would take care of them if she had died today. Dolores had fought all her adult life for her children. She had found all kinds of ways to feed them when they didn't have any money. They had survived on table salt alone one day in Mexico because there wasn't any food. She always found a way to solve their problems, to get around their poverty and keep them healthy and happy. But now she thought, what would they do without her? She couldn't bear it. She drew her hand up to her left temple and let her finger trace the edges of the red ring where the gun had been. It was the first thing that Enrique saw when he came home from school and found her asleep in bed.

It had rained the night before and the East Montgomery football field was a muddy mess. The white eagle painted on the fifty-yard line looked like a fossilized pterodactyl frozen in the muck. The whole middle of the field was a mud bowl. When the boys took the field their cleats stuck in the deep pockets of soggy earth. It would affect the game. They needed to keep their balance and control the ball more closely to their bodies. During our warm-ups, I told the boys to line up at the far end of the field. Then we walked down to the opposite end, checking out and getting to know the soggy and slippery field.

Enrique did not come to the game and I was worried about him. Edi didn't want to tell me what had happened at first; I teased the story out of him and learned that Enrique had stayed home to be with his mother. I told Edi his mother was going to be fine. But he was angry.

"If I ever find him, Paul, I'll kill him," he said, the tears his eyes drying up quickly.

I knew that Edi meant it. He was a sweet kid, but the family had been through such tough times, they had become fiercely protective of one another. That's why he needed soccer so much. He needed to get out his aggression on the field or else he risked finding another way to release it.

The game started the way the last game against the Eagles had ended; with both teams attacking and going at each other. But mid-way through the first half, we began to dominate and control the ball. Caballo slipped through on the right wing and went straight toward goal. He fired a ripping shot that was too strong and too fast for the Eagles' keeper, who tried to block it but let it slip through his outreached arms. The goal lifted the team, infused them with confidence. From that point on, the Jets were on fire and the game was ours.

Loco stole a ball, quickly sprinted up the left side of the field, and sent a shot toward the goal. The keeper was ready this time and deflected the ball. But Lobo, our left forward, got the rebound and slipped it past the keeper to put us up two to nil. The Jets scored a third goal when Chuy sent a lofted pass across the field to Caballo, who calmly headed the ball in. The game was effectively over. At the half, we held a commanding lead of 3–0. The Jets tagged another goal in the last minute when the Eagles let Loco slip through and fire a rocket shot to the upper right corner of the net.

With the game over, the boys celebrated their 14–2 record by throwing themselves into the mud and sliding on the ground. They laughed and cheered and piled on top of one of one another as they played *la bolita*. Then they looked for Ricardo, Matt, and me and smeared mud on our faces and heads. We had finished the season strong, with eight straight wins and three consecutive shutouts. We were prepared for the play-offs. But even as we celebrated and I tried to outrun the guys intent on bathing me in mud, my thoughts drifted back to Enrique. Celebrating without him there left me feeling a bit empty. I wanted to get back to Siler City quickly and see how he was doing.

It was almost midnight by the time Edi and I pulled up to his white house on the outskirts of town. Edi got his book bags out of the trunk of my car and we went into the house. I didn't know what to expect but hoped that Enrique was awake. I just wanted to make sure he was okay. I knew Dolores would be; she was a strong woman. But Enrique was a sensitive kid, the classic parentified child, the boy who was forced to grow up early and had always felt the weight of the world on his shoulders. We went inside and found him sitting at the round kitchen table in a white T-shirt and jeans. I asked Edi to let me talk to him alone for a minute. When I sat down next to him I kept my eyes off the black-and-brown shotgun on the table. Best not to acknowledge that right away. I started by asking what was up. Enrique wouldn't look up from the table. It was hard for him to get the words out. I asked again. "What's up, Enrique?"

"Nothing" was all he said.

I persisted. I wanted him to tell me what happened. It would help if he could verbalize it. Enrique wasn't like Edi. He had trouble expressing his feelings. Edi lived in the moment. He could be sad one moment and then happy the next, as if the bad feelings had never existed. Enrique brooded. We talked about the game and I told him what had happened, how we dominated them, how the guys threw themselves and slid across the muddy field, and how they tried to smear mud on me. He laughed, imagining the scene. That loosened him up a bit. Then he started talking about what happened to his mom. He apologized for not coming to the game but said he needed to stay home with her.

"Listen, man, you did the right thing," I said. "Don't worry about the game. We won it. You'll be there for the play-offs. Your mom needed you tonight and you were there. And that was more important than any game. How's she doing?"

He nodded. "She's doing okay. She's sleeping. She's been sleeping all afternoon and night," he said, obviously worried.

"She'll be okay. Sleep is good for her after what she's been through. I'll talk to her tomorrow." Enrique was her son, but Dolores couldn't tell him everything. He was still just a kid; I knew she wouldn't unburden herself to him. Enrique leaned back and let out a huge yawn. He was exhausted with worry and emotion. A heavy weight had been lifted from him. He was starting to crash. He would sleep now.

"Hey, man, you know I got to take that gun with me now," I said, slipping the words in as I got up. It caught him off guard. He didn't want to let his gun go. "I can't leave here without it. I'll give it back in a couple of days, but I got to take it now."

"You're going to take my gun, Coach?"

"Yeah, can't leave here without it."

He was upset and thinking dark thoughts and then he let it all go. "I just want to kill him, Paul. I want to go out there and find him and shoot him. I don't know where he is, but I could find him. The police won't do anything. I just want to do something, you know. I have to . . ." He was crying now and I wrapped my arms around him and told him it was okay. I knew he couldn't find the perpetrator if he went out into the night, but he could find a lot of trouble.

"I know," I replied softly. Acknowledging that I understood what he was feeling was all Enrique needed in order to release his anger.

"Okay," he said, closing his eyes. He was too tired to argue. I gave him a hug and picked up the gun, surprised at how heavy it was. I had never owned a gun and didn't want one. Enrique kept it because sometimes strangers would come to the house drunk, looking for the people who used to live there. I could understand. When you live in the country, you feel alone. There is no way help will get to you in time. People feel the need to protect themselves.

I popped open the trunk of my car and placed the shotgun next to the five-gallon watercooler I brought for the games. I closed it and climbed into the car. It had been a long night and it wasn't over yet. I still needed to clean up some things in the Jets football locker room.

The Jets Hangar was located on the far east end of the football field between the home and visitor stands. The front of the building had two large windows that swung out to allow for concession vending. Inside, the hangar was divided in two. One side was reserved for the home team, with lockers, chairs, closets, bathrooms, and showers for the players. The other side was set up the same for the visitors. There were four entrances into the building, the front concession-stand door, the visitors' locker-room door, the home locker-room door, and the football coaches' door, which led into their small office.

Although we did not use the locker room, we did use the ice machine located in the coaches' office for our watercooler. Before each game in the afternoon, I went in there to scoop ice into our watercooler and fill it up with water from the locker-room drinking fountain. Often, the football coaches would be there, jawing about their players, the team, the game, and the long hot practices. I didn't say much, just went in and did my business and was as polite as I could be. We were the new kids on the block and I understood what that meant. We had a place and we had to respect theirs. This was *their* facility.

As the months passed, our friendly greetings slowly grew into small conversations about how the team was doing and who we were playing. The head football coach was a decent man, kind and polite. He had a heavy burden being the football coach. Most people don't know how much importance is placed on the shoulders of a coach in a small community. People love you when you are winning and despise you when you are losing. And then you have to see them at church on Sunday morning.

Putting together a winning program in our first year had opened a lot of eyes at JM and won us a certain amount of respect. Students, teachers, and the community had seen that soccer was a good thing. It had been a positive addition to the school. Brushing shoulders as I did with the other coaches in a small office had softened the perception that soccer was a threat to football.

Which was why it came as a shock that night when I saw one of the flyers that were posted above the desk of the head coach. Stuck in the middle of sheets that read "Excellence Demands Preparation" and "The 6 Ws: Work Will Win When Wishing Won't" was one neatly made flyer that featured two photos of one of the coaches throwing one of our soccer balls. The caption below the photos read, "El Lowmano. You not throw the soccer ball, you keeck it, eh?"

My heart sank. The flyer was posted for all the football coaches and players to see. It was offensive on a number of different fronts, but what stung me the most was that the men who put it up were also the boys' teachers.

The boys were already so self-conscious about their Spanish accents. I felt as if I had been thrown down a dark well. Were all our pleasant conversational exchanges just a front? Were all the polite words that passed between us just a facade? Crawling out of the hole I felt I was in would require a lot of effort and I felt so *tired* of having to deal with this. These slights did more than make you feel bad. They cut into the core of your values, made you question things like faith in people and God's goodness.

I knew I needed to respond to the flyer immediately, but I didn't know how. I reached out to grab the piece of paper and tear it from the wall. Anger seemed the most obvious direction. I could throw a fit and make demands. But that would only make me more enemies and harden feelings further. I could go to Moody and let him deal with it. But the coaches could lose their jobs and this situation didn't merit such harsh consequences. If there is one thing I have learned in writing about race, it is that things can get explosive real quick. Going to Moody would only bring this simmering issue out in the open and create deep wounds at the school.

So often in Chicago, I had seen groups, Latinos and African-Americans, cry foul about race and discrimination. They had rallied and challenged the authorities and filed lawsuits. Those measures were successful in many cases, but they had also left the city raw and divided. Confrontation worked to correct unfairness, but it always came at a deep human cost. There had to be another way.

What did I really want from the coaches? An apology? No. I wanted them to take the flyer down, and I wanted them to learn something. I wanted them to learn to think before they opened their mouths. I wanted respect. Respect can come from fear or from love. Fear was easy to achieve. Love was so much harder. The civil rights movement had used both, but what remains today seem to be tactics that emphasize fear and confrontation more than love. Love

required everyone to put aside their pride and to grow. And standing there in the office with my hand on the flyer, I wanted growth.
Scorching the earth only left everything bare, black, and smoldering.
I knew what I wanted to do. This was a coaches' thing. Football and
soccer. And the coaches had to work it out.

The next afternoon, before practice, I entered the Hangar and
the coaches' office where the ice machine was kept. I scooped my
usual amount of ice into the cooler and listened to the other coaches
make chitchat about their upcoming game. They asked when our
first play-off game would be held and I told them the next Wednesday. The head coach was seated at his desk on the phone. The flyer
was still tacked up on his bulletin board. I kept waiting for an opening, for him to get off the phone, or for one of the other coaches
to stop pestering him. The room was too crowded. I wanted this
to be just between us. Finally, he got off the phone and I saw my
opening.

"Coach," I started. He looked at me. "Coach. That needs to come
down now." He looked at what I was pointing to and his face turned
ashen. He knew right away that the flyer was a mistake. It had been
a joke among them and they had assumed it wouldn't get out of
their locker room. It hadn't been meant to be seen by someone
from the soccer team. He acknowledged that it needed to come
down and he was embarrassed. I wasn't about to let him off that
easy.

"Coach. That is highly offensive and disrespectful. You know the
kids have a hard enough time trying to talk in English without
being made fun of. It needs to come down." But Coach was way
ahead of me. He snatched the flyer off the wall and immediately
crumpled it and threw it in his wastepaper basket. We looked at each
other and he understood the problems that the flyer presented for
him at JM. I asked him where it came from. He said that one of the
newspaper guys had made it and brought it to them. That made
sense because the pictures had been professionally scanned or copied. The whole thing was too neat. That an outsider made it didn't
excuse it. "That may be, but you are the head coach and you can't

have that on the wall for everyone to see," I said. "Having it on your wall means you endorse it." He got the message. He had gotten it the second I pointed it out to him. And he had realized the problems it could cause if word of the flyer went out of the Hanger. I thanked him for taking it down.

The whole exchange had lasted only a few seconds, but the coach and I had come to an understanding. I wasn't going to rat him out; he took down the flyer, and we both knew it didn't need to go further than that. It was just something between the coaches. I turned and talked to one of the other coaches in the room. They asked me if we were going to win our first play-off game. None of them had even witnessed my exchange with the head coach and that was okay. But out of the corner of my eye I saw Coach take the wastepaper basket out of the Hanger and go outside. Later, after the football coaches and players went to their practice field I hung around and looked for the flyer. It was nowhere to be found in the large garbage bins located outside the Hanger. But I had taken a picture of it the night before.

We won our first state play-off game at home on a cold night in November, defeating a school from the northwest region of North Carolina, 4–0. The state play-off system was designed to reward teams that finished high in their conference. Albemarle had finished top in the conference and we had finished second. Both teams were rewarded with having their first games in the play-offs at home against teams that had finished lower in their own conferences. As a second-place team, we could expect one home game and possibly a second depending on the rank of the other team. In order to reach the finals, a team had to play only four games at the 1A state level. Home field was a big advantage. After we won our first play-off game at home, I gathered all the boys together in a line and we turned to our fans and lifted one another's arms above our heads. And then we took a bow. I held Enrique's hand. He had played a tough game on defense that night. We had achieved so much during the first season. We had come in second in our conference and won our first play-off game at home. We were for real.

9

The school bus groaned from the strain of climbing up the Blue Ridge Highway on our trip to Hendersonville High School for our second play-off game. The steep winding road was carved directly through the Smoky Mountains, exposing the jagged outcroppings of rock on either side of the bus. The boys marveled at the mountains as we cut through them. "It looks like Mexico," Lechero said from the back of the bus. With their faces pressed against the cool glass, some of the boys looked back across the valleys of time and distance to when they were just kids playing in the great *campo,* or open country, of their native lands. But the vision lasted only for a moment and then they were back in the United States, back to their new reality. They sat back into the seats and passed the time sleeping, playing cards, and listening to *rancheras* on their CD players. It was a five-hour trip to Hendersonville and we still had two hours to go.

I got up and sat next to Caballo. He was awake and nervous. At eighteen, he was already a man in many ways. Older and more experienced than the other boys, he'd had a rough life as a migrant. His eyes held that dark brown color of deep soil. We talked about his life and he told me about all the jobs he'd had since moving to North Carolina. He'd picked blueberries in Duplin County, the little money he earned being tallied by the number of baskets he loaded onto the truck. "I have been to the mountains too, Cuadros," he said, and looked at me with his small, knowing, thin eyes. "Tomatoes," he whispered.

There'd been a summer when his family picked tomatoes in Swain County, packing the fruit in white cardboard boxes and stacking them in the middle of the rows of plants to be picked up later. Swain County, at the time, frowned on migrant kids going to school, and so many worked in the fields with their parents. From there, the family headed to Christmas-tree country, where they would trim Fraser firs and cut, bundle, and throw them onto trucks to be sold all over the country at local supermarkets and by private vendors. I had reported on Christmas-tree workers in Sparta, North Carolina, and found that some workers had been living in a school bus much like the one we were riding during the season. Americans never really understood where their food or other agricultural products like Christmas trees came from. If they fully grasped the work, the sweat, the long hours for little pay, the cold that the workers endured during the hard winter months in the mountains of North Carolina, they might begin to view their Christmas mornings differently.

The boys were a bit restless, and decided that it was time to measure how strong Dominic, our German exchange student, was. Dominic was not very tall, about five ten, but he was solidly built, with strong muscular legs, a thick neck, and a cinder-block-shaped head topped with a crew cut. He struck terror into the legs of our opponents.

"*Ja,* okay, I do it," Dominic told them when they wanted to arm-wrestle. He took them all on and won. The boys would call out one another's name and one by one each fell to the sturdy Dominic. When they ran out of Mexicans, they finally called for Oso and his six-four frame. If any of the Latino boys could defeat the German, it would be the Honduran. They cheered and laughed as the two young men squared off. Oso was a big kid but he was not unusually strong or muscular. He had lost a lot of weight during the season but had toughened up, so he had that going for him. But Dominic proved to be the heartier of the two and beat Oso in a long, red-faced match that tested the will and endurance of both boys.

We arrived at Hendersonville High School in the late afternoon when the sun was quickly settling under the mountain skyline. It was getting cold and the wind whipped around us. The boys shivered in their shorts.

The Hendersonville Bearcats arrived dressed in white and red. They were tall mountain boys who took to the field and began to warm up. The Jets were a bit intimidated by their size but shrugged it off and started to stretch out. When the referees arrived, the starters took their positions and the teams faced each other for a brief moment before the center referee blew the starting whistle.

Indio touches the black-and-white ball forward to Pee Wee, who stands with him in the middle of the field. The game begins. The Hendersonville Bearcats surge forward to pressure the ball immediately. Pee Wee deftly dribbles around the first attacker and passes the ball off to the right side of the field to Chuy, the ball spinning clockwise. Chuy collects the ball with some space between himself and the Bearcat defender. He knows where he is going. He cuts to his left inside toward the middle of the field and then quickly cuts the ball back out with the outside of his right foot, the ball close to his body, faking the Bearcat defender and leaving him in the dust. The small crowd of Jets supporters scream, *"Olé!"*

Meanwhile Caballo has opened himself up to Chuy on the right side next to the sideline. Chuy sees him and sends a choppy pass; the ball bounces toward Caballo. I think, "Jeez, we got to keep those balls down on the ground." Caballo gets the ball, his back to the goal: the Bearcat defender is pressed against his back, his arm wrapped around Caballo's waist. A clear foul, but the ref doesn't see it. Caballo turns on the Jets. He's got it now. The game is on. Caballo goes one way and then turns and cuts back the other way, finally turning around and facing the goal. He burns the defender and cuts in, racing for the eighteen—the point where the penalty box begins. He has one thing in mind—penetrating, shooting, and scoring. But as Caballo sprints down the field, he is immediately attacked by two Bearcat defenders. He can't get through both of them, he tries dribbling one way, then another, he is moving like a spinning top in the right corner of the field. No one comes to help him. I am standing on the sidelines watching as he desperately tries to get out of the box the defenders have put him in. Finally, he carves out some room for himself and sends the ball cross field toward Indio, but before the ball can get to him, a Bearcat defender heads it away. Pee Wee is there to head the ball back into the attacking third, but the ball is lost.

Now the Bearcats press, controlling the ball. They work their way down the left side of the field and string together two wall passes, burning Loco on the right. Loco quickly recovers and sprints back to defend. The Bearcat player passes the ball to one of their forwards. Bomba is there to pressure the forward, but the player is too big for the freshman and he gets around Bomba. The Bearcat player penetrates into the eighteen, and just as he is about to shoot, Edi races at him like a bullet, cutting through him and stripping away the ball before he can get the shot off. Edi is fearless, he doesn't think about colliding with the player, his eyes are on the ball and nothing else. He pushes up the field, standing erect, his head up, looking for open players, and, after spotting Pee Wee in the right middle of the field, sends the ball in a high arc above the heads of other players and straight to Pee Wee, who heads the ball to the right side of the field for Chuy, who quickly touches the ball up on the right to Caballo.

The attack is on again. The defenders push up their line, shortening the field and setting up the forwards for an offside trap, if needed. Caballo receives the ball and again he has two defenders on him right away. I now know that the Hendersonville coach has scouted us out, has pinpointed our strengths and weaknesses. He knows that Caballo starts our plays, is the top goal scorer, and our main weapon. We attack from the right. Coach has two defenders on Caballo, shutting him down. We will have to find a way to get Caballo open and another way to win.

The Bearcats win the ball again and come at us, attacking from our left. Bomba is allowing too many guys through. He is like a sieve. We can't stop them on the left. They are staying away from Dominic—his size and strength—going after the freshman. This time the Bearcat forward slips past Bomba. Edi launches himself at the player, knocking the ball loose. The ball bounces at the top of the eighteen, a dangerous situation for any other attacker to pick and fire a shot, but Fish comes off his line in a flash, and before a Bearcat forward can get to the ball, Fish pounces on the loose ball, wrapping it up in his arms and hugging it close to his chest. He tucks his head in to avoid getting kicked. It is obvious that the freshmen on the team are having a tough time. They can't compete against the upperclassmen on the Bearcat team, despite their talent. We will have to make a lot of changes during the half.

I substitute out Bomba and insert Lechero into the defense. The game is an even match, with each team stymieing the other. The Bearcats are taking more chances and penetrating on our left, but Fish and Edi are making up the difference. With just fifteen minutes left in the half, disaster strikes. On a hard run down our right side, the Bearcat midfielder crosses the ball to the left side to a forward. Lechero jumps but is unable to head the crossing ball away. The ball spins in the air and a Bearcat forward gets a head on it, but not all of it. Fish comes off his line. He knows the dangerous nature of the play and he sprints to the ball to get there in time to punch it out. But Lechero is there and Fish holds his ground for a second thinking Lechero will get it. The ball bounces off the head of the forward and weakly dribbles into the corner, beating Fish. The Bearcats draw first blood. That may be the game, I think. One goal could win it.

You can feel the boys tense up as they walk toward the middle of the field to begin play again. They know they have to respond. But the Bearcats double their resolve on defense and we are unable to penetrate for clear shots on goal. The forwards are getting frustrated and Caballo is literally disappearing from the field. The first half ends and we are only forty minutes from being eliminated from the play-offs.

We desperately needed to make some adjustments. The coaches got together for a moment while the boys rehydrated. We decided to keep Bomba out. Sometimes the game is too much for the freshmen. Indio was also useless up front, but that didn't hurt us as much and we would keep him there. There wasn't much we could do to help Caballo. Chuy would have to support him; and we would have to rely on Chuy to break through. He was capable but had a tendency to send his shots high and over the goal. Those were the adjustments. The boys would have to do the rest. We'd have to wait and see. There were no ties in the play-offs.

The play-off ratcheted up the intensity of the game. There was nothing among the private leagues, their tournaments and shoot-outs, that came close to a high school play-off game. The stakes were much higher and the games were single elimination. You lose, you go home. You are not guaranteed the three games club tournaments allow. The games were also very public, played at night, under the big lights, and in front of your whole community. You played for pride, for your school, for your town. When you lose on a club team in a tournament, no one calls you a loser at school the next day. When you win, girls don't smile at you in the hallway. Pressure? Club teams didn't know what pressure was.

The second half starts with the same intensity that the first ended on. Each team attacks the other with reckless abandon. The game gets tough and dirty. The Bearcats begin to outmuscle the Jets. They push, grab, and slide-tackle our boys. The referees make some calls, but miss too many. And each time the referees call a foul on the Bearcat team, the home crowd goes crazy. They yell at our players and try to intimidate them. Lechero feels the brunt of the abuse on his end of the field. But the adjustment proves to be inspired; Lechero takes out the attacking right forward of the Bearcats. The forward can't get past him, and with each win of the ball, the crowd screams insults at Lechero.

But then the game takes a dark turn for the Jets. A Bearcat forward slips through the midfield and gets past Edi into our defending third of the field. The breakaway is on. Fish sprints off his line and makes a bead directly for the feet of the attacking player. He knows a second goal would finish us off. But he sees a weakness in the attacking player. The ball is too far in front of his feet. Fish has room to snatch it away. The two players run straight at each other. Seeing a charging fearless Fish, the Bearcat forward loses control of the ball and it bounces out in front of him, he can't reach it now, he knows that Fish will get it, and instead of letting it go, he slides with his cleats up. Fish goes down, wrapping his hands on the ball, but the forward's cleats gash into his right knee. His knee is burning and pain shoots through him. The defenders push the Bearcat forward away. The ref blows his whistle. I scream on the sideline at the foul. The referee pulls out a red card and the forward is ejected from the game. The home crowd shouts out their indignity at the call even as we head out to check on Fish. He has to come out. He has taken a bad blow and there are red welts on the side of his knee. The spiky cleat could have scarred him had it slashed his face. But now who will play in goal? It's up to Indio. He played goalkeeper for me on one of my club teams. He knows the position and has shown talent. Indio it is. We help Fish off the field.

The game resumes with the Bearcats now playing one man down. They are unable to replace the red-carded player. Our attacks become more pressured. The Bearcats crouch into a defensive position. The game has become a question of whether we can score and whether or not the Bearcat defense can stop us. They crowd the goal with all their players and the field shortens. It becomes almost impossible to score. In essence, twenty-two players barricade the small space. But we continue our attacks. And then it happens. Caballo finally breaks away on the right side of the field. He charges at the goal like a train. There is no stopping him now. He has the ball, he has the speed, and he knows where he is going. And just as he crosses the eighteen—unchallenged—he sends a wicked shot high, and on target, for the upper V, or corner, of the right side of the goal. I can see the ball zoom for the corner and I know there is not much the keeper can do about it. But suddenly the ball knuckles out and bends off to the right, hitting the near post on top and deflecting out of bounds. That's it. The game is over. When the whistle finally blows, the boys throw themselves down on the field, crushed by the defeat. We get them up and they shake the hands of the Bearcats, feeling less than thrilled to do so.

The boys threw themselves back on the field, scattered like fallen soldiers. They were devastated. Many of them sat crying. They took the loss hard. The seniors took it the hardest. Pee Wee held his head and wept. Even Oso had tears streaming down his face. Fish looked stunned. They all looked so broken. I knew I had to bring them back somehow.

"*Bueno, chavos,* this was a tough loss," I said. "But you have to re-member what all of you accomplished this year. Look at how far we have come. Look at what you have achieved; this is the first year of our program. Something that many people didn't want to see and look at how far you have made it. No one will take this program away now after what you achieved in our first year. I know this is hard on you seniors, but I want you all to know that whatever hap-pens to this team, whatever the future holds, nothing could have been done without your dedication. You wanted this team. You made this team."

We got on the bus and started on our way home. The bus was dark and that was okay because some of the boys were still crying. They hadn't wanted anyone to see them. I looked behind me and noticed Fish was now weeping too.

I left my seat and went to the back of the bus. I sat down next to Lechero and Chuy. I took Lechero's hand and told him what a wonderful season he'd had and how next year would be better. Then I embraced him. I turned to the seniors, to Chuy and told him how grateful I was for all his hard play this season and embraced him. I then sat next to Pee Wee, whose electric smile was always lit, and embraced him. I told him if there was anything I could do, all he needed to do was ask and I would help. Oso was next and it was hard getting my arms around him. I made my way down the aisle to the front of the bus.

Two hours after we left Hendersonville, music could be heard from the back of the bus. The tinny sound of the *norteño* music floated through the bus. Ricardo shined his flashlight back there and we caught a glimpse of the boys dancing. They were all elbows and spinning bodies. I smiled.

Second Season

10

Alberto Cuadros arrived in the United States in 1960, alone, with little money in his pockets and an undefined plan of how he would live. He had left Peru, his wife, and two boys behind in search of an opportunity to improve his family's situation and find greater freedom. He had been orphaned as a boy, and had made his living on the streets shining shoes until he was finally placed in a Franciscan monastery by an uncle. Alberto married late in life, at thirty-seven, and had a family. Even with his Franciscan education, he could never make ends meet. When his sister received a scholarship to study dentistry at the University of Michigan, he made the decision to join her.

My father found a job as the janitor of St. Mary's Student Chapel in Ann Arbor. It was difficult, but he got used to the cold winters and strange new foods. He worked hard cleaning the church by day and then working nights at Drake's Candy Shop as a dishwasher. When he had earned enough money, he brought my mother and two brothers to Ann Arbor. I was the first member of my family to be born in America. We lived in a little room in the basement of St. Mary's, underneath the chapel and the altar. I can recall faint images of the tiled floors, the little yard in back with the statue of the Virgin, and the cool walls of the stairs leading to the basement.

After three years at St. Mary's, Dr. Benedict R. Lucchesi, a renowned cardiologist and part of the team that originally developed the cardiac pacemaker at the university, found my father a job as an animal-care technician in the pharmacology research department. Dr. Lucchesi had been the son of Italian immigrants; he saw his own father in my dad. My father was responsible for all the animals on which the researchers were experimenting. In time, my brothers and I all helped to care for the dogs, cats, mice, rats, and guinea pigs. The job transformed our lives. We bought a house, my family had health benefits, and my father earned a pension. But he hated the job. He was responsible for the feeding and cleaning of the animals; and it was hard, dirty work, which he deplored. My father was a learned man, one who had studied ancient Greek and Latin. Needless to say, the job did not challenge him intellectually.

On his days off in the spring and summer, he would take me and my brothers and our cousin Willie to Michigan Stadium—the Big House—and we would kick a soccer ball around on the green carpet. In those days, the stadium was open to the public. I can remember receiving passes on the big Maize and Blue M on the fifty-yard line. My father taught us how to play the game. He showed me how to trap, turn with the ball, pass, and shoot. We loved it. By my senior year in high school, I was varsity team captain. My father came to all my games. He was so proud but at the same time he spared me no criticism on the field. I can remember him always telling me to "Stop the ball!" and "Control it." He nagged me about three things in life: stopping the ball, practicing the violin, and writing. To his last days, he always asked me what I was writing.

He played with me throughout the years, even into his seventies when he was still strong. We were mirror images of each other. I became the man he always wanted to be and his life always inspired me to be the man I had always wanted to be. Funny how fathers and sons can pick up the same thread in life and weave a single cloth from two lives.

I grew up very much like the boys I coached. I knew the immigrant experience here. I felt the same pain and embarrassment of not speaking English when I started school. The sting of being alienated, separated from a home, had left its mark on me as well.

I spent my days in school educating myself, navigating the system on my own terms without my parents. I applied to college by myself and found the money to attend. I always worked my way through school. And I felt the cold slap across my face of racial prejudice. After college, when I lived in Los Angeles, I wanted to be an advertising copywriter. I developed an excellent spec book and dropped it off at some of the biggest ad agencies in the city. They loved the book and without fail would call me in for an interview. But when I walked in the door—short, brown, with dark hair—all of a sudden there were no openings for me. Many of them told me to try my luck with a Spanish-speaking agency.

I was young and naive and didn't know I was being steered away from a white-dominated business. I was undaunted. I eventually found a job as a copywriter, but after a year I became disillusioned with the business. Who wants to write about pizza all day long? My father sensed something was wrong and he asked me one day, "What are you doing with your pen?" I thought long and hard about his question. That's when I applied to graduate school in journalism. But I made myself a promise. If I was going to be a journalist, then I was going to be the kind I wanted to be. I didn't want to be a beat reporter. I wanted to write longer pieces and I wanted to write about the people marginalized in our society.

So, when I looked at these boys kicking the ball on the field, I saw my family, my father, and myself in their eyes. I wanted to teach them how to kick a ball, but I also wanted to help them through this life. I knew what they were going through and what was ahead.

It was a cool spring morning when about a dozen of the boys from the first-season team plus a couple of new ones joined me in the parking lot of St. Julia's Catholic Parish on Highway 64.

The church had changed significantly since the David Duke supporters had vandalized it almost two years before. The congregation, both English-speaking and Spanish-speaking, had worked hard to build a new church along Highway 64, eight miles outside of Siler City. The new church was magnificent to behold. It was built in a Spanish Mission style with a canted tower, slanted on one side, that stunned the locals.

Father Dan had included a soccer field for the Latino congregation. The field itself still needed some work. The grass was thick and uneven and one side of the field was up on a slope. But there was enough level space for what I wanted the boys to learn and do.

I had called the boys together to form a challenge club team through the Chatham Soccer League. I had spent many nights thinking about the Hendersonville game and what we had done wrong that first season. We were ready for a change. The boys had to crank it up to the next level. I wanted to teach them a new system of play, one that would complement their strengths with the ball and hone their attacking style.

The high school rules prevented me from coaching more than nine boys from the high school team during the off-season. That was okay. I made up for the deficiency with boys from other places. On the club team were Fish, Lobo, Lechero, Bomba, and Loco. Like the high school team, this was a team of brothers. Fish's brother Guero joined us, as did Enrique's brothers, Edi and Arabe, the youngest. Indio's little brother Perico also joined the team. Rounding out the team were Santos, a young man who had the potential to be a great player, and two non-Latino boys, Brett and Anthony, who had played on a club team of mine.

The guys were already taking shots on goal, sending the balls flying over the crossbar into the parking lot and bouncing them off the parked cars. The boys quickly realized they needed to move their cars. Many were already learning how to drive and some of them already had licenses. The lack of a driver's license didn't stop them from driving. Rural kids drive; there was no way to stop them. States that were clamping down on their driver's-license restrictions for immigrants after 9/11 didn't get this. You can't get anywhere in Chatham without driving. It made more sense to find a way to include them in the system. They were on the road with you.

I blew my whistle. I was a whistle coach. I needed the whistle to bring them in, to tell them to move, to get their attention. I had previously considered throwing the whistle away, but it was too hard to yell at them to come in. The boys gathered around.

"*Bueno, chavos*" I repeated the greeting in English. "We are going to work on only a couple of things this spring. We are here to learn how to possess the ball and play the four-four-two. That is all we are going to do."

"*¿Y la cascarita?*" Servando asked. He was new. He didn't know that we had put that behind us. I looked at him, but before I could say anything, Fish handled the question. "We don't play that anymore."

"Okay, we are going to play *puro* possession. Pure possession. This is how we are going to do it," I said. I divided the boys into three teams, each team with different colored pinnies. Two teams always played against one team. In this case, it would always be eight boys against four boys. There would be no goals, no shots, just possession. The two teams controlled the ball with the pass, keeping it on the ground, while the four other boys attacked and tried to take it away. If they were successful in stealing the ball, the team that lost it would defend against the other two teams. The guys didn't totally get it at first. They lost the ball a lot. Their passes were dull and slow. They got confused about who was on whose team. But slowly they began to come around.

We played possession for three hours that day. There was no *cascarita,* no shots on goal. It was all possession. The guys began complaining like goats.

"Cuadros, I am tired of this," Loco said. "Let's play." I told him we *were* playing. By the end of the practice, the guys were all exhausted. The heat and the constant movement of the drill were both very intense. The drill accomplished several things. It forced the boys to make better passes. It forced them to be aware of who was on their team. It made them keep the ball down. It made them run to open spaces. And it taught them that they could control the game simply by possessing the ball among each other.

The guys stripped off their shirts and changed into new ones.

Their bodies were rapidly changing. They used to be skinny. Now their chests were bronze colored and puffy with new muscle. Their legs were like chiseled slate. They got in their cars and took off. Enrique, Edi, and Arabe got into mine and I drove them home.

The family had been evicted from their previous home. Not for the first time, their landlady had raised the rent without notice. Finally, Dolores complained bitterly of the increase, the *third* in a year. The landlady evicted the family in January 2003. After they left, they found a little country cinder-block house with three small bedrooms near the highway, in back of a chicken and cattle farm. The house was bitterly cold. It had no heat and broken windows. It was a disaster. The previous tenants, also Mexican, had left a lot of junk in the house and outside. But Dolores had raised an industrious family. She and the kids scrubbed the place down and fixed it up. They found new windows and taped them in. They built a porch for the front of the house. They repaired the roof. I found them a screen door to keep the flies out.

They had that immigrant drive to better themselves with whatever they could find. If it was cold, they slept together to keep warm, the girls with the girls and the boys with the boys. If they needed a porch to keep the mud out, they found the plywood and built it. If they needed new clothes, they went to the PTA or Salvation Army to find bargains. They were proud of their savings. If they were hungry and had no money, they would pick a few ears of corn from a cornfield and feed themselves. Dolores had learned to make a game of life and she had passed this onto the kids. They found a way.

But while the younger kids like Edi and Arabe loved the little house, Enrique had a harder time. He was seventeen now, a senior at school, and he was sleeping with two younger kids. He had no privacy, an excruciating circumstance for any adolescent, and now he was choosing to stay home alone more to escape feeling suffocated by his family. One night the pressure was too much. He flew into a rage and slapped poor Arabe. Dolores had come to her youngest son's defense. Enrique smashed a door in and yelled at her. There was so much repressed anger in him. He had been abandoned by his father and forced to endure terrible poverty. He didn't have very many friends. He didn't even know how to have fun. And now he was sharing a room with these two boys, with no privacy. It was too much and he exploded.

Dolores thought of calling the police that night. But Enrique calmed down. The kids were growing up and it was growing harder for her to deal with them. It had been easy when they were little. But teenagers were different. She and I talked about it and I told her that all teenagers go through this kind of thing, especially someone like Enrique. He would grow out of it. He would get better. I said it with certainty, even though I knew that sometimes they didn't.

I had lost my mind. I was insane. I couldn't believe I was doing this but I was. I pulled into the McDonald's parking lot in Siler City in a large white cargo van I had rented to take the boys to the North Carolina Youth Soccer Association State Challenge Cup tournament in Jacksonville. The van was a sixteen-passenger vehicle, long and wide, with seat beats for each of the kids. Laughing and screaming, the boys climbed in and I realized that I had become a bus driver. It was the one thing I had sworn I would never do. I had volunteered all my time to coach, to prepare them for games, but I made a personal promise never to drive a bus. But we needed to get to our tournament and try out our new system. So I had rented the van knowing full well what it meant. Sometimes you have to just yield to the absurdity of a situation. I had yielded. Bad.

"I can't believe I am doing this," I told Indio, who sat up in front with me. He nodded solemnly, looking back as the guys started punching one another.

"It's the passion, Cuadros," he said. "The passion for the game. It makes us do crazy things."

We arrived in Jacksonville, home to Camp Lejeune, a Marine Corps base, and trekked out to the soccer fields where the tournament was being held. More than a hundred teams were playing in all different age groups. There were teams of young girls in ponytails deftly managing the ball in a game. Boy teams going at each other. Parents cheered their kids on and had snacks waiting for them when they finished.

The State Challenge Cup was one of the premier tournaments in the state. And even though we were playing in it, I felt that the club teams were becoming a deterrent to good soccer in the United States.

The giant club organizations, like Capital Area Soccer League in Cary, North Carolina, were too large and too regimented to develop good creative soccer. The system was such that only the affluent kids could afford to play on the teams, and it was even a stretch for the middle class. So they were the ones ultimately coached and seen by the college coaches and scouts. Each year, parents shelled out hundreds of dollars for uniforms and matching backpacks from the top soccer attire companies like Adidas. Parents paid $200 for uniforms *alone,* not including shoes, league fees, separate tournament costs, transportation, and hotel accommodations.

Once their kids had joined in these leagues, parents found themselves sucked into the world of club soccer, but ignoring all the inherent elitism, the club system in the United States didn't necessarily produce the best players. With all the money and all the resources and all the coaches, the players were overcoached. Their game was too regimented, too robotic.

These club players understood the game and the rules, they had some moves, knew positions and what to do, but could they think on their feet, *literally,* when cornered? Soccer is a game of ideas. Players have to solve the complex field problems of time, space, speed, the rhythm of the game, all while generating enormous physical effort. That means that in spite of the best coaching, it is always a players' game. The player has to come up with a way to win. And that meant players had to be creative.

All over the world, the best players learn to be creative while playing with their friends in their backyards, on the street, sneaking onto tennis courts, or at the beach, playing with balls made from nothing but socks tied together, or grapefruits, or whatever. These players, who were very much like my players, didn't need a coach or uniforms as prerequisites for play. They taught themselves. Playing *was* practicing. They played all the time, every chance they got.

Coaches in the United States think in terms of American football: get the biggest, get the strongest. But soccer has always been a wonderfully democratic game. Diego Maradona was five feet nothing. Pelé *maybe* five nine. Ronaldhino? And all of them grew up poor.

I believe this erroneous American approach has made many people dubious about the American style. America is the home of rock and roll, but American soccer has been played more like a dirge. American soccer should be bold, it should be brash, and crazy, and creative, and wonderful. And it should be open to everyone.

All this was foremost in my mind as we stepped out on the field at the tournament. It featured more than a hundred teams from all over the state, yet we were the only team to have Latino players.

We quickly won the first two games of the tournament and were looking to make the final four if we won the third and decisive game. But disaster struck during the second half.

Enrique was coming into his own as a defensive player. He was stronger now and more determined. He maintained his good nature, but he wouldn't allow anyone to come into his area unchallenged. Enrique was our anchor. Built like a bullet, he headed balls away and ran down attackers. The guys on the bench called out "Mosca! Mosca! Mosca!" or "Fly! Fly! Fly!" every time he cleared the ball.

Partway through the second half, Enrique chased down a loose ball with an opposing player on him. Just as the two were going to reach the ball, Enrique went down. He rolled on the ground, grimacing in pain and clutching his left knee. I felt a hot electric surge along my spine. I quickly ran out onto the field; it was clear he was in agony. A trainer supplied by the tournament examined and determined that he had torn his ACL (anterior cruciate ligament), one of the main ligaments that hold and keep the knee tightly together. No, was all I thought. I knew what a torn ACL could mean, and I didn't want Enrique to go through it.

The injury to Enrique took the life out of the team; we lost the game and were eliminated from the tournament. The guys had never seen an injury like this before. We left Jacksonville a bit dejected. We hadn't won the state cup. That was okay. I was more worried about Enrique. But he seemed to have lightened up, and the pain had subsided. The guys seemed to be recovering from the loss as well. They were blowing spitballs at one another in the back of the van despite my yelling. We dropped off Enrique and his brothers and headed to Siler City to drop off the rest. On the way back, I pulled into a car wash and made the remaining boys clean the van out. You can't let them get away with anything.

Dr. William Taft was one of the best-known orthopedic surgeons in the state. He was *the* expert in sports-related injuries at the University of North Carolina Sports Medicine facility. A tall man—balding, exacting, and experienced—Taft was a sharp as the corners of his bow tie. He took Enrique's knee in his hands and performed the ACL test, pulling the knee out to see if it was loose. "Yep, he has a torn ACL," he said, sticking a knife right into my chest. That meant surgery to repair it, and that meant money Enrique's family didn't have.

Access to health care was a serious problem among the Latinos who had migrated to the South. Many had no health insurance. Their jobs were the not the kind that offered many benefits. The poultry industry initially did not offer plans or plans workers could afford.

But the worst off were those who became injured and thus a liability to their company. If they were undocumented, they would usually be fired. I knew plenty of guys who had lost their jobs because they got injured. In one case, a man named Luis was injured on third shift, the cleaning shift, at a poultry plant. He had slipped and spilled chlorine and ammonia, and hadn't been informed that mixing these cleaning chemicals would produce a toxic gas. The entire plant was evacuated and several workers were taken to the local hospital. Luis had inhaled the gas and gotten sick. He was treated but continued to suffer terrible headaches, sensitivity to light, and an inability to stand up for very long. Eventually he was fired. He moved back to Mexico.

When I inquired about the spill at the plant with the North Carolina Department of Labor, I was told no investigation had been conducted even though the plant had been evacuated and people had been sent to the hospital. Officials said the department did not conduct investigations unless three people were admitted to the hospital. I saw several people at the hospital being treated, but only two were admitted. The crucial third admission necessary to set off an investigation did not occur. That the department requires three hospital admissions as a prerequisite for an investigation was no secret.

The worst case I came across was a young man of nineteen who was living in Snipes Trailer Park and had been working at a sawmill. His right pant leg had gotten caught in a bark stripper and it sucked him in, tearing off the flesh below his knee. The mill was so loud no one could hear him screaming in agony to turn off the machine. Finally, in desperation, he took off his gloves and threw them at somebody, who turned around, saw in horror what was happening, and shut the machine down. The young man was medevaced to UNC hospital, where he was treated. His leg was reconstructed from flesh from his buttocks and thighs, but it looked like a bloated mess. The flesh was uneven, skinny just below the knee, and then swollen, as if he was wearing a boot made of meat. He could barely bend his knee. The bark stripper had not had a safety guard to prevent such an injury. This young man lost his job at the mill and could not find another job. I lost track of him over time and suspect he moved back to Mexico.

Families did eventually begin to seek out health care, but only when their situation became dire. Many didn't want to take unpaid time off from work to see a doctor. Others didn't know where they could go in order to see someone who could understand them. Still others went to *curanderas* or *sobaderos,* curers and massagers, for their injuries and ailments before going to a clinic or doctor. Eventually, a network of comprehensive community health centers began to serve the Latino community. Their charge was to help the poor obtain access to care. At first, many of these clinics served the African-American community, but as the Hispanic migration intensified, they became crowded with pregnant Latinas and their children. Black folks stopped going to those clinics.

Clinics had to hire translators or teach some Spanish to their employees in order to deal with their new patients. They found the Latin American custom of using both the paternal and maternal family names confusing. A Latino might give his name as Luis Gonzales Martinez. Gonzalez would be the paternal or family last name. Martinez would be the maternal name and not the last name.

Names were a perennial source of confusion. Then there was the use of "work names." Undocumented Latinos would use their work name or alias. This would confuse health care administrators to no end. Many Latinas were afraid to reveal their real names, and afraid too that their babies would be born with their work names. Others had a hard time explaining why they needed a work excuse note from the doctor in their work name and not in their real name. These workers and families searched for clinics and health care providers who understood that many of them were undocumented.

But the real challenge these community health centers faced was the decline in Medicaid-reimbursed patients. As African-Americans moved out of the chicken plants and into health care, education, and government work, their benefits increased. These clinics saw a drop in Medicaid reimbursements—their main source of income for this at-risk population. When the Latino population began to explode, they didn't have health insurance and were ineligible for Medicaid. Clinics began to find creative ways to get reimbursed for serving this population.

With pregnant Latinas, they relied on something called "presumptive eligibility," which allowed them to bill for a couple of procedures during a pregnancy under the presumption that the patient was eligible for Medicaid. When as was often the case, they found the patient was ineligible, they could no longer apply for reimbursement, but the strategy did help offset some costs. Instead, the clinics charged sliding-scale fees. Latinos are very good at paying their bills and obligations as long as they can pay them over time. But despite the sliding-scale fees, many clinics were struggling with lower reimbursements. All of this was, of course, classic cost shifting. Companies didn't want to pay for adequate health care for their workers and so society picked up the tab. Communities were basically subsidizing these industries' workers and paying for them to have a disposable and pliable labor force.

Enrique was one of the lucky ones. He had been born in the United States and qualified for Medicaid. His surgery bill would be completely paid for. But what would have happened to him if he hadn't been born in the United States, as was the case of many of the other boys on the team? I shuddered to think of it.

Enrique's operation took more than three hours to perform. I sat in the waiting room with Dolores, who prayed quietly for her son in Spanish. I tried to calm her as best I could and called Gloria Sanchez, the Chatham County basic-needs coordinator, as well. I had to explain to her what was happening. First, Dr. Taft had been unavailable to perform the operation, so Dr. Elwood Garrett, a renowned orthopedic surgeon, would do the job. Dr. Garrett had a thick Southern drawl and had been the surgeon for the U.S. national soccer team. He knew what he was doing. A strip of Enrique's patella tendon would be harvested as the new ligament. Then Dr. Garrett would drill into the femur and tibia and thread the tendon piece through and anchor it with screws. The tendon would be stronger than the old ligament. Everything went fine, and when Enrique came out of surgery he was groggy but looked good.

But then something went terribly wrong. He began to feel horrible pain in his knee. It was so bad he bit and tore into a towel. The nerve block he had been given ceased to work. The nurses rushed to give him pain medication, but it seemed like forever before they finally injected him with something to ease his suffering. Enrique calmed down, but then he couldn't move his lower jaw. It had gone numb. He couldn't swallow and he couldn't talk. The nurses summoned the anesthesiologists and an intern, all of whom were baffled by what was happening. After another minute of uncertainty and fear, Enrique recovered and could speak normally.

I took him home with Dolores to the little farmhouse and we put him on the couch. He had his leg bandaged and wrapped in a leg brace. After two days, I changed his dressing and looked for signs of infection. The dressing was bloody but the wound and sutures looked good. I checked on him frequently, and in a few days I took off the brace, per Dr. Garrett's instructions. Dr. Garrett believed in getting the athlete up and about as soon as possible and moving the leg and knee. Enrique was on his way to recovery. But he would need lots of physical therapy in order to be able both to flex and extend his knee normally. Despite the pain and frustration of not being able to move well, all Enrique thought about was getting back to playing during his senior year. I didn't pull any punches. Given his recovery time, I told him he had lost his chance.

11

It was another hot day in July as I prepared to gear up for our second season of soccer. I got out of my car, slung the black bag of balls over my shoulder, and walked toward the baseball dugout. There had been a lot of changes since the previous season and it seemed as though life was moving in fast-forward, a blur of images good and bad.

Ricardo would not be coaching this season. He had gone home to Chile for the summer and wouldn't be back in time. Big Oso had returned to Honduras after graduation, succumbing to frustration at his inability to attend college here because of his undocumented status. Chuy made floor manager at the fast-food restaurant and seemed to be turning his life around. Caballo was still going to school and was in his junior year even though he was nineteen. He was ineligible to play. Also ineligible to play were Fidel and Pepa, the two freshmen who had almost been dropped from the team during the first season.

The news that struck me the hardest was learning that Pee Wee had dropped out of school in his last semester. He was one math credit shy of graduating but he said that he just couldn't do it. He had completely lost interest in school. His parents had moved back to California and he was living in Siler City with an older sister. Pee

Wee was a citizen and he had the greatest chance of anyone on the team of making it, but it seemed for some reason, that the Chicanos, the citizens, had it much harder than the immigrants. They found it harder to fit in and find a place in school and in life.

I could sympathize with Pee Wee. Growing up, I had also felt like a fish out of water, the only Latino at my high school in Michigan. I led a double life, like many of these kids do. Speaking my "secret" language at home and switching to English once I walked out the door. My best friend in high school was a Taiwanese-American kid with whom I'd bonded because of our mutual feelings of alienation from and angst among the Anglo kids.

But many Latino kids hurt themselves by dropping out. They reject the world that rejected them.

This is where Latino parents can fail their kids. The options for success are less defined for Latino kids and their parents. It can be harder for Latino parents, especially immigrants, to guide their kids through the American high school experience when they themselves have never been through it, don't understand it, or are too busy working to try. For many immigrant parents, when a kid reaches sixteen he is on his own, he is a man, able to make his own decisions about his life. That worked in Mexico but it can have disastrous results here.

As I got to the dugout to open the closet door, the baseball coach was there, sitting down, his arms across his chest.

"Hello, Coach," he said, eyeing me. He got up.

I knew what was coming.

"Coach, I don't understand why y'all need to be out here," he said, staring at me. He was pissed. He wanted his field left alone.

"Coach, I ain't happy about the arrangement either." I had a plan to try to placate him. "Now, what I was thinking is we develop that little field out in back of the football field and that can become our practice space."

He smiled. "Now that's something I would like to see done."

Coach was warming up now. We both agreed that it was a terrible situation. We did need our own space. The baseball outfield was inadequate. It lacked width and we couldn't keep permanent goals up.

The solution was expanding the little auxiliary field. Coach liked the idea a lot. He even patted me on the shoulder. I added the field to the list of things to be done.

The boys were now arriving. Indio sidled up to me and inquired about my conversation with Coach. I gave him a look. The guys didn't like the fuss Coach kicked up about the field. It made them feel like interlopers. I tried to explain to them that it was his field. He loved it. And that they would feel exactly the same way if another team used our field.

"I'm going to burn it, Paul," Lenin said, shaking his head. "I'm going to come out with some gasoline and burn it."

Ugh. This was not what I needed to hear. I knew it was an empty threat and Lenin would never carry through on it, but still I raised my eyebrows. He was smiling now, that big jack-o'-lantern grin on his pumpkin-shaped head. Despite Lenin's goading, it was good to see him. He'd spent several months in Mexico with his parents after graduating two years ago, than had returned to Siler City, bored and a bit lost. Over the summer, I had found him a job doing what he loved best, coaching soccer. He was now working as the recreation coordinator for the North Carolina Youth Soccer Association. Of all the kids from JM, Lenin was the most assimilated, the one who could work with anyone and succeed in anything.

Lenin was now my assistant coach and it was great working with him. He knew what he was doing when it came to coaching, and had the skills to show the boys what needed to be done. We had brain-stormed together and we were now ready to put our intense planning into effect. It was going to be a very exciting season.

The boys were already setting up the practice goals and taking shots. The balls flew at Fish, who deftly deflected them, chuckling all the while. Some of the new boys sent their shots high, over, and outside the ballpark. Back were the underclassmen from the first season. This was an extremely young team filled with vitality and vigor. The first year's team had been older, serious, talented, but lacked the youthful swagger and confidence that underclassmen gave to a squad. This team was brimming with it. They were a confident—if not downright cocky—bunch.

We got back an excellent core team from the first season, including Fish, Bomba, Indio, Edi, Lobo, Loco, Lechero, and Enrique, who, despite his injury, was still on the team. To this complement we added some new faces; Beto, a talented ball-control artist who could stop on a dime; Nemo, a bullet-shaped Guatemalan who everyone said looked like the little clown fish in *Finding Nemo* because of his smile; Alex, a doughy freshman who wanted to lose some weight; Douglas, or "Dougie-style" as the boys called him, a Colombian-American kid who was an army brat and a senior transfer; and Anthony, from my club team.

The rest were the younger brothers of the older boys, including Perico, the little dart of a player who could leave you in the grass; Guero, who had developed into a penetrating left-footed player with a mean shot; Pony, Caballo's younger brother who could one day become the best player the team had seen; and two more Lechero brothers. The Lechero family consisted of seven children, mostly boys, and a new one seemed to come to JM every year.

There were a couple of other kids to round out the team. "Ro-Ro," a skinny freshman with absolutely zero self-confidence problems; Servando, a quiet kid, but gifted; and finally Tereso, a tall, well-built player who was seventeen and had finally passed into high school this year. He'd had terrible disciplinary problems in middle school and could never move on to the next grade. I took one look at him and knew that he would be the best player on the team. He was fast, strong, an excellent dribbler, and had a wicked instep shot that sent the ball screaming and moving in the air like a swallow.

Tereso would be a handful. He hated authority and didn't listen to anybody. He would be at JM only as long as he was having fun. The minute the school imposed rules and restrictions he'd be gone. He would never be eligible for the following year. I wasn't sure he would even make it to the next semester. But I still believed that the team could help him, focus him, give him something in which he could excel and distinguish himself. Maybe it would turn him around.

I still felt bad about Pee Wee. I had formed the team with the idea of helping these kids stay in school. If Pee Wee had played for more than one season, maybe he'd have turned out differently. I wanted Tereso to have that same chance.

Lenin and I gathered the guys around and I went through my usual speeches about the rules of the field and the team. The guys were eager to get back on the field and play a *cascarita*. Instead, I pulled out a white marking board and set it in front of them. I was going to explain our new system. There were some groans but also some show of interest.

"Last year, we got beat in the play-offs because we were too one-dimensional. Too easy to shut down. We were not well organized and our game was predictable. Talented, but predictable," I said. I knew I had gotten their attention by reminding them of last year's defeat. These boys wanted to win.

The first season we had played a 4-3-3 system that gave us four defenders, three midfielders, and three forwards. But this hadn't worked well. Our three forwards, our attackers, were underutilized and our midfield struggled. We had talented ball controllers and our success as a team would depend on making the best use of them. We would control the middle of the field and work our attack through the midfield either on the flanks or through the center. This was where our strength lay. The *cascarita* had taught the team to play a tight ball-controlled game with good touches, flicks, and passing. That was the good thing about the *cascarita*. The bad thing was it taught them to be selfish—to be individuals and to hog the ball. We needed a system that brought the strengths of the *cascarita* to the middle and eliminated the egotistical play.

"This year we are going to play a new system, the four-four-two," I said, then paused for effect. Some of the guys knew the system and had been seeing the pros play it for years. They were familiar with the concept but no one sitting in front of me and Lenin had ever really tried it. It would take discipline and smarts to master this professional style.

The 4-4-2 system had four defenders in the back, four midfielders, and just two attackers. The strength of the system lay in the middle. Four midfielders allowed a team to better control the game and set up the attack. On the surface, it seemed that two attackers were not enough. But when the four midfielders also pushed up on the attack, the team could then attack with six players and not just three.

The boys were used to the 4-3-3, and it was an easy system to understand. Everyone had their place on the field. The midfielders could pass the ball to the forwards and let them attack. But in the 4-4-2, the midfielders could no longer do that, they needed to also push up and attack with the forwards. This meant a lot more running and better-conditioned players. With my 4-4-2 system, I wanted the boys in a straight line across the field, two wingers and two interior center midfielders. Some 4-4-2 systems called for a "diamond" of midfielders, two wingers and one attacking midfielder up top and one defending midfielder below. I liked the straight-line midfielders. It created natural triangles between the forwards and midfielders. The system would play to the strengths of our players, and I knew if we could make it work we would be unstoppable. But . . . could they learn it fast enough?

Here's how Lenin and I set it up. In the middle we would have Edi starting on the left wing; with his natural left foot and speed, he could burn defenders on that flank. Inside of him, as left center midfield, would be Guero. He was also left-footed and was exceedingly adept at controlling the ball. On center right midfield would be Indio. He had flunked out as a center striker. I knew Indio was extremely talented, but he was not a natural forward. Instead, he was a midfielder who could attack. On the right midfield wing would be Loco, with his great speed and strength. The two forwards would be Lobo on the left—another left-footed player—and Bomba, who possessed a devastating shot.

In the back on defense would be Anthony on the left wing, Dougie-style on the right wing, Lechero as the last man sweeper, and Tereso as the central defender. Having Tereso as the center defender was an inspired choice because he possessed the ability to penetrate into the midfield, attack with a dribble, and send a rocket shot on goal. He would stop opposing teams' attacks and start our own. With Tereso as center defender, we could switch from a 4-4-2 system to a 3-5-2 system, depending on how well he was playing.

Having a fifth man in the center who could still get back to help defend would crush unprepared teams.

Over the next two weeks, I was happy with the way things were going in practice. There were some problems with Tereso but we were working on them. He was frequently late for practice and I urged him to understand the consequences. In the end, the slacking would be reflected in the amount of time each player got to play during actual games. There would be a day of reckoning. I wanted the boys to learn that even though the coach, or boss, didn't seem to care or be paying attention, he was actually doing both, and there would be consequences.

Lenin and I met at San Felipe's Mexican restaurant in the new shopping complex where a Wal-Mart had been built. Siler City was changing fast. There were new stores, new restaurants, the Wal-Mart superstore, and new banks and homes rising daily. The town was thriving and it was a direct result of the new buying power of the Latino population. The Latinos had reinvigorated Siler City's economy—there was no mistaking who had triggered the growth.

Lenin loved tacos à la diabla, spicy tacos that came in a dark red sauce that resembled lava, both in texture and "temperature." I had a couple with him and my eyes started watering. Peruvians eat aji, a spicy sauce, on their foods that made some Mexican sauces seem tame. But when I was growing up in Michigan, my mom could never find the right kind of peppers to make Peruvian ajis. My tolerance was good but not great. Lenin and I had horchatas and sodas, tacos, plates of fajitas, and an occasional chela, or beer, after a hot day. We always brought pen and paper and ended up doing some of our best planning over delicious meals.

One night, Lenin and I were sitting in a booth at the restaurant when we spotted Fish and his girlfriend, Elisa, on the opposite side of the dinning room. The young couple looked distraught. Elisa, a pretty Latina with long straight hair, sat crying. I suspected they were having problems. After a short while, Fish came over and sat down next to us.

"*Este,* Cuadros, um, I have to go to Mexico," he said softly, as if not believing what he was saying. Fish was never one to mince words. He was extremely mature thay way. There was no hemming and hawing with him. He said his grandmother was sick and his mother wanted him to return with her. "I have to go," he said, playing with a straw wrapper, twisting it.

"Okay, how long do you have to go?" I asked slowly, knowing that I wouldn't like the answer.

"I don't know. She is sick. When she gets better, then, I guess, I will come back," he said, looking across the restaurant to Elisa.

We were going to lose our star goalkeeper. We all knew what the loss of Fish would do to the team. Lenin and I were devastated. "When are you leaving?" we asked. There was about a month before school started. He answered, "Tomorrow." That was why he was having dinner with Elisa. He was saying good-bye.

Many Latino kids have their education interrupted because of family needs. Sometimes it was family in L.A. or Chicago, but often it was pressing family issues in Mexico. They would leave the United States and spend months in their home country, destroying any chance of resuming their education once they came back—if they came back.

But Fish's trip was about much more than leaving Siler City with no idea when his grandmother might be well enough for him to return to North Carolina. Getting back would not be easy and there was a serious possibility that he'd be risking his life. Crossing the border had become much harder and more dangerous since 9/11. People died in the desert of dehydration, exposure, or were killed by unscrupulous smugglers.

The added security at the border had not prevented migrant workers and their families from coming. All it did was lock them in once they got through. Talk in Congress by men from immigrant families themselves, like Representative Bill Tancredo from Colorado, about building a fence at the border and deporting people, would never stop the tide of immigrants from risking everything to come to the United States. Tancredo and others like him never fully understood why people came here. They were desperate for a better life and they were willing to risk their own lives and the lives of their families to find it. Neither a fence nor the United States Army could stop what was beating in their hearts. Human beings will find a way to improve their lives, no matter what obstacles are thrown in their path.

What I found truly ironic about the migration of Latinos to the United States, was that it was motivated by a truly American desire. Only a *real* American would weigh the uncertainty against the possible gain and attempt to come to the United States. Perhaps only an immigrant son could understand this. But "Americans" are born every day, everywhere in the world. They are born in Bangladesh, they are born in Morocco, they are born in Brazil and in China, in England, and in Mexico and Peru. Many just never get the chance to actually get here. Being an American is so much more than just having citizenship. It's that beat in your heart to be free, to be your own man, to have control over your own destiny. America has always been an idea. It has nothing to do with papers, documents, or immigration laws. It has a lot to do with ideals and dreams. And our country needs Americans like these. It makes us a stronger nation, more adaptable and smarter, and fosters unique and creative talents. Siler City had been transformed from a sleepy town that was slowly dying into a robust and growing community. It was renewing itself. And America has always relied on its immigrants to revive it.

The mood at the table had grown somber. Fish would be giving up a lot to help his mother take care of his grandmother. He was an excellent student, loved going to school, had goals, he was smart, had a beautiful girlfriend with whom he was deeply in love, and he desperately wanted to play on the team. He was giving up his whole world.

"Maybe I will be back in time," he said, attempting to cut through the dark feelings.

"Yeah, that's a possibility," I lied. I knew that when these kids went back to Mexico, it usually took them more than three months to get back. Fish would return, I knew this, somehow, if he survived the desert, but he would miss the season. He knew it too.

He got up and said good-bye. I stood up and embraced him. Then I sat back down and thought that this might be the last time I'd ever see him.

"Well, there goes the season," I said.

12

It had been a hot sweaty day at the chicken plant for Fish. He'd spent hours vaccinating flocks of young chicks that would then be delivered to anxious growers. His hands were sore from grabbing the birds, cradling them, and inserting a needle into their downy coats. When he stepped into the white clapboard house, sticky and tired, feathers still clinging to his clothes, he knew instantly that something was terribly wrong. His mother, short and stout, stood in the dark living room and told him his grandmother was gravely ill.

The news hit Fish hard and he stood there frozen in thought. The little white feathers on his shoulders and sleeves shook loose and floated quietly to the wooden floor. His mind raced back to the blue shores of Veracruz and the last days he had spent there by the beach. He had only been thirteen when his family was finally ready to join his father in Siler City. They hadn't seen one another in three years and now they were all going to cross the border, and hopefully, God willing, be reunited as a family. But first, they had to say good-bye to the *abuelita,* Fish's grandmother, but Fish hadn't been able to do this. He thought he could walk over to her little wooden house with the corrugated metal roof as he had done hundreds of times before, but his feet would not move.

His mother scolded him, tried to reason with him, but he still refused. He shook his head and kept his eyes down. He couldn't face saying good-bye forever. He was her first grandson and she doted on him—making him tortillas just the way he liked them. He felt ashamed about his inability to go see her. What would she think of him when everyone but him showed up at her house? He couldn't bear to think of it. But the pain of having to say good-bye was too great for him and he ducked his duty, dodged it, and left the next day without seeing her or giving her one last *beso,* one last kiss.

But Fish hadn't escaped anything that day. In the back of his mind, he always thought of himself as a coward. He talked to his grandmother, on the phone but it wasn't the same. She said it was okay, she forgave him, but Fish's guilt stayed with him. So when his mother said that she would be going back to Veracruz, Fish didn't hesitate. "I'll go with you," he announced. It was his last chance to see his grandmother and his last chance to finally say good-bye to her the way he should have done four years ago. He knew it would be risky. He would be risking his chance to finish school, losing his girlfriend, Elisa, the team, and maybe even his own life or freedom. It didn't matter. He needed to see his grandmother one last time.

Fish's grandmother had been bedridden for several days. She was exhausted from her long life and tired of living alone. All her family had left for America, but she had been too old to make the journey and start anew. Her life was here. Her people. Her world. She could never go to El Norte. But as each family member had gone north, one by one, she began to feel abandoned, left behind. She endured four years on her own, but now she had given up. She wanted to die.

That was how Fish and his mother found her. She was gaunt, her tiny body, stretched thin and her eyes were hollow. But when she saw Fish she smiled. A glow came into her eyes as if someone had turned the wick up on a lantern. By the end of the day she sat up. After a couple of more days, she rallied and got out of bed and

walked to the kitchen. When she was strong enough to walk farther,
Fish and his mother took her to a doctor. They had brought the
dollars that would be necessary for her to receive treatment. There
was no health insurance for the poor in Mexico. You paid for treatment. If you didn't have money, you suffered until you either got
better or died. But with a relative living and working in the United
States, a family could survive in Mexico; they could have food,
medical care, a new house, or even a business.

Abuelita was on the mend when she insisted on cooking for
them. It seemed like the old days, his grandmother in the kitchen
slapping tortillas between her hands and tossing them on a tall stack
on the table for Fish to eat. To pass the time, Fish played *cascarita* with
the older men from the village. He tended to the animals that had
grown bold from lack of attention and made sure his grandmother's
house was secure and sturdy. Some days he went to the Gulf and
swam in blue waters after kicking the ball around on the sandy
beach. He'd return smelling of the sea and lick the back of his hand
to taste its saltiness. His body was getting darker by the day, the sun
burning his arms and legs. People from Veracruz were often much
darker than other Mexicans. At night he'd lie in bed looking at the
blue-black sky and the stars. He thought of Elisa, and the team, and
home.

"AAAAHHH!" Ro-Ro screamed as he dove for the ball and
came up with dirt in his mouth. He had stood in goal, his legs
spread apart, pulling his shorts up, hunkering down low, coiling
himself for the shots that were being sent toward him just like a real
pro. But his efforts to block the ball weren't exactly the stuff of
legend. He seemed to be swimming instead of flying toward the
ball. His legs were floppy; there was no spring to his leap, and his
arms flailed wildly. A ball would have passed right through them
even if he got a hand on it. The guys hammered shots at him, hitting
him. They laughed. Ro-Ro had brought it on himself, bragging he
could be a better keeper than Fish. "Watcha, Cuadros, I can do it,"

he said. His self-confidence was a good—if occasionally hilarious—thing.

But most of the guys washed out at keeper. Most weren't as amusingly bad as Ro-Ro, but they were pretty bad. Indio was excellent; he had played keeper for me on the club team and I knew he could do it. But I didn't want to give up such a talented player in my midfield. Guero, Fish's younger brother, was another excellent possibility for keeper, but again, I already had him positioned in the midfield. The guy I was looking to now to take over goal was a young player named Chisco, a powerfully built kid, mean-looking, with spiky hair. He was tough; he thought of himself as a *cholo,* a gangster.

There were a number of kids at the school who were into being *cholos.* They were generally good kids but were usually having some trouble at home. Chisco was a *cholo,* as was Nemo, Ro-Ro, Guero, and Pony, all the new kids. They'd all had some trouble in middle school with discipline and they had arrived at JM thinking they could pick up where they left off. But Moody would never tolerate such behavior. He maintained tight control over the school and did not stand for any nonsense.

Still, my kids thought they were smarter than everybody. I was constantly after them, outthinking their little games and excuses, offering witty retorts to their jokes. Once, when some of the guys said that some of the *cholos* were too sick to come to practice, I knew they were just being lazy. So I left Lenin in charge and drove to Bray Park, where I found them loafing around. They were actually going to play a *cascarita.* The look on their faces was worth the effort of searching for them. I hauled them back to practice and ended that silliness right there. "*Oye,* Siler City is a small town," I told them in the car. "Don't think I can't find you. I am a reporter. Finding people is what I do." The guys just smiled when I came back to practice with the other boys in tow. They knew me.

The *cholos* were never really serious about being gangsters. They didn't know what a real gang was. They talked about being *vatos locos,* but they had no idea what gangbanging was all about. Enrique and Edi could have told them. But the *cholos* just copied what they saw on television and the movies.

Lenin and I ate many tacos à la diabla talking about Chisco and his ability to play goal. In the end, I felt the defense would be strong enough to overcome the weakness in goal. And the opposition would have to get past our midfield first.

A month had gone by and Fish was still in Veracruz. School had already started and he knew that his eligibility to play and even to attend school was in danger with each passing day. He had only two weeks left of eligibility. He missed Elisa. He missed his family and friends. He missed school. And he missed the team. He knew from his brother that the team was already practicing and perhaps had played a game or two. He tried to take it all in stride, but inside his stomach he felt a constant churning, a nervousness that wouldn't go away. No matter how hard he tried, he couldn't shake it. He decided it was time to go home. There was nothing left for him in Mexico. His grandmother was much better. He talked to his mother and they agreed it was time for him to go back home. Fish found a "coyote," a smuggler, who would guide him across the border.

The time had finally come. He had put off this moment for four years and now he had his second chance; this was the reason he had left Siler City. His grandmother was much better and she stood up to receive him before he left. *"Cuidate, mi'jo,"* she said to him. "Take care of yourself, my son." Fish took her in his arms and said good-bye. He was crying openly now. He knew this would be the last time he would see her ever. *"Te quiero.* I love you," was all he said to her. They stood together for a moment and then she let go of him. He left, and didn't look back.

Fish arrived in Agua Prieta on a Thursday, prepared for his crossing. Agua Prieta is a small town on the Mexican-U.S. border located in the Mexican state of Sonora. It had become an entry point for many undocumented migrants to cross over into the United States. There were more crossings there during the 1990s when the U.S. Border Patrol began clamping down on other entry points in California and Texas. The town of Douglas, Arizona, also found itself a major crossing point for migrants and also at the center of debate about illegal immigration. Crossing at Agua Prieta was extremely dangerous; people had to cross over the Sonoran desert. Many got lost, were left behind, and even died under the burning sun.

Fish had bought a dozen cans of beans and other food supplies and stuffed them into his school backpack. In his hand he carried a three-gallon plastic jug of water for the journey. He wore a sweater and a coat that could be rolled up even though it was August and the desert would be hot. He knew the nights would be freezing. The little money he was carrying was stuffed into one of his shoes. His family had contracted with a coyote they trusted, which was saying a lot. Many coyotes were bandits and robbed the people they were smuggling once they'd gotten them into the desert. They would cruelly abandon their charges and leave them to fend for themselves, to live or die without help. Women and young girls were especially vulnerable; coyotes or bandits had been known to rape them or sell them into prostitution.

Fish's group consisted of a couple dozen men, women, and children guided by a single coyote, a thin-framed, wiry man with a white cowboy hat with the sides folded in like two breaking waves. They started out on a Friday night and walked into the desert. The coyote wanted to push far out into the Arizona desert and put some distance between his charges and the border. They walked for six hours before stopping to rest. Fish sat down in the dirt where he stood. He dug into his backpack, pulled out a can of sardines, and peeled back the lid, exposing the little fish drenched in oil. He took out his plastic bag of tortillas and pulled out two. He slapped the fish into the tortillas, folded them, and took a bite. The fish were oily and warm but delicious. He could feel them nourishing him, giving him renewed strength as they slipped into his belly. The other members of the group had brought food in giant plastic bags. The coyote, dressed in black jeans and a white shirt opened to his navel, went around the group telling them, "Don't eat so much, only a little." He didn't want people stuffing themselves and then getting sick and having to be left behind. He would not stop for any stragglers. The coyote got them up and they started walking again. They walked this time until three in the morning, when the coyote stopped them again and told them they could rest for a few hours.

Fish could tell the older men were struggling to keep up. He felt good. The first day hadn't been bad. He knew that being an athlete was helping him. All those laps and practices he had gone to during the spring and summer for the club team had made him strong. He felt he was ready for what lay ahead. But he was worried about some of the other people in the group. He resolved to keep to himself like he had been told. Better not to get to know anyone too well. After only three hours of rest, the coyote again got them up and the group resumed walking.

They walked for another six hours and watched the sun rise over the Sonoran desert, illuminating the rocky terrain in burnt orange and rust. It was the most beautiful sunrise Fish had ever seen. The sky was a fresh robin's-egg blue and it seemed to stretch forever. Beneath the shell of the sky lay a tan serape thrown over the earth, threaded with deep wooly layers of browns and reds stitched across the ground. And the sun, still a friend, glowed thinly behind the low bronze mountains, the knuckles of God. Fish looked up at it and his heart grew lighter.

The group stopped periodically—rested, ate, if there was time—and then got up and walked some more. After the second day, people were beginning to run out of food and water. They discarded their containers along the trail until it became a graveyard of plastic milk jugs. By the third day, many people were out of food and water. Fish's supplies were low as well. He'd never realized how quickly he could go through food and water. Hunger began to be a weary companion to him with each step. The group came across three deer and several of the men, including Fish, decided to go after them, but the deer were too fast.

On the third night they ran into trouble. They had been walking for more than two hours when they were spotted by the U.S. Border Patrol—*la migra*. The group quickly scattered as the green-shirted patrol agents descended on them. Fish hid in a ditch, where the *migra* couldn't see him. But while the *migra* couldn't see him, he could see the migra. They were chasing the coyote through the desert and the coyote kept stumbling over rocks or stepping into ditches, cursing. Fish found it funny. When it was clear that the *migra* had left, Fish found himself alone and in the dark. He didn't know where he was and could only guess which way to go. In the confusion of the raid, he had lost his bearings. The next decision he made could cost him his life—if he made the wrong one. The sun would be coming up in the next few hours and he would be alone and on foot in the desert. He backtracked from the ditch and thought he found the group's original path. He wasn't sure, but he had spent the night tracing their steps. He was on his own.

Fish had been walking for only two hours when the *migra* caught him. The Border Patrol agents were nice to him. They loaded him up in their white vehicle, took him back to Agua Prieta, and dropped him off at the border. Fish was lucky. Other migrants were taken to a detention facility and held for some time. Central Americans usually had a tougher time because they couldn't be so easily released. They had to be deported to their countries.

After the Border Patrol left Fish in Agua Prieta, he met a man who said he could help him cross again. Many migrants did not make it on their first try. Fish wasn't sure if he could trust the man. He might leave him in the desert, rob him of what little money he had left, or simply kill him. There were all kinds of people who preyed on migrants. But the man was older, in his forties, he had a kind face, and there was nowhere else to turn. Fish had to trust him. Sensing Fish's fear, the man bought him food and water for the journey. He told Fish he didn't routinely smuggle people; he did it only when he needed the money and he only took very small groups to ensure success. With his new provisions, Fish started out again to cross the border, this time with just five other people.

The new coyote had a different route from the previous one.

This time, they would not go outside and around Douglas so much—this new way was safer, short. Getting across the border really depended almost exclusively on knowing the terrain. Several years ago, I crossed from Mexico into the United States with a friend of mine near Nogales, Mexico, and its sister city, Nogales, Arizona. We had driven into Mexico in his Jeep and spent the day sightseeing. On a whim, we decided to cross the border on the way back. He drove me through the desert, using a small dirt road that ran through both countries. We didn't run into any trouble on our way. When we reached the border, all that separated the two countries was a rickety fence and a sign that read YOU ARE ILLEGALLY ENTERING INTO THE UNITED STATES. My friend opened the fence door and we drove through. That's how easy it was.

Many migrants don't know the area; they don't know the country, or terrain. If they did, they wouldn't have to pay thousands of dollars for a coyote to guide them. The ease with which we crossed belied the notion that you could render two thousand miles of rugged terrain secure. Congressmen who voted for building a fence to shield the border had clearly never been to the border.

This time, it took only a day of walking in the desert before Fish and his group arrived in Douglas. They were taken to a safe house. The ranch-style home's white walls were lined with green shaggy brittlebushes and orange Mexican poppies trailed the walkway. It was the first real shelter Fish had known in more than a week.

Inside, the house was gutted. No furniture, just mattresses on the floor to accommodate the migrants who used the house as a way station en route to Phoenix. But that didn't matter. It was the most beautiful house Fish had ever seen.

The house was stocked with a large supply of food, and Fish dug into the plates of meat and beans and the stacks of tortillas. He ate all he could and drank so much water he could feel his sides press against his ribs.

When he couldn't eat any more, Fish stepped into the bathroom and took off his dusty clothes, laying them on the toilet, and climbed in the shower. He stood with his hands on the tile wall and let the warm water run down his body. The water turned dark brown and it seemed as if Fish's body was streaming chocolate. He watched the brown water swirl into the drain, erasing the miles of desert dirt that had baked onto his skin. Outside the little bathroom window, in the backyard, there was a tall lemon tree whose branches made the shape of a hand. He had lost weight on the crossing and was skinny now. He bowed his head into the wet stream and waited as the water soaked into his dusty hair.

Fish emerged from his shower reborn. For the past six days he had thought of nothing but survival: finding water, hoarding his food to make it last, enduring hunger when it eventually ran out.

But now he had one burning thought. When he contacted his family by phone in North Carolina to pay the coyote for smuggling him across the border, there was only one thing he wanted to know.

"Have the practices started?"

Fish was worried about his eligibility. He knew he couldn't play if he got back to school too late.

"Yes," Guero told him. "We have the first game in four days."

I t was the first day of the second season for the Jets. We were scheduled to play at home against our county rivals, Northwood High School, a larger school with an excellent soccer team. Northwood had the advantage of having a nice feeder system in place with Chatham Soccer League, where kids played and developed as they grow. My kids didn't have that organized feeder system. The Northwood players were also physically bigger than the Jets.

There were a million things to do before a game. I needed to bring the game balls, the practice balls, the keys to the lights if we needed them, the corner flags, and check on who'd been present during the school day to make sure no one played who had skipped school. Today was also the last day that Fish would be eligible to play. Even if he showed up tomorrow, he'd be out for the rest of the season. I had hoped he would show his face before today, but it hadn't happened. I had spent the past few weeks asking Guero if Fish was on his way, but all Guero would do is shake his head. So, here we were, without our star keeper. No matter, Chisco would have to step up. My buddy Matt, who had been a keeper for Dartmouth College, had been training him.

I was sitting in John Phillips's office going over the tardy and absent lists, checking to make sure everyone could play when I heard Phillips say in his booming voice, "Mr. Cuadros! So, how does the team look this year?"

"Well, we'd be better if we had our keeper," I said, sitting down for a moment. The athletic director's office was something of an inner sanctum at JM. The coaches and Moody gathered there to jaw and swap stories about the teams and the students. It was like being in a barbershop where all manner of topics were open for discussion.

"What's wrong with your keeper, Mr. Cuadros." Phillips barked my name out.

"Well, for one thing, he's in Mexico."

Phillips laughed. "Not going to do you much good from there."

Moody stepped into the room from the side bathroom. He'd overheard our conversation. "Who's your keeper?"

I told him.

"Well, he's here," Moody said. "Yeah, he came in today," I couldn't believe it. I made sure he had the right name. Moody confirmed it. I hadn't heard anything about Fish's return. I grabbed a physical examination form there and left.

"Go get him, Mr. Cuadros," I heard Phillips say as I ran out the door.

I drove straightaway to Fish's house and found him on the living-room couch. He seemed a little thinner, gaunt actually, but in pretty decent shape. I could only imagine what he had been through to get here. I asked him why he hadn't called and he said he hadn't had any time. He had literally just gotten home and enrolled in school, barely making the school deadline.

"You want to play tonight?" I didn't know if he had the strength. He looked at me and a smile trailed across his face.

"*Sí*, Cuadros," he said, putting a hand on my shoulder. "I want to play."

"Well, let's go," I said, and we left with his goalkeeper gloves, shorts, and cleats in his hands. "You need to have a physical to be eligible," I told him as he dressed in my car. I drove like hell to a local health facility, where I had worked out a deal for the players to get their physicals at a reduced rate. It was five o'clock when we got there, and it was closed. I banged on the door, knowing the doctor was probably still inside. He came out, a young man in his thirties. I asked if he could do one more physical. He looked at me like I was kidding. No, here he is, I said, and held out the form. The doctor looked at Fish for a moment and then asked, "You in good shape?" Fish nodded. He may have been a bit dehydrated and undernourished, but he was young. "Okay, you look physically fit," the doctor said, and signed the form.

Fish and I laughed about it in the car. As we entered the parking lot where the Jets Hangar was located, I asked him, "*Bueno*, how was the crossing?" He didn't answer and just looked at me and smiled. He had grown with the miles, I thought. He turned his head away.

On a field of lush dark green where the boys were running and jumping, kicking the balls high in the air and taking shots, Fish turned toward me and said softly, "*Es como un sueño*, Cuadros." "It's like a dream, Cuadros." I knew not to inquire further. All the boys had their crossing stories. They had all been through the "desert" in one form or another.

I put my hand around his neck and patted him. "Like a dream of home, no?"

13

The South Stanly defender gets to the ball ahead of Pony and sends it high and up the field, clearing it out of danger from the Jets' attack. Tereso puts the ball back into play for the Jets with a high header that keeps it in the defending third of the Rebels' field. But the Jets just watch the ball land and bounce. They don't run to the loose ball. Instead, they let the Rebel defenders get the first touch on it and they clear it again. The Jets are dominating the Rebels on the attack, but their game is completely disorganized. The Rebels have hardly been able to penetrate the defensive third of the Jets. The Jets defense has pushed up to the midfield line, confident that they can shut down any attacks. I scream at them from the sidelines, telling them to settle the ball down, control it, possess it like in our practices, pass it around, and set up their attacks properly. But no one listens. They are playing like they play in La Liga, where every player plays for himself and seeks his own personal glory. Gone is the disciplined game of possession that we have worked hard on all season long. They know they are dominating the game, but are frustrated that they can't score. Tereso is a madman on the field. He displays tremendous skill on defense, sending high balls back into the attack with towering headers or trapping the ball and dribbling up into the midfield,

attacking the Rebels defense. But he also screams at his teammates, pissing them off, yelling things like, *"¡Oye, pinche pendejo!
¡Sube!"* "Hey, you shit, move up!" The words cut through the
other players and seem to infect them. They answer with equal
vulgarity. Everyone starts to get mad at everyone else. It's as if the
Rebels aren't even there on the same field.

The game is tied 1–1 and in overtime. Fish is not himself and
has allowed one goal on an error when he came too far off his line
and the ball sailed in over his head.

But then the Rebels get a long through ball over the heads of
the Jets defense and the Rebel forwards press their attack, penetrating quickly and deeply into the Jets defensive third of the field.
Fish is caught off his line, having pushed up too far to watch and
track the Jets' attack. The Rebel forward sees a vulnerability and
sends a lofted shot at goal, catching Fish off guard. The ball sails
over Fish's head and outreached hands and goes into the goal. The
Rebels, despite having few scoring opportunities, score again. The
Jets' cool collapses and all the players scream, blaming one another
for the goal. The game ends with the Rebels winning 2–1.

"This team did not beat us tonight," I started. "We beat ourselves tonight. The screaming, the cusswords, the anger.
That's what killed us. You were playing against two teams.
The Rebels. And yourselves." The guys sat there, some with their
heads between their knees. Lechero and Tereso just looked away.

"*Pinche, vatos* don't want to play," Tereso said.

"That's one of the worst things we did tonight. We are not going
to call each other names out there. I don't want to hear any more
insults, bad words, or anything. That's what killed us."

I broke it down for them. We didn't play our game. We played
selfishly. Everyone was out for himself. There was no organization.

"We cannot beat Albemarle if we are going to beat ourselves like
this," I said, turning my head around to look at each of them. Bringing up Albemarle had caught their attention. They had beaten us

once already this season, 2–0. They had become our main rivals. We had lost twice to them last year and now once this year. We had played an excellent game against them at home—keeping up with them, possessing the ball on them, and attacking brilliantly. But we had given them a penalty kick that had put us behind.

"Okay, those were the bad things we did. What were some of the good things we did?"

"*Nada*, Cuadros," Lobo said. "Nothing, Cuadros."

"Well, you're probably right. We didn't do a lot of good things. But we did tie the game. That's at least something."

The guys laughed. There wasn't much else to say after that. Part of coaching is reading not only individual reactions but the collective emotion of the team. A coach needs to tap into that. If that emotion is negative, a coach needs to turn it into something else. I didn't want to leave them feeling sullen and pissed off at one another. In such cases, you find a way to bring them back. Levity is usually the best answer, but the moments after a game aren't the best time for recriminations. Emotions are too high, especially if you've lost miserably the way we had. You can't fix things there. Fixing things would come during the practices. We got on the bus and went home.

O ur new team hadn't come together yet, they weren't playing as a team. One of the biggest hurdles to bringing them together was getting rid of some of the bad and destructive habits they had learned playing or watching La Liga games.

La Liga was created in the 1990s by the chicken workers who were bored on their day off. They gathered on Sunday afternoons and played a *cascarita*. Those *cascaritas* eventually grew into teams. Soon a private organized league was formed—La Liga. The number of teams quickly swelled as the number of migrants increased in the region. In a few years there were hundreds of teams with thousands of players. Mexican teams would play Salvadoran teams or Honduran teams or Guatemalan teams. La Liga was eventually divided into three divisions, the first division having the very best and most talented players. They played for pride, prizes, and giant trophies.

Many of the boys' fathers played in La Liga. The games were often raucous, shoving, fouling affairs of junky soccer, especially in the lower divisions. In division three, players routinely tackled from behind, bringing talented players down and injuring them. Emotions and tempers always ran extremely high. Referees sometimes took their lives into their hands at the games in attempting to break up fights. Local police officers were eventually hired to provide security for the games. On the field, it was not unusual for teammates to yell at one another, curse one another, argue with one another, and generally get pissed at one another. This was not the "beautiful game."

Teams in La Liga were always scouting new talent. Coaches would approach the talented younger players and try to persuade them to join their team. The teenagers would generally start off well, but over time, the players on other teams would hack at them, knock them down, and injure many of them. It was hard for a young teen to compete against a twenty-five-year-old man who played dirty. I hated it. No one ever learned how to play the game there.

When the boys who'd played in La Liga showed up at practice, I would have to spend time undoing all the damage they suffered there. I would have to teach them organized ball, possession ball, teamwork, and erase all the hacking and foul play they had experienced and learned to inflict. I had seen talented young players with tremendous potential come out of La Liga as hacks.

But La Liga did help in some ways. It toughened some players. They came out of the league hard and strong. Fish, for example, was a product of La Liga. He had seen it all by the time he got to his junior year in high school. He had been through shoot-outs, won games by blocking penalty kicks, and made tremendous saves. All that served the Jets well. But other La Liga players did not have the same good fortune. A player who was talented with the ball might find himself constantly knocked down and end up leaving La Liga with a torn ACL, his career effectively over.

After losing to South Stanly, I feared the Jets had degenerated into a La Liga team. The new players, the *cholos,* who had all played in La Liga, had brought that game with them to our team. I'd seen all the same elements at the Rebels game. The shouting, the cursing at one another, the insults, the arguing, the foul tempers, and the selfish play. And the one player who seemed to be leading the others in La Liga behavior was Tereso, perhaps the most talented player on the team next to Fish.

Tereso came from a good family and his father worked hard. But unfortunately, his parents let Tereso run wild. A big kid with a round baby face and dark hair that hung down in bangs to his eyebrows, Tereso defied authority at every turn and generally didn't care what punishment he received. He was like a cat walking away from you. You had less than a 50 percent chance of getting him to turn his head when you called his name.

There was something about his headstrong personality you had to admire, but it was also incredibly frustrating to be his coach. Coaching sought to bring kids together to achieve something greater than themselves. Tereso was interested only in himself.

When it came time for team pictures, Tereso, as usual, arrived late. He wasn't even dressed in his uniform. When the team was all ready and the photographer had positioned us in rows in front of one of our goals, Tereso was still languorously putting on his socks. It was infuriating. He made the entire team wait while he got ready at his own pace. I almost threw him off the team right then and there. Lenin talked me out of it.

Meanwhile Fish had obviously come back from his border crossing a changed player. He wasn't his old self. He was thin, gangly even, took foolish risks, and was overconfident. He had cost us the game against South Stanly by coming out too far off his line in goal. It seemed as if he was trying to be the player he used to be, but he was overcompensating for having missed practices, drills, laps, and being in poor shape. As a result, he was making bad decisions.

The team seemed to be coming apart. There was disharmony in the ranks and no one seemed to be having any fun. The game had to be fun or why even bother? I spent many sleepless nights thinking about how to get the team to come together again. Coaching for me had to be enjoyable, and if the team wasn't happy, I wasn't happy. Things had to change.

The first thing I did was to ban all the swear words. The words were a big part of the problem. Gone were all the curses, the insults, and the four-letter words. No more *chingas, vergons,* or *putos.* If I heard one bad word from someone, it was ten push-ups. Now, ten push-ups is not a lot. That wasn't the idea. The idea was that it was an immediate punishment. Say a bad word, you had to drop and do ten. If you didn't want to do it, the practice stopped until you did. If a guy complained too much about it, I would drop and do ten with him to challenge him. They did push-ups on the practice field, they did them in the dugout, they did push-ups on the field at away games, they did them in the bus on the floor, they did them anywhere and everywhere until the guys themselves started to police the *groserias,* the cursewords. But I would never let them rat one another out. The rule was either I, or Lenin, had to actually hear the word before anyone had to do push-ups. I didn't want any tattletales on the team. They knew I was serious when I had Loco do ten push-ups in the middle of a game for swearing when he got kicked.

In addition to the cursewords, I no longer tolerated their foolishness. I was not going to waste my time if my players were not there to practice and work hard. If they failed to focus I simply left, taking the balls with me. The first time I walked away the guys didn't know how to take it. They knew that without me there was no team. The next day, my heart was uplifted when each of the boys came up to me individually, shook my hand, and said he was sorry.

Despite the extra effort, though, the team continued to struggle. We lost to East Montgomery by a single goal even though we had dominated the game. It seemed as if the team could not endure any adversity without breaking apart. They were fragile mentally. If they went down even one goal, they lacked the capacity to fight back and win the game. Instead, they turned on one another.

It was early afternoon on a Thursday when I spotted Lenin in downtown Siler City. It was odd; Lenin should have been at work in his office in Greensboro, with the North Carolina Youth Soccer Association. As the recreation coordinator, he was responsible for signing up recreational soccer leagues around the state. He should not have been hanging out in downtown during the middle of the day. I wondered if something was wrong but waited to ask him until after our next practice.

We met after practice in the parking lot of a church on the outskirts of Siler City. The Vínculo Hispano was having an event at Loves Creek Baptist Church and Lenin had volunteered to help out. I got him to take a break and we sat on a bench outside the church's parking lot. I asked him what was up. Lenin always had a smile on. He met tough moments with laughter and tried not to show his real feelings. But he knew he had to talk to me and he could no longer avoid it.

"I don't work there anymore, Paul," he started. "I quit two weeks ago."

"But why?" His answer stunned me.

"I couldn't take it. That office work was too 'white' for me. I didn't get along. I didn't like being in the office all day. I wanted to be outside. Sitting in front of a computer was not me," he said, and looked out at the cemetery next to the church. Many of the Latino kids saw America in terms of brown and white. It was white to work indoors at á desk. It was brown to work outdoors. It was white to study hard and do well at school. It was brown to get by. White people didn't work hard, Latinos were hard workers. Many of the young Latinos took pride in their differences from mainstream society.

He explained that he had done his job, going to other leagues to persuade them to join NCYSA. He had to be out of the office to do his job, but his boss didn't like the fact that he was never around. She told Lenin that he needed to tell someone where he was going before he went. He didn't see why this should be since no one else had to do it. Why just him? After a while he began to think everyone was watching him as if he were a criminal. The other employees were not mean to him, he said. It was just a feeling he had. When he couldn't take it any longer, he quit. He didn't give two weeks' notice, or ask for vacation pay, or anything. He quit Mexican style. He just up and left.

I tried to explain to him that he couldn't just do such a thing. He needed to give notice. He wasn't on a construction job. This was a real office job, one with benefits, and with expectations about appropriate behavior. That didn't matter to him.

"I wanted to tell you, Paul, but I couldn't," he said. He was tearing up now. He felt he had let me down. He was feeling really vulnerable, not an easy thing for a Mexican man to show, even one as Americanized as Lenin. Mexican men were supposed to be strong, never cry, and be macho.

"That job was too white for me, Paul," he said again, regaining some of his cheer. He shook the whole experience off. He had found a new job as a teaching assistant at the middle school. That was a good fit for him. It was an active job and he could work with kids. He loved kids.

I thought about what Lenin had said to me for a long time after we left each other that day. I was troubled that someone like Lenin couldn't succeed at an office job that was centered around something he loved, like soccer, and it made me wonder if many of the other Latino kids couldn't as well. Lenin was the most assimilated kid on the team, next to Enrique and Edi. He spoke perfect English, was bright, and could get along with anyone. But he felt isolated and alienated at his job. I knew what he was describing. I have been the lone Latino in an office many times; it's not usually the easiest experience.

For the first time, I began to have fears about what would happen to all these kids. How would they assimilate into this society? If Lenin had trouble, how well would someone like Indio do? I realized that the idea that some of these kids could break out of their socioeconomic status might be a pipe dream. Perhaps Enrique had found a better way. He didn't set his sights too high. He simply wanted to be a cop. He didn't want to be a lawyer, just a cop on a beat working on a twenty-year pension. This was the natural transition for the children of immigrants. That generation became cops and firemen, plumbers and electricians. The girls became nursing assistants, comesticians, hairstylists, or teaching assistants. If they worked hard they became teachers. Hopefully their children would move up the ladder. But there was no guarantee with Latinos. For some reason, many of our kids got stalled on their way up.

The kids felt different, left out in some way. But exclusion wasn't the only force at work here. I had often heard immigrant Mexican families speak with derision about being ambitious, *ambioso*. They said it as if the ambitious person was selfish, self-absorbed, and doing wrong. Humility was looked upon more favorably. Latino immigrants—like any other group of immigrants—survived, at least at first, by relying on one another. But gaining wealth, acting "white," assimilating, and not speaking Spanish separated people from the community. The values and prejudices of a society they were not a part of were all different fingers on the same hand of alienation. And those feelings of alienation translated into many kids feeling lost, lost in themselves and lost in their communities.

You could see that clearly in the halls at JM among the Latino students. There were generally three groups of Latinos at school. There were the "newcomers," kids fresh from the border who didn't speak a word of English and were placed in the English As a Second Language classes. Then there were the "immigrant" kids, like Fish and Indio, who'd come to the United States when they were younger and could speak English. And finally there were the "Chicanos," kids like Enrique and Edi who'd been born here and could often speak both languages fluently. Sometimes the kids would mix, but often they didn't. A newcomer had little in common with a Chicano who perhaps couldn't speak Spanish well. We had all three groups on the team—one of the few places at the school where they could come together for something that they all loved.

Loco is on fire. He makes several runs down the right wing with the ball, penetrating deep and fast into the South Davidson defense.

The fans yell hateful things at the players. "Go back to Mexico!" But it doesn't stop Loco. He continues to hammer their defense and scores a second goal off a corner kick. The rout is on. But even as the Jets dominate, their behavior begins to deteriorate. Maybe it is because of the heckling from the Wildcat bench and from their fans, but the boys begin to lose their cool. Lechero is screaming at his teammates. I pull him out and sit him down on the bench. All the work we have done on team unity falls apart. Tereso begins to insult the other players when they miss or send their shots wide. We are crushing this team, but the guys can't pull it together.

The stadium becomes a cauldron of hot-tempered feelings from the players and the fans. The Wildcats start to knock down my players in what looks to me a hopeless attempt to try to knock us off our game. I fear some of my guys might get hurt. I make some substitutions to protect some of the younger players. Everyone seems to be fighting everyone else. The Jets are fighting among themselves, insulting one another, name-calling, the Wildcats are fighting us with hard tackles, and the Wildcat fans are nasty. The game becomes unsavory. The referee ejects a Wildcat fan for unsportsmanlike behavior. And then, thankfully, it ends without any on-the-field fights, shoving, or violence. The guys line up and shake one another's hands. But the fans can't get over the drubbing we have given them, 6–0. I can see several of them together, one of them cups his mouth and yells, "Wait til y'all git up here!" We have to climb up through the fans' seating area in order to leave the stadium. I take the words as a direct threat to the safety of my boys. I decide to keep them on the field until all the fans have left.

"Why do we have to wait here?" Guero asked, shuffling around. The guys were tired of waiting. But I held them there until the last of the fans have exited the stands before we started to go.

"Because I say so," I said.

"Eh! *Pinche gueros!*" Lechero screamed at the fans, throwing up his arms in disgust.

"*Cállate,* Lechero!" I screamed at him. "Shut up, Lechero!" The last thing we needed was to provoke those men. We still had to get out of the stadium and onto the bus safely. The boys didn't know how nasty people could get. I didn't want a confrontation.

The crowd finally seemed to be clearing, with only a few stragglers left. I asked Ms. Leary, our bus driver, to please bring the bus right up to the exit at the top of the stadium to avoid any contact with the fans. She agreed. She was scared for the kids too. This had been the most verbally vicious game I had ever participated in. We had endured stupid fans before, but had never been threatened.

Ms. Leary was a talented young African-American teacher at JM. She had a smile that could light up a room. She had once told me that teaching was an extremely stressful job and that teachers had only a couple of ways of coping with the tension. "It's either the Bible or the bottle for teachers," she said. She never told me which one she'd chosen. She was fearless behind the big wheel and always got us to our games on time. That night, when she went to get the bus, she encountered the same unruly and rude group of fans. One of them gave her the finger and another stated simply, "We're rednecks here," implying that she had better watch out or they would "take care" of her. She took the threat to heart.

South Davidson High School was located in the small town of Denton. The town did not have a large minority population, either black or Latino. There had always been some trouble between folks from Denton and African-Americans. The JM basketball team had problems with their fans because of the black players. Now it seemed that attitude had also found purchase with the newcomer Latinos. We had gotten a good dose of it tonight and unfortunately so had Ms. Leary.

When we saw the bus, I told Lenin to escort the boys at the front while I took the rear to make sure no one got hurt from behind. I also wanted to be sure I could see everyone. When we finally made it up to the bus, the crowd had thinned out and we didn't have any problems. I got on the bus and told Ms. Leary to step on it, and at that moment I noticed that something was wrong with Edi. He was visibly upset.

It seemed that when Edi had gotten aboard, he found Tereso in his seat. Edi was a team captain and his bag was still on the seat, but Tereso wouldn't budge. The two exchanged some words and Tereso got up and shoved Edi. Not a smart thing to do. But Edi stood his ground. Tereso then smacked Edi across the face. Edi later told me that he felt the sting on his cheek and then a deep well of anger rising in him, but he remembered all those times when he had been provoked to fight and how he had always been punished for it. He did not strike back, and Tereso finally gave up the seat. Edi sat down and held back the tears. He had come so close to losing his temper, as he had done so often in the past. But he had fought against those feelings and mastered them at last. He wasn't going to be provoked anymore.

I told Moody about the threats to the team and Ms. Leary and he took it very seriously, but nothing he could do would change the fact that the game had been a disaster: from the fans' taunting to the threats against Ms. Leary to Tereso and Edi nearly getting into a fight, it was obvious that this game was one more sign that the season was spinning out of control.

I decided to start with Tereso. He was the best player on the team. He had size, speed, an uncanny way with his head on the ball, and he could dribble past opponents. But he was also disruptive, insulting, disrespectful, and now apparently, he'd started punching his teammates. Sometimes your best player can also be your worst player. I had created the team in part to help at-risk kids, and give them the chance to succeed. But how far was I willing to go to help one kid? How much would I sacrifice? In the end, I thought about the violent nature of Tereso's act against Edi and I knew what I had to do. Other coaches might not have done it for a slap, but I felt that all the kids had to feel safe and secure on the team. I couldn't tolerate violence of any sort.

Before practice the next day, I called Tereso over in the parking lot.

"You know why I'm calling you over here, right?"

He knew. I asked him if he had struck Edi the night before on the bus. He admitted it without any excuses. That was Tereso. He was his own man. I told him that at the start of the season we had all gone over the rules of the team and the punishments for breaking them. There was a rule on fighting.

"I will not tolerate violence on the team for any reason."

"Are you throwing me off the team?" Tereso never flinched.

"Yeah, you're off the team. Turn in your uniform," I said. He looked away for a moment and then offered me his hand. I shook it. I then called Lechero over.

Lechero came over with his eyes wide. All the guys could see that something major was happening in the parking lot. I explained to Lechero that his behavior at the game and on the bus had been too unruly. I had told him time and time again to control himself, but he just couldn't seem to do it. I suspended him for one week.

I then called Edi over. Now all the guys were worried. They had seen Tereso leave and Lechero sulk off as well.

"Edi, you are real lucky you didn't hit Tereso back because you would be off the team too right now," I said. "It always takes two people to have a fight."

Edi nodded and said, "I know, Coach, that's why I didn't hit him. I learn, Coach." Last year, Edi might have struck back; this year he had shown incredible self-restraint.

"You're suspended for one week."

"Okay, Coach," he said, accepting his punishment. Then he turned to me, his eyes wide. "But I'll miss the Albemarle game."

"I know."

An anti-immigrant supporter in front of City Hall in Siler City (©PAUL CUADROS)

The 2000 anti-immigrant rally was a precursor to the anti-immigrant rallies that have since become popular as the immigration debate sweeps the country. (©PAUL CUADROS)

David Duke and Richard Vanderford (©PAUL CUADROS)

Progressive Siler City residents wage a counterprotest (©PAUL CUADROS)

Getting the team ready for the big game (©JEFF DAVIS, *CHATHAM NEWS*)

The Jets prepare to take on Lejeune (©JEFF DAVIS, *CHATHAM NEWS*)

The Jets on the attack (©JEFF DAVIS, *CHATHAM NEWS*)

Halftime speech and forty minutes left
to win the championship
(©JEFF DAVIS, *CHATHAM NEWS*)

The final whistle blows and the Jets begin to celebrate (©JEFF DAVIS, *CHATHAM NEWS*)

The Jets receive the state championship trophy (©JEFF DAVIS, *CHATHAM NEWS*)

Naming the most valuable player of the game (©JEFF DAVIS, *CHATHAM NEWS*)

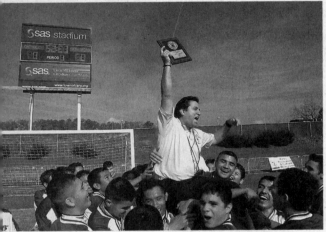

On the shoulders of the Jets, the coach raises the championship trophy (©JEFF DAVIS, *CHATHAM NEWS*)

The fans congratulate their heroes (©JEFF DAVIS, *CHATHAM NEWS*)

On the sidelines acknowledging the fans (©JEFF DAVIS, *CHATHAM NEWS*)

Fish and Elisa take a break after the state championship final (©PAUL CUADROS)

Edi with his state championship medal during the last *cascarita* (©PAUL CUADROS)

The Jets with their medals at Indio's house (©PAUL CUADROS)

14

The tension during the practice was palpable. The boys wanted to know what had happened to the three missing players. I ignored them and kept running the practice as usual, concentrating on shots on goal, which I knew would hold their interest.

But the tension level increased after the practice when Tereso suddenly showed up. I was putting balls and other equipment into my car when he pulled up in a blue Nissan. Tereso got out of the car quickly and approached me. Bundled up in his hand were his uniforms. He didn't say much and didn't seem angry. He just handed them over and thanked me for letting him play. Then he left. I threw the uniforms into my car. That's when I noticed the entire team approaching me. They had seen Tereso turn in his uniforms. I turned to Lenin and said, "This doesn't look good."

At the head of the pack were Fish and Dougie-style. They were among the oldest players and they were visibly upset.

"Why is Tereso off the team?" Fish asked directly.

"Tereso is off the team for disciplinary measures," I responded. I wasn't going to get into explaining my reasons to them. This was none of their concern. This was between Tereso and me. He had accepted it. They needed to deal with it too.

"'We want to know why. That's not asking much," Fish said, holding his ground.

"Actually, Fish it is. This is none of your business. This is between me and Tereso."

At that point Dougie-style stepped in. "Look, Coach, we're concerned about the team. That's why we're here. We want to know what he did. And why he needed to be punished the way he was," he said. Doug was a smart kid. He was sharp and could sweet-talk his way through most things. I liked him a lot. But now he was trying to finesse me, play good cop to Fish's bad cop.

"Look, the punishments are personal and private. I will not discuss them with the team. I appreciate your concern, but this is not between you and me. It is between Tereso and me. That's it." I liked a good argument. Confrontation didn't bother me. I kept my cool, as always. Showing anger meant you had lost an argument.

"We don't think it's fair, Cuadros," Fish said. "Why wasn't Edi punished the same?"

The guys thought I was playing favorites. They thought that I had not thrown Edi off the team for the same offense as Tereso because I had known Edi for a long time. "Edi is being punished. Lechero is also being punished for his behavior. That is all I will say."

"Come on, Coach," Doug said. "We know that Tereso and Edi were fighting. We want to know why the punishments were different."

This finally got to me. "Come on, Doug," I said, lifting my voice. I hardly ever raise my voice in anger, but now I did and it got their attention. "Tereso has been a disruptive influence on this team since he got here. But I will not tolerate violence on this team. And I will not discuss individual punishments with everyone else. You can ask them, but I will not talk about it."

"This is unjust, Cuadros," Fish said, taking a step forward and putting a hand on my shoulder.

"You know, all season this team has struggled, to work together and support each other," I said, taking a step back and removing Fish's hand from my shoulder. "And the one person who has done the most to destroy team unity is the one person you all finally come together to support. Think about that. Now, I know what you guys are worried about. I am too. But we're just going to have to deal with it."

Fish turned and started to walk away. The other guys turned around with him and walked to their cars. Doug stayed behind.

"This is a chance, Doug, a chance to come together."

"I don't know, Coach," he said. "You may have lost the team."

"I know."

Sometimes you have to be willing to lose everything in order to gain everything. That's the way I felt. The team needed to be shaken up and changed. We were turning into something we couldn't be proud of. I didn't want the team to become a bunch of thugs. We were not going to be La Liga at JM. The boys needed to aspire to higher things. I couldn't understand why they had come together to protect the one guy who had been a constant source of frustration to all of us. It wasn't just because of Tereso's talent. I asked Lenin why they were backing him up.

"I don't know, Paul," he said. "But they are finally coming together like a family."

Family. I thought about family long and hard on the way home from practice that evening. I wanted the players to think of one another like that. And they did. They had grown up together, sharing so many of the same experiences. They had faced being segregated in this community together. They had all shared the hot embarrassment of saying a word or phrase in English incorrectly and being laughed at. They had endured the stares and the muttered words behind their backs. They played soccer with one another for hours on hot days in the summer or cold afternoons in the winter. They knew one another well. Many were related by blood in some way. One of their own was expelled and they rallied around him like family. It didn't matter what he had done. He was one of them. It didn't matter that he had brought them down; he was a brother, a *carnal*. When a boy hooked up with someone else's sister, they called each other *cuñado,* brother-in-law, as if they were married and real family. They felt that way about one another. They were all entwined with one another. I wondered as I pulled into my driveway whether any of them would show up tomorrow or if they would just all up and quit in support for their *carnal*.

The boys were upset that the punishments had come right before the Albemarle game. The loss of three strong starters would mean we would lose badly to the Bulldogs. The boys had been looking to finally beating them after three games and a year and a half of rivalry. They had not even be able to score a single goal against the Bulldogs. They begged me to punish the players after the Albemarle game. Not a chance. Edi and Lechero were suspended a week. No more no less.

On the bus trip to Albemarle, the boys sat quietly in their seats. There was no music, no dancing or horsing around. Fish wouldn't even look at me. I was getting the cold shoulder from other players as well. That was okay. I wasn't there to be their friend, I told myself. I was there to coach and to help make them into good decent young men. If I had caved, they would never respect me again. Even Indio was quiet. I was going over the special lineup for the match when Bomba, the quiet kid from El Salvador, came over and sat next to me. He offered his hand.

"I'm with you, Cuadros," he said, not looking at me. "You taught me everything about how to play this game. I just wanted to tell you I appreciate you."

I shook Bomba's hand and thanked him. He must have sensed the tension on the bus and my own isolation. There is no more lonely feeling than being in a group of people who are unhappy with you. I had thought that none of them would show up for the game. But they had. They always would. They would always come for the game.

Our second match of the season with Albemarle—our archrivals—was close. It was the kind of game where everything went right for us but nothing went right for us. We shot wide of the goal or sent balls crashing into the posts or crossbar. We somehow couldn't seem to complete a goal. As off as we were, Albemarle was finding the game equally as tight. They couldn't score or penetrate our new defense.

The new lineup featured Lechero's younger brother "Lecherito" playing in Edi's position on the left wing in the midfield. Most of the boys in Lechero's family played defense. They seemed to be born for it, one right after the other. When the three older brothers tried out for the team, I noticed that two of them would come on alternate days. I found out later they were sharing soccer shoes. That's what happens in a family of seven children in which all five boys play soccer.

Lecherito was skinny, but like his older brother, he was sturdy like a whipcord. He had been born in Mexico with a cleft palate that had been poorly corrected. He had a crooked scar that ran from his nose down to the top of his lip and his face appeared to be broken. The palate prevented him from speaking, he could manage only grunts, and mumbled garbled speech in Spanish. A teacher had once asked him to read a paper in front of the class, unaware of his impediment. He stood there and cried. Even though Lecherito couldn't speak well, he was an excellent student with good grades.

At the sweeper position was Nemo, the bald-headed kid who fancied himself a *cholo*. He was short, stocky, and built like the tip of a torpedo. He had laser vision for loose balls, which he would sweep with long clearing kicks. But he also had a devastatingly wicked shot.

In front of him, in Tereso's old position, I put Bomba. I knew Bomba had the brains to play both defense and push into the middle and attack.

The boys played their best game of the season against Albemarle. They frustrated them, scared them with shots that came close to scoring, and closed them down on defense. And they didn't fight against one another. It was as if all that negativity had never existed at all. There was cooperation, teamwork, sweat, sacrifice, and real encouragement for one another. Gone were the insults, the recriminations, the yelling, the anger. The game was tied, 0–0, at halftime. When my players came over to the side of the field and I sat them down to discuss the first half and what we needed to do in the second, I opened up with a wide smile on my face. They needed to see my emotion to understand that what they had done was what I had expected of them all season long.

"That was the best half you have played this season," I said, clapping my hands. They knew it too. I could tell they were tired from the exertion of playing a tough game against a hard opponent. But they were unbowed. Indio was filled with determination. He sensed they were close to finally cracking Albemarle and he wanted to seize the moment. They all did.

The Jets took it to Albemarle in the second half. We outshot them and beat them to the ball. The boys were playing inspired soccer when they set up plays. The game went back and forth in the middle with neither team dominating. We had several crosses from the wingers, mostly Loco, who sprinted down the wing and sent the ball across the field and goal for one of our forwards. But the strikers couldn't get there in time or were blocked out by the Bulldog defense. We were inching closer and closer to scoring, but just when we had the momentum, the Bulldogs would show how their size and strength could win games. An Albemarle attacker picked up a loose ball just outside our eighteen and with one touch cracked a cannon shot that found the upper right corner of the net for a goal. There was nothing Fish could do. The shot was perfect. Despite the loss, the guys came over to the sidelines after the final whistle as if they had won the game.

I met them with open arms. They embraced me and slapped my hand. The boys knew we had turned a corner this night. We were finally a real team. No matter what would happen during the rest of the season, we would all be in it together. The atmosphere had changed with the suspensions and expulsions. The boys could feel it. They knew they had played their best game of the season, losing only by one shot. And they had done it without three of their strongest starters. Fish came over and held out a big white cartoon-size hand; he still had his gloves on. I grabbed it. He pulled me in and I slapped him on the back.

"*Es todo,* Fish," was all I said. "That's all, Fish."

Enrique grunted as he extended his left leg straight out. He was sweating profusely and he could feel a single tear wiggle down his back. He let his leg fall and heard the heavy clank of the black steel weight crash against another disk. It had been five months since Dr. Garrett had cut into his knee and reconstructed his torn ligament. He bore a red pinkie-thick scar down the middle of his knee. His leg felt good.

Dr. Garrett had a fast protocol for getting ACL-torn knees back on the field. He said that Enrique could go back to playing after about five months depending on how well he healed and rehabbed. Other doctors would have told Enrique nine to twelve months before returning to play. But Enrique had worked hard to get to where he was today. The first few weeks had been the hardest. Bending the knee caused terrible burning pain. He didn't want to do it, but his physical therapist pushed him and he pushed back. After a month, his extension and flexion were pretty good. After three months, he could run straight ahead, not too fast, but he could manage a decent trot. Turning and twisting were another matter. The ACL was designed to hold the knee together. It could endure tremendous pressure to twist but was not designed for the extreme force that some players put on their knees.

Enrique had been patient through it all. He had lain awake in bed, crying, lamenting the end of his soccer career and missing his senior year. He knew that he would have been a starter, a leader on the team, and had been looking forward to it. But most of the time he kept this pain private, showing it only occasionally and only to Dolores. She would tell him, "God knows why this happens." There is a saying that God never gives you more than you can handle. If that is true, God must have thought Enrique one of His strongest children for all the things he'd had to endure in his young life.

After five months, Enrique was ready to ask Dr. Garrett if he could play again. I worried that it was too soon. But Dr. Garrett was the expert. He looked over Enrique's knee, taking it into his thick hands and turning it this way and that. It seemed solid enough. "What are the chances of him hurting the knee again? It is weaker?" I asked. Dr. Garrett explained that the patella tendon used to substitute for the original torn ligament was stronger than a normal ligament. Enrique's left knee was in essence stronger than the right knee. If he felt he could play, run, and cut, then he could get back out on the field.

Enrique was ecstatic. He had helped me coach all season long, getting the guys together, carrying equipment when he could, and keeping Lenin and me company on the sidelines. I gave him an official coaching polo shirt and cap, which he loved, but he missed the uniform. He missed being a player.

Our next home game was against Chatham Central. The Bears were not as strong as they had been the previous year and this would be an excellent team for Enrique to return to play against. I would sub him in as a forward and not on defense, his usual position, to see how he did running and turning on the field.

Before the game, as the players were lining up to take single shots on goal, I asked Enrique how he felt. He nodded and adjusted his athletic glasses. "I feel good, Paul," he said, taking a couple of steps to intercept a pass.

The game against Chatham Central went as planned. We jumped out to an early lead when Edi sprinted down the left wing and crossed the ball for Perico, who tapped it in for a goal. The little freshman had been disappointed that he wasn't starting and wasn't getting much playing time. But he was young and he needed time to mature. By the half, the score was 5–0.

With a comfortable lead, Enrique's time had finally come. I decided to sub him in the second half. He was surprised to be put up front, but that's where I wanted him. He crossed himself as he stepped onto the field. In the stands, Dolores put her hands together when she saw Enrique jog out.

The Jets played around with the ball, passing it from player to player, controlling the game and not allowing the Bears a chance to touch it. I had taken Fish out of goal and put in Pony in order to give Fish a chance to play forward with Enrique. The two worked well together. They were two of the older kids on the field and were friends.

The ball was eventually passed to Guero in the middle, who turned and dribbled past one defender. He passed the ball off to Enrique at the top of the eighteen. Enrique didn't hesitate; he turned his defender around, dribbling in a circle, a classic Hadji maneuver, so named for the player who invented it, but instead of continuing to dribble, Enrique hammered a shot on goal with his right leg. The keeper hadn't expected a hard shot and the ball went through. It was Enrique's first goal. The team erupted in cheers. The boys on the field rushed over and embraced him, jumped on him; he took it all in stride and trotted back to start the game again. He was pumped up. I could see him in the middle of the field jumping up and down. It had taken courage and strength to make it back onto the field. But it had taken something else for Enrique to score a goal.

For all the cloudy days that he had seen in his young life, there were moments of shining glory as well, when the warm rays of the sun would touch his brown face. No matter what would happen to him, Enrique would always come back. He had proven that he could take adversity and turn it around into victory. When the game ended and Enrique came off the field to the sideline, the guys from the bench called out his name, "Mosca! Mosca! Mosca!" They embraced him and slapped his hands and he smiled behind the big black glasses that I had worn when I was a player. Right then and there, he ceased being Enrique and returned to being La Mosca, the Fly. He was a player again. And he was happy.

15

The Jets came in second in the conference behind Albemarle for the second year in a row. Although we had lost twice this season to our archrivals, we were heading into the play-offs with a newfound sense of unity and play.

We beat our first opponents in the state play-offs, 4–0. The boys were elated, but their joy was tempered by the knowledge that the first play-off game was designed to be easier than the later games. They were aware that the second game would be tougher. And since we had come in second place, we would be traveling.

It was on a Saturday afternoon that we gathered at JM for the two-hour journey to Elkin High School, home of the Buckin' Elks. The Elks had come in first in their conference and had the home-field advantage.

The game was a fast-paced match with both teams battling for possession of the ball. But midway through the first half, we started to control the ball in the midfield and set up plays for the forwards. Indio was showing his strength as a player and leader as he dribbled through defenders and sent passes to the two hungry forwards.

We scored the first goal on a penalty kick when Pony was brought down inside the box after beating two defenders. It was all Elkin could do to stop us. We struck again and the game seemed almost over when the Elks came back in the second half and scored a goal. Each minute seemed an eternity as the clock ticked down. When the game ended, the boys ran out onto the field and piled on top of one another in a *bolita*.

I didn't have much to criticize after the game—they had played so well. "I only have one word to say to you all." I looked into their eyes and held their attention for a moment. We had gone farther than we'd been able to do the previous first season, and we'd done it with a younger group of players. "Only one word . . . ALBE-MARLE!" And with that, the boys jumped up and crowded together, yelling their heads off. We would be playing against the Bulldogs on their field for the third time this season. We had made it to the quarterfinals of the state play-offs, one of only eight teams left. We were peaking at the right time and the boys were eager to play Albemarle.

The small city of Burlington had begun its life as a collection of shops that catered to the railroads for the North Carolina Railroad after the end of the Civil War. A fitting origin for what is now known as the "Outlet Capital of the South." In 1990, the Latino population of Burlington barely registered at 1 percent. Ten years later, it had risen to more than 10 percent and was continuing to grow.

Burlington was well known to Latinos in several counties, including Chatham, not only because of the bargains on clothes and other goods but also because of a nightclub. El Club started as a Mexican restaurant but later evolved into a club featuring Mexican music, cheap beer, and pool tables. It gained a reputation among Latinos as the kind of place where anything could happen and often did.

Latino kids from Jordan-Matthews soon discovered El Club and quickly learned that they would be served beer there. In Mexico, the drinking age was sixteen and a teenager could get drunk all he wanted. El Club simply adopted that ethic. No one seemed to care.

The club was making money. The police either didn't have a clue or didn't want to.

So, when the *cholos*—Nemo, Guero, Ro-Ro, and Chisco— walked into the dark club the night before our big game against Albemarle, they didn't get carded. The quartet went to tables on the side and sat down, taking in the ambience. The club was filled with Latino men dressed in silk shirts and fancy cowboy hats. The tinny sound of Bachata melodies played loudly as couples danced on the floor. The boys ordered some *chelas*—beers—and eagerly celebrated the victory against Elkin. They started tipping back the beers and catching glimpses of *las rucas,* or the girls, trying not to stare or start any fights.

The next day, when the boys boarded the bus for the big game against Albemarle, the back of the vehicle was unusually quiet. I didn't think much of it and turned to Lenin to discuss the strategy for the game. Although we had lost both games we'd played against Albemarle, the second game had been close, despite our playing without two starters. We would be at full strength tonight.

The bus bumped along the two-lane road as we passed the farms and small towns of the Piedmont. Across the aisle, Enrique sat listening to his Duranguense music and looking out the window. He had been born here in North Carolina, in the U.S. but he was still very Mexican and he clung to those things that reminded him of the rancho, the farm back in his mother's pueblo. He loved to dance the traditional dances and cherished his cream-colored cowboy hat and tan Cuadra ostrich-skin boots and matching leather belt and buckle. He wore them with white pants and a black shirt when he went to the Sports Arena, a dance hall erected in the country outside of Siler City that catered to Latinos on the weekends and featured *norteño,* ranchero, and Duranguense music. It was a wild place that featured private dancers, lots of men, and even the occasional wrestling or boxing match.

Behind Enrique, Dougie-style sat quietly working on his calculus homework. He had plans after this season of going to college and living abroad. His father was in the military and he had lived at one time in Africa and wanted to return there. Dougie-style had been completely accepted by the other Latino boys and he took to them like family.

Across from him, two of the Lechero brothers silently traded blue socks. And directly behind me, Loco stretched his legs across the aisle, asleep, his brown arms covering his eyes.

The football field at Albemarle High School was one of the best in the conference. It was long and wide, with beautifully maintained Bermuda grass that stretched from one green corner to the other. It was impeccably manicured and it was flat. The stands were well-constructed levels of concrete with a high press box. On a green sloping hill on the northern end of the field, beyond the track that encircled it, was a white paw print and the word BULLDOGS painted boldly across it. More students had attended the school in the past, but several years before, the population of the town had dwindled and the school dropped to the 1A level.

The Bulldogs were champs in practically every sport and dominated in high school 1A football. When I walked into the football locker room at JM and told the football coaches whom we were playing in the third round of the play-offs, they were very excited. They wanted us to beat them bad. It was that way with Albemarle. All the coaches, players, and students at JM just wanted to beat them in something. And Albemarle knew they were good too. When the Albemarle soccer coach came over to exchange rosters for the game, he wore a T-shirt that announced the six conference championships they had won—in a row.

We warmed up in our usual way, running our possession game until the boys' bodies began to glisten with sweat under the bright lights, and taking shots at Fish to get him mentally prepared. The referees called the captains over and Doug, Fish, and Edi went over to toss the coin in order to find out who started with the ball. The refs explained what kind of game they wanted—what they would tolerate and what they wouldn't.

There wasn't much to say to the boys before the start of the game. They knew the stakes, and they were nervous but determined.

With pregame tension running so high, I felt that any kind of inspirational pep talk wasn't necessary, but I was still a coach and it was a moment to pump up as much adrenaline as possible. "*Bueno, chavos.* Well, boys, the third time," I said. They smiled. "The other games are history. They don't exist. Only tonight exists." I paused for a beat and let my words sink in. "They've always beaten us, but tonight, you will change that. Tonight, you will erase the past." You could feel the energy in our circle rise. They were jumping up and down now. "Tonight . . . this night . . . will be ours!" And with that, the guys gathered together, linking arms, and Edi—our captain—started us off. "One, two, three, let's go, Jets!" The boys took the field.

The whistle blows and the Bulldogs start the game with a slow pass back to their midfielder. Pony flies at the midfielder who's got the ball, putting immediate pressure on him, forcing the player to move to his right. Pony is there and pokes the ball away, stealing it and turning upfield. He cuts out and then cuts in, leaving a defender in his wake, but then two Bulldogs go in on him. He can't dribble his way out. Loco has come up on the wing and is shouting at him to send the ball wide, but Pony can't hear him. The Bulldogs are on top of him. Pony goes flying, as if hit by a missile; he rolls on the ground. I shout at the ref, "Hey, where's the card, ref? That's outrageous!" No foul is given; the ref merely holds his arms out as if his holding a baby. Okay, that's the way it's going to be. I look at Lenin. The game is on, all right. Albemarle wants to win and they will do anything it takes to get the job done.

High school ball is fast and furious. The fields are shorter and narrower, making the game quicker, harder, and rougher. There is not a lot of room to slow the pace down and hide. There are no comfort zones in high school ball.

Indio gets the ball on a wild bounce in the midfield. He can do it. He can control the game. He penetrates up the field dribbling around one player. The fans who have come out for JM shout, "*Olé!*" He fakes left and then cuts back out right. Another "*Olé!*"

comes from the fans behind me. Pony, our striker, checks back toward Indio as he is making his run, creating space behind him. Indio sees him and passes the ball to the freshman; he doesn't stop but keeps running toward goal. Pony hits him with a wall pass, a give-and-go pass that is a devastating play that cuts through defenses. Meanwhile, on the left, Lobo sees Indio and his run and he sprints inside, reaching the eighteen. Indio draws the defense to him, and just when they commit, just when they are on him and are going to steal the ball or send him to the ground, he sends a sweet soft pass on the ground in front of a charging Lobo, who takes it inside the box. Fear grips the Albemarle defense. The Jets are in. The keeper comes off his line, it is his only choice to prevent a goal from Lobo. The move forces Lobo to his right and he shoots. The shot sails but goes wide. The Jets have sent a scare into the Bulldog bench. Across the field, I can see the coaches screaming at their players.

The game is at a stalemate. With each passing second, the tension builds, layers of nervousness pile on top of one another. This will not be a high-scoring game. One goal will do it. The boys on the field trade blows, elbows, and shoves off the ball. The Bulldogs are playing rough and using their superior size to knock my guys off the ball. The Jets counter with excellent ball control and tricky plays. But there is no decisiveness in the game yet. No one is controlling it and commanding it. It just goes back and forth, with both teams desperately trying to control the ball and set up a play. I pace the sidelines, waiting, hoping for that decisive moment when we will break through. Suddenly Edi gets the ball on the wing.

He has done it all season. His speed is inspiring, his strength frightening, when Edi has the ball he is a race car in fifth gear. He sprints down the side with abandon, there is no fear in his eyes or legs, he takes it to the Bulldog defense. And just when the tackle comes in to take the ball or him out of the play, he passes it inside to Guero. The Bulldog defense instantly converges on Guero. Guero is stealthy, he has a bag of tricks, but it is no clever move that he pulls out on the Bulldogs. No. It is a disciplined play, a wall pass back to Edi, who has continued running down the wing.

Now I know. This is it. It is Edi who will take the game into his hands. It is Edi who will make his mark. He cuts inside toward the eighteen and his destiny. And just when the defense is on him, he rips the left-footed shot. The ball flattens as it is struck and then punches out and takes off. It seems to be moving slowly in the air at first, in super slo-mo, and then, with surprising speed, as if it someone had hit the play button, it picks up velocity and finds the frame. But the ball is just wide and it strikes the white post and bounces hard and high away across the end line. That was it. We had it all there. But we were just wide.

The Bulldogs respond. They come back hard and furious at Fish. But this time, Fish will not be caught off guard by a ripped shot from outside the eighteen. He is ready, poised, and prepared to hold his line or come off it and scoop up loose balls. And he finally comes through in the waning minutes of the half. The Bulldogs penetrate into our defending third. A large curly-haired fellow has the ball and gets around Bomba. Lechero is there and closing fast. But the player shoots a blistering ball toward the frame. It should have beaten him, it should have crushed him, and sent the Jets down into oblivion, but Fish is there. Fish is a giant. Fish can fly. He throws himself back, his legs bent at the knees and then kicking out to stretch, his right arm extends, and with the flat part of his palms he deflects the ball out beyond the frame. His body continues to roll in the air, parallel to the ground. He lands hard on his side but keeps his head and eyes turned toward the ball. It is a spectacular play. And I know that the old Fish is finally back on the field. The Bulldogs are awarded a corner kick and Lenin and I are nervous. We are not as tall as the Bulldogs. It is a weak point, but our defense is strong.

And that's when I notice something strange. A photographer is there on the end line just behind the post with his thirty-five-millimeter camera and flash. He snaps a shot as the corner kick comes into the box, blinding Fish for a split second. The ball goes out for another try. It is an outrageous affront to the game. Most photographers use a zoom or telephoto lens for their sports shots. I don't know any who use such a short lens, and no one uses a strobe, or flash. Being a reporter and an amateur photographer, I know this isn't right. He is interfering with the game and putting my boys at a disadvantage. I worry that this is a setup. I point out the photographer to the sideline ref and complain bitterly. He sees the guy taking flash shots as the second corner kick is taken.

When the half ends, I go out to the center ref, the man in charge of the game, and complain about the photographer disrupting the game. I tell him that other coaches have complained about this and that no real photographer would use such a short lens and a flash during a night game. The ref is convinced. He calls the photographer over and tells him he cannot position himself near the goal. The photographer is irate. "Look, I know what you're up to," I tell him. "I'm a reporter, no one uses that flash at a night game."

"Mind your own business."

"It *is* my business." The ref allows him to shoot from the sideline but bans him from taking shots near the goalposts. I walk back to my team.

"Okay, tell me what's going on out there?" I asked the guys.

"They're fouling us all over, Cuadros," Lechero said.

"What do you mean?"

"Okay, like, one of the guys keeps grabbing me," Anthony said.

"Okay, if they're playing like that, I want the captains to take note and tell the refs. That's your job. Do *not* retaliate. That's what they want. They want to provoke you so we get a yellow or red card."

I looked around. The guys were unbowed. They had played a hard half and had come close to scoring a goal. The defense was holding despite the rough play.

The guys were ready. Bomba seemed a bit down and I substituted him out for Enrique. Enrique would help to anchor the defense. I looked over at Guero and wondered what was up with him. He seemed sluggish and hesitant, almost as if he were afraid of these guys.

The second half starts with the same intensity. Both teams are determined to be the first to score a goal. We get a break when Anthony wins a ball in the defensive third of the field and moves it up. He passes the ball up wing to Edi on the left. Edi takes it and passes it inside to Guero. Okay, the boys are touching the ball, moving it around. Guero cuts inside while Edi continues to run down the wing. Just as a defender goes in hard on Guero, he cuts out and lofts the ball toward the sideline for a waiting Edi. The play is on. Now, if the guys can only figure out how to penetrate for the goal. Edi goes up and passes off to Lobo inside and makes a bending run. Lobo knows what Edi is doing, the bending run will be slow and keep him inside, he hits Edi with the ball as he comes out of his bending run. Edi is free for a moment. A defender closes on him and he remembers the drill where he goes to the end line and then crosses the ball back in front of the goal. It is a perfect play, and one designed to kill teams. Edi sends the ball low and fast on the ground in front of the goal. Guero is there. The play has been performed perfectly, but Guero can't get there in time. He is late and short by a couple of seconds and his first touch on the ball is poor. There is pressure from a defender. Guero's shot is wide, not on target. What should have been a simple tap with the inside of the left foot into the right corner goes horribly wide. It was a game-winning play but we didn't finish it. I don't understand Guero's sluggishness. And then he disappears on the field. We play the 4-4-2 system, but Guero is nowhere to be seen. He hangs back, preferring to play defense rather than attack.

"*Oye! Guarda ese, vato!*" Lechero yells at Enrique. "Hey, guard that, guy!" Lechero takes over the defense. He stands the last man on the defence and he can see the whole game unfold in front of him. When a ball squirts through, Lechero comes out and clears it. But he bears the brunt of the ruthless play of the Bulldogs. He is knocked down, pushed, and tripped up. A Bulldog grabs his shirt, spins him around, sends him to the grass, an obvious foul. The play is dirty and Lechero is doing everything he can to restrain himself. He holds out for as long as he can before he starts to dish it out as well, shoving players, tackling hard, and not letting anyone get the better of him.

With each passing minute, the game grows tighter and tighter. Both teams know that now any little mistake or sway in luck will decide the outcome. The Jets have played a better game, but that means nothing. All that matters is the scoreboard. And then it happens. The Bulldogs penetrate through the defensive line. An attacker shoots the ball and it is blocked, deflected by Lechero. The attacker gets a final foot on the deflected ball and sends it high in the air and off to the left. A Bulldog winger is there. He can hardly reach the ball but just gets there and the ball bounces off the top of his head, a poor header, but it is enough to send the ball on a high arc toward goal. Fish is out of position. He desperately moves to his right to cover the arching ball but he is too late. With only four minutes left in the game, the ball bounces through, a poor fluky goal, but a goal nonetheless.

The Bulldogs celebrate on the field. The Jets can't believe it. Lobo desperately tries to convince the refs the winger was offside on the play. But the ref tells Lobo to back away. He doesn't; he is pissed. The referee pulls out his yellow card. This sends Lobo into a fury and he takes off his shirt as he walks off the field. The ref now pulls out a red card and he is ejected from the game entirely. "Lobo! What are you doing? Just go to the bus and stay there!" I yell. We are starting to lose it. I want them to finish the game but they know it is over. They now only wait for the clock to finish them off.

The game resumes and the Bulldogs press their attack more easily now that we are down a man from the red-card expulsion. With a one-to-nothing lead, the Bulldogs do not let up their rough play. Lechero feels an elbow in his back. He's had enough. He goes in hard to retaliate and sends the player down on the ground. As the player falls in front of him, he jumps over him, and as he sails over he gives the player a little back kick that doesn't connect but the intent is there. The referee sees it and immediately yellow-cards Lechero. The Bulldog player gets up. There are strong words exchanged and a shove. The *cholos* on the bench go crazy. I hold them back. We don't need a fight after losing the game.

Lechero comes over, throwing his arms up. He's had enough. It is one thing to lose a game. It is another to lose like a bunch of punks. I am furious, the guys have lost their cool. It's like the whole season was encapsulated in the final four minutes. The anger, the loss of control, the immaturity and lack of class all come out in the final four minutes. We show our true character when we hit the wall.

After I send in Nemo to replace the disgraced Lechero, I notice that there is one player who has not given up. Indio will not be broken. He wins a ball and with only two minutes left, he races up the field with it. He is dribbling past defenders on a swift run. And then, before he reaches the eighteen, he is brought down by a foul. We get a free kick. It is no doubt our last chance to tie the game up. Nemo will take it. He has a devastating shot. He steps up to the ball and slams it. It is strong enough and low enough to beat the keeper, but it just goes wide. The game and the season end. The boys are crushed. They fall where they are as if the whistle had swept their legs out from under them. Indio is beside himself, he is inconsolable. The other guys are weeping bitter tears. I put my arms around Indio as he sits on the ground.

"I want you all to remember this feeling right here, right now," I said, looking around at the devastated young men. "I want you to remember how you feel right now. And I want you to save that feeling for next year. We will be back. I promise you."

The guys were starting to come around, they were beginning to lift their heads. "We played strong and hard and gave these guys the best game of the year. That said, the final minutes were a disgrace. I never want to see this team lose its control again. We have to learn to win with honor and to lose with honor. If you can't do that, then we can't have a team."

Mr. Moody, who had come to watch the game, stood looking at Indio and a couple of the other boys who were still wiping away their tears. He turned to me and said, "It's good, Paul, to see them crying. It means they care. I wish some of our other athletes took it this hard."

The boys loved the sport and they had wanted to win. They had wanted to be champions. But I knew tonight's loss would do so much for the next year in terms of growth, maturity, and determination. An older team that had already learned those lessons beat us that night.

Lechero and his brothers needed a ride after we got home. They lived in one of the trailer parks that had been constructed in the past two years. I was glad to give Lechero a ride home because it gave me a chance to talk to him about his temper. "You need to change that, Lechero. When you let the other team make you angry and lose your cool, they win."

As we approached Lechero's trailer park, home to many Latino families, I saw the blue lights of the police cars.

"What's this?' I asked.

"They always do that, Cuadros." Lechero said matter-of-factly.

The local police routinely set up driver's-license checkpoints in predominantly Latino neighborhoods to catch migrants with no licenses. I could see three men already by the side of the road being held by the police. I rolled my window down as I approached the roadblock. The officer asked for my driver's license. Now it was my turn to hold my temper. We had just come back from representing this town in the state play-offs and the boys had to be treated to this on the way home? Weren't they tired and bruised enough?

The police officer looked at me as I handed over my license. He didn't say anything.

"I think this is an outrageous violation of my rights," I said, looking him in the eye. "This is selective enforcement. How can you set up a block right in front of a predominantly Latino neighborhood?"

"You have the right to say that," the officer said.

"How do you think this makes these boys feel? You better believe I am going to complain to Chief Phillips about this." That was the advantage of living in a small town. You got to know everybody.

"You have that right," he said, handing me back my driver's license. I drove off and into the trailer park. I looked at Lechero and his brothers in the back. "That's just wrong," I said. "You want to get angry about something, Lechero? Get angry about that."

Third
Season

16

Enrique adjusted the shiny royal-blue gown. He couldn't figure out how to zip it down. I lent him a hand and grabbed the zipper and pulled it all the way down to his knees. The gown fell a little short. Enrique had borrowed it from Lenin, who was shorter. He laughed. He wore black pants and a white shirt with a black tie. I noticed how his arms and shoulders had filled out. He was very much a young man now, strong and solid. I couldn't help but be proud of him. He was the first in his family to graduate, and it had seemed, just a short time ago, that he might never reach this hour.

It had been a tough year for Enrique. He'd always been a good student, but this past year he had slacked off and was in danger of failing English. That's when I learned the real reason he wasn't paying attention to his schooling.

"I don't know what to do, Paul," he said. "I was thinking maybe I could do another year in high school."

It was hard to believe that he wanted to spend another year in school, but many of the Latino students were nineteen and still in school. Doing another year didn't seem so bad to them. It was easier to flunk out and come back. It was certainly a lot less intimidating than going into the real world. School had provided them the structure they needed in their peripostatic lives. They were settled in school.

"Look, Enrique, I know it's scary leaving school," I told him. "It's your world now, but you have a lot to look forward to—you have a plan. You want to be a police officer."

Enrique had to graduate from high school. There were four other brothers and sisters behind him. He had to set the precedent for them. It wasn't fair that all the responsibility fell to him, but that's the way it was.

We spent several days going over papers and assignments. It was as though he had run a long race and now barely had the energy to put one foot in front of the other. He made it, just barely, and earned enough credits to pass.

When he received his diploma in the JM auditorium, his rather large family roared and cheered, causing members of the audience to turn around and look. Enrique flipped his tassel over on his cap. He hadn't been able to afford the fifty dollars for the tassel, so I had paid for it. He needed one. You can't be a graduate without a tassel.

Outside the auditorium, the graduates crowded in the long hall-way, their parents and friends snapping pictures. We didn't have many players on the squad who graduate that year. Besides Enrique, there was Doug, who had already been accepted at the University of North Carolina–Chapel Hill, and Lobo, who would soon find a job in construction. We only had one dropout this year. Tereso didn't make it to April. The last I heard he had gone back to Mexico.

When the crowd filed out of the hallway into the cool spring night, I stayed behind. The auditorium and the gymnasium were located in the main hallway, the one where all the school's trophies were displayed in wooden cases. Across from the trophy case were the pictures of the school's champions. The photographs were gi-gantic, eight feet by four feet, encased by a wooden frame. They showed the golf team, two basketball teams, a cross-country team, and two women's tennis teams. There was not a Latino face among them.

I wondered about the fate of next year's team. The new kids this year hadn't done so well. The *cholos* had all struck out; they got into trouble seemingly every week. Their grades were pathetic or they simply didn't show up for class. They shaved their heads prison style.

Pony was one of the best players at the school. He was on the verge of breaking out and doing something with his game. He was a smart kid, but he had skipped too many days. Ro-Ro was also going to fail. He was too immature and acted out in class too much. Behind them, Nemo, Chisco, and Servando would also not be eligible.

But the one case that broke my heart was Loco. He had dropped out of school one month before the end of the year. He wasn't failing a single class, and he wasn't acting out at school. But in April he started having trouble at home.

He lived with his older brother and sister outside of Siler City in a beaten-up trailer. His mother lived near Atlanta and she occasionally came to visit the family in North Carolina, but his siblings were his guardians. Loco never knew his father. In the spring, Loco's mother found herself in a terrible situation. She had become involved with a drug dealer in her trailer park. The police arrested him and put him in jail. But no one knew where he had hidden a stash of drugs. Now his comrades wanted to find it too. Loco's mother found herself questioned by the police and sought out by the drug dealers, but she had no information for either of them.

Loco loved his mother. She was the only family he had, aside from his brother and sister. He began driving to a nearby state on the weekends and coming back to Siler City on Sunday nights. She needed his help, his protection. That's when he decided to drop out of school and move to be near her. He spent the next few weeks with her and failed to re-enroll in school. He didn't have any friends there and he felt lonely and afraid. He awoke in his mother's trailer one night to pounding on the front door and threats by the men who'd been involved with his mother's dealer boyfriend. He was scared for his life. One weekend, Loco came back to Siler City and called me.

"You need to make a decision, Loco," I said. "You need to decide where you want to be. Now, I know you want to help your mother, and that's a good thing, but you can't really help her with her problems. Those are` *her* problems. Not yours. You're only sixteen. What can you do? It isn't safe for you. You are in danger while you are there."

"Paul, I don't know what to do. She's my mother," he said. He was beaten. I could tell that he wanted to stay in Siler City. It was his home. He just needed someone to tell him. I didn't want to do that. I wanted him to realize it for himself.

"Look, Loco, I can't tell you want to do." He was a good-looking kid, generally happy and upbeat. As I sat across from him, he looked to me to be tired and confused, "But I will tell you a story. There were two brothers fishing. Suddenly one of the brothers fell into the lake. He couldn't swim. His younger brother looks at him and he's scared. He doesn't want to lose his brother, but he can't swim either. Meanwhile his brother is drowning. So what does he do?"

Loco brightened up. He was into the story now. "He jumps in and saves him anyway?"

"He jumps in, that much is true. But his brother grabs him and pulls him down under the water. The older brother tries to climb on top of the younger. The younger brother is now fighting his brother to save his own life. Eventually, both brothers became so exhausted that they both drowned. You see, sometimes you can't save the people you love without them bringing you down. Now, you're in way over your head here. You can't help your mother out of her problems. But you have to decide what *you* want to do."

Loco thought about it a moment. He knew that he couldn't do anything other than get himself in trouble.

"I want to stay here," he said at last. I was relieved. He had made the best decision of his young life. It was a mature decision.

I spoke with Moody about Loco and he understood his situation and was compassionate. A kind teacher at the school had also spoken on Loco's behalf. Moody cut him a break and allowed him to make up his work in two of his classes for the last month. He hadn't flunked them; he'd only received incompletes. But he was still shy one class. Loco was ineligible to play.

In most places in the South, summertime is a time to slow down and find shade from the stresses of life. But Siler City had not gone fishin'. It was a town abuzz with activity. The town had changed so much since the David Duke rally. Amazingly, it seemed that the resentment and hard feelings had subsided dramatically. The rally had had a cathartic effect on the town. If dealing with the migration was like moving through the five stages of managing grief, then Siler City seemed to be in the final stage, acceptance. It wasn't a secret as to why people in town were more accepting of Latinos. You could see it all in the new businesses and money that was pouring into Siler City. Along Highway 64 there was now a new Food Lion, a new bank, a new pharmacy, a new auto-parts store, a Sonic, a Bojangles Chicken, two barbecue restaurants, two new hotels, a new Subway, a new Wendy's, and the one thing that everyone pointed to as being a sign of real progress, a new Wal-Mart Supercenter.

In addition, a housing boom was occuring in Siler City. Several new trailer parks had been constructed as well as new apartments and single-family homes. Whole neighborhoods were being built. And longtime residents found the values of their homes increase. "The city in the country," as Siler City was known by the local radio station, was finally coming into being.

The immigrants had infused the town with new blood that quickened its pulse. In just fifteen years, its population had almost doubled, from 4,808 in 1990 to 8,078 in 2004, according to the U.S. Census Bureau. The town was fast becoming predominantly Hispanic. By 2000, the town was 39.3 percent Hispanic; 39.8 percent white, non-Hispanic; and 19.7 percent African-American. It was as if the world had leaked into Siler City and transformed it.

Nowhere else has the migration of Latinos to Siler City had a more profound impact than on the town's overall age. What was once an aging and dying town is now thriving with children, youth, and vitality. Siler City has been revitalized by the influx of Latinos. The most dramatic example of this is in the median age of the town. In 1990, the median age for Siler City was 36.8 years, according to the U.S. Census Bureau. By 2000, that age had dropped to 31.4 years, an overall decrease of 5.4 years. Among demographers this is considered a dramatic decrease in just ten years.

When comparing different racial and ethnic groups a clearer picture develops of Siler City's future. The median age of African Americans in Siler City in 2000 was 34.6 years, the median age for whites, non-Hispanics, was 45.9 years. But the median age of Hispanics was just 24.7 years. More Hispanics in Siler City are in their prime childbearing years than any other group. This demographic reality portends that the future of the town and many other towns in North Carolina that have seen a similar influx rests among the Latino population. Towns that were once growing older, aging out, seeing its young people move to larger urban areas, declining business growth and spending, are being reborn, revitalized, and given a new chance at life by the migration of Latinos and their children.

America is also growing older as the baby boom generation begins to enter into its retirement years. The influx of Latinos, whether authorized or unauthorized, means that the country, like Siler City, can also be revitalized and re-energized by this migration. The question remains whether the country can accept this demographic reality and work with it to help these immigrants assimilate or whether they will be left on the fringe of society, never able to reach their full potential.

In addition to lowering the median age, the economic buying power and impact of Latinos in Chatham County is in the hundreds of millions of dollars. Chatham County and Siler City could not operate without the spending and income Latinos produce. Hispanic buying power in the county was estimated at $110 million in 2004, according to researchers at the University of North Carolina's Kenan Institute of Private Enterprise's 2006 report on Latinos in the state. Latino economic impact is estimated at $98 million.

In North Carolina, the migration of Latinos was having a similar impact. Latinos contributed about $9 billion to the state economy in purchases and taxes, according to researchers at the Kenan Institute. Latino spending alone led to 89,600 jobs. Latinos did cost the state money in terms of health care spending and education. The state spent $817 million on Latinos in 2004, while only $756 million was generated in corresponding tax revenue. If recent migration trends continue, the total economic impact of Latino spending in North Carolina could increase to $18 billion by 2009, according to the institute's study.

The school had also been transformed. Jordan-Matthews was not the school it had been three or four years earlier. Moody had made significant changes for the better. There was a new rhythm, one led by a more disciplined drummer, and the students appeared to respond to it. The teachers also seemed to respond to the new JM—they were optimistic about the future. There was genuine warmth at the school for all the students. Moody could be heard to exclaim, "I love our kids. These are *good* kids." And I believed him. It was as if you could put your hand on a wall at JM and feel it humming with life.

My relationship with the football coaches had also changed. They were now genuine friends and the problems from the first season seemed to have completely faded away. They truly accepted these kids and were involved in their education. There is nothing like winning to change people's attitudes.

The boys were changing too. Fish had moved to Greensboro and found a job working in the construction industry. It seemed as if all the Latinos in the state worked in construction. He shared an apartment with friends and worked most of the day hanging drywall or framing a new house or building.

One day in June, he got a desperate phone call from his girlfriend, Elisa. She needed to move out of her mother's house. They were having problems relating. She was a nice quiet girl and she was deeply in love with Fish. The couple had met at a *quinceañera,* a party given to girls who turn fifteen, a time in Latino culture when a girl became a woman. They had taken to each other immediately and started dating. Their relationship had grown over two years and was very serious.

When Elisa called Fish and told him she wanted to leave her mother's house, Fish did not hesitate. He drove there immediately. When he pulled up, she was already walking out the door with her belongings. She had made up her mind that she was no longer going to live at home. She was moving in with Fish. Many Latinas feel the pressure of living in two cultures and want to adapt to the American one. They want to be free from having to stay at home all day after school, cook for their families, and tend to the smaller children. Many dream of finding their own jobs, making money, going out on dates, deciding their own futures and destinies.

But frequently their parents are still living in the old country and want them to stay home and definitely not have boyfriends. Sometimes the pressure is too much for the girls and they hook up with an older man and leave their parents. Sometimes they allow themselves to be "robbed"—taken away for a week or two only to come back "married." Then they discover, much to their dismay, that their new husbands require them to drop out of school, stay home, and wait on them when they come home from work.

Robbing girls, or *robando,* occured with some frequency at many schools in North Carolina. Older men in their twenties would troll around the school looking to pick up young Latinas, and adventurous girls, or those desperate to get out of a bad situation at home, often fell prey to them. There was a lot to appeal to the girls: the men had cars and money from their jobs, and the girls often believed they were in love. All of a sudden they'd be showing up at school with new clothes or gifts from their boyfriends. Eventually the girls would disappear for a week or month. Their parents, distraught and upset, knew their daughters had been robbed, a practice not wholly uncommon in rural Mexico. Everyone understood what was happening. The girl would return "married," or *juntado,* with the man and some kind of accomodation would be worked out between the families. But the girls would never be allowed to come back home. They were married and had to live with their husbands, which usually meant moving into his parents' house. Then the girl would quickly find she had traded a set of parents for a set of in-laws.

Fish couldn't take Elisa back to his apartment in Greensboro with the other guys. So he brought her home and talked to his parents about his intentions and Elisa joined his family. He was now considered Elisa's husband and it was expected of him to provide for her.

Many Latino husbands and wives are not formally married; they are simply *juntado,* as they would have been in rural Mexico. Couples who could not afford a wedding ceremony simply join together in common-law marriages. But these couples take their commitment as seriously as if they had been married in church.

Latino immigrant couples in North Carolina found it difficult to get formally married. The state required that couples put down a Social Security number on their marriage license. Undocumented couples didn't have Social Security numbers and so they didn't get legally married. The state, in its effort to promote marriage as an institution, wisely decided that undocumented couples could still sign a marriage license without a Social Security number, but they would have to reveal the reason why they didn't have a number on a separate sheet—a completely impractical nonsolution. Father Dan, my friend at St. Julia's, had told me he sometimes drove couples to friendly counties or into South Carolina to get a marriage license.

At school, Fish had often arrived late to class because he'd walked Elisa to her class first. The American kids couldn't understand why the Latino boys escorted their girlfriends to their classes, why they were so attached to them. Latino kids couldn't understand why the American kids had a problem with such affection. American girls thought that the Latino boys were smothering their girlfriends, keeping them on a leash. The Latinas loved the attention and affection. The rules for dating were wildly different for each group. The Latino boys wanted to show everyone that this was *their* girl; they were in love and they were together. To the Latinas, this meant the boys really cared for them. But the Americans couldn't grasp why the girls would give up their independence so easily.

I was home reading when I received a call from Indio. His voice sounded urgent and stressed. Usually when he called he was jovial and good-natured. I liked getting calls from him. His attitude about things never failed to lift my spirits.

"Hey, Paul, I have to talk to you, man," he started. "*No manches, no way*—I have to go to Mexico."

He had my full attention now. "Why? What's going on?"

"My grandmother is very very sick. I don't think she will live, you know. I want to see her. I want to go back," he said, straining to get the words out. He was choking up.

I knew this was tearing him up inside. He was fond of his grandmother. I had met her many times when she lived with the family in their row house. She was a slight, short woman in her sixties with wiry hair like a Brillo pad. She'd suffered for years with diabetes and couldn't quite grasp how to modify her diet. She moved back to Mexico to live with a daughter, and there, her condition had gotten worse. She was having terrible headaches and her eyesight was beginning to dim.

"You can't do it, Indio," I told him honestly. "You have too much to lose. Your education, Indio. You might never get back to finish school." I was worried for him because Latino families often let a teenager decide his own course in life. That's the way it was in the rancho, the country. Indio was a rising junior, he was going to be seventeen this year, a man in Mexican culture. I hoped that his parents had the good sense not to let him go.

Two days later I got another phone call but this time it was from Indio's father, Don Indio. He wanted to come over to my house and talk about the situation. When he arrived I could tell he was nervous. Don Indio and I had become friends. I had coached his kid for more than five years and knew the family well. He was a tall man by Mexican standards, lean, strongly built, and I could tell that Indio would one day fill out and look like him. He was a smart man despite having only completed the sixth grade. He commanded the respect of his peers. He had spent five years in the *pollera,* the chicken plant.

"Cuadros, I wanted to tell you I am going to Mexico," Don Indio started. I ushered him into my office. He explained that it wasn't right for Indio to go. This was his mother who was sick and he needed to be the one to take care of her. Unlike Fish's case, when his mother was going and needed company, Don Indio could handle this himself.

"I want you to help me. I know you are a writer and I want to write a letter to my children before I go. You know, Cuadros, you know what can happen. I want them to understand," he said, and paused for a moment, holding back tears.

"It's okay, man," I said, putting my hand on his shoulder. "I can write any letter you want." Don Indio wanted the letter typed and written professionally. I sat at the computer and let him dictate what he wanted to say. When we were done, he signed it, and I sealed it in an envelope. Then he looked at me and his dark eyes penetrated mine.

"Cuadros, do not give them this letter unless I do not come back," he said gravely. "Only then."

I understood. These were his last words to his kids before he embarked upon a perilous journey that had no guarantees that he would be back. I offered him a beer and we drank together and talked about his trip, kidding ourselves that it wouldn't be so bad. I told him that he didn't need to worry, that he would be back soon enough. When he left, I placed the letter in a book on my bookcase. It sits there to this day.

17

The narrow avenue cut through downtown Siler City and went up a hill to the old cemetery in what used to be the western outskirts of town. Many years ago, it had been home to the families of millworkers who labored in the old textile factories, stitching and cutting fabric for the country. That Southern industry fell on hard times and was now on its deathbed—a victim of globalization. But what globalization taketh, it also giveth, and when the Latino migration began in earnest in the mid-1990s, an enterprising man known to the community as "Pelucas" because of the toupee he wore, took it upon himself to provide housing for the growing number of workers in the chicken plants who were coming from Latin America. He owned a number of little run-down row houses along the avenue and he rented them out to Mexicans, Guatemalans, and El Salvadorans. The houses were all in a state of disrepair, with no heat, broken windows, no air-conditioning, and roach infested. They were little more than boardinghouses where workers could bed down after pulling two shifts at the chicken plant.

"Avenida Pelucas" or Pelucas Avenue, as it came to be known, became an entrenched enclave for Latinos and their families as the years passed and if the avenue had possessed a heart, it would have been found in Indio's backyard. There, behind his little white row house, was *la cancha,* the field. There was enough space in the backyard to accommodate a soccer field.

It was the birthplace of soccer for all the Latinos in Siler City. Boys from all over town would come to Indio's house to play. But if the small field attracted the boys in the barrio, it also brought the men from the plants to play a *cascarita* on Sundays or after work and drink some *chelas.* When the boys got old enough, everybody mixed it up on the field. To improve the condition of the field, Don Indio erected two goals, hammering several pieces of long two-by-fours into the red Carolina earth. The wooden goals didn't last long, and he eventually got a friend in the plumbing business to donate and weld several long pipes as sturdier replacements.

The field was no longer than thirty by twenty yards and it was uneven, sloping uphill toward the cemetery. There were obstacles too. On the north side was an old shed and on the opposite side was a small wire fence and trees. The obstacles didn't really matter, there were no boundaries; if a player had possession of the ball he just went around the shed, disappearing for a moment before reappearing on the other side. Sometimes, during the game, one player with the ball would be seen to briefly disappear behind the shed and another would reappear, coming from the opposite direction, the second having stolen the ball from the first.

I met Indio in the shed that he and his father had converted into a room. He, his brother Perico, and his uncle slept there to escape the overcrowded conditions of the main house. Indio loved the shed. He could stay out late at night and come home to what was basically his own apartment.

"Okay, tell me about John the Savage," I asked him. We had been studying and preparing for the coming school year, especially for his AP English class, which he needed to do well in if he wanted to go to college. His summer assignment was to read Aldous Huxley's *Brave New World.*

"Well, John Savage kills himself because he cannot fit in," he said.

"That's right, but tie that into our discussion about Darwin and evolution. What did we say about survival of the fittest?"

"Darwin said that animals needed to adapt to survive," he said, and paused for a moment. He was figuring out where I was going with this. "John Savage did not adapt to his environment."

"That's right," I said. He was almost there. "Now, did he not adapt or did he *choose* not to adapt? What do you think?"

He got it. "He *chose* not to adapt when he killed himself."

"That's right. You have to adapt to survive in your environment, but first you have to *choose* to do so. Now let me ask you this. Are you John Savage? You come from another place, but have you adapted to the U.S.?"

"Yeah, I've adapted in some ways. I am still Mexican but I am learning English. I go to school here, play soccer here. My life is here."

I wanted to challenge him a little more. Make him think. Indio's mind operated best on concrete levels; abstract ideas and themes did not come easily to him. If he was going to pass AP English, he needed to respond to literature in a different, less hidebound and literal way. "Okay, let me ask you this. Can you play soccer for the United States?"

He took up the question with gusto. "Yeah, I could play for the United States. It would be a chance to show people what a Hispanic could do, how a Hispanic could achieve and do good things."

I dug deeper. "Could you play for the U.S. against Mexico?"

He threw his head back and laughed. He thought about it a moment, but just laughed some more. He couldn't answer that question—yet. It cut awfully close to his dreams. Then, finally, wiping the smile from his face, he started nodding. "Yeah, I could," he said. "I could play against Mexico. But maybe I would just sit on the bench."

Five years prior to this day, Indio had been living in Mexico City with his mother, brother, and sister. His father had emigrated to the United States more than three years earlier and the eleven-year-old boy missed him terribly. He was an excellent student in school but nearing the end of his education by Mexican standards. In order to continue beyond the sixth grade, the family would have to start paying for his schooling, but it was unlikely that they could afford the uniforms, books, and other supplies.

Indio missed his father; the emptiness, the vacancy, in his home and in his heart was growing bigger and bigger with each day. It consumed him and plagued every waking moment of his young life. He was a very focused kid, one who could zero in on a goal and keep his eyes on it until he either achieved it or failed to achieve it. He begged his mother to let him go to the United States to be reunited with his father. She talked it over with her husband and he made the arrangements for Indio to be brought to North Carolina.

It was on a Tuesday when he boarded a bus to the Texas border. He was scheduled to meet with a cousin of his father who would accompany him. A reliable coyote had been contracted and Don Indio had paid well for his son to cross safely. But the cousin didn't make it, and little Indio found himself alone as he joined the group and began the trek across the desert. His family was desperate to learn what had happened to him, but there was nothing they could do now that the crossing had begun. In North Carolina and in Mexico, his father and mother held their breaths and waited to hear word about their oldest son.

His companions were mostly men and they walked through the desert with packs of sardines, tortillas, and cans of beans stuffed into their bags. Indio crossed a river on horseback, and when he reached the other side, he thought he was already in the United States and the journey was over. He was wrong. By the third day, the group was out of water and food. Once, they came close to being crushed by a stampede of cattle and only avoided death by ducking behind trees. Another time, thirst became too much for the men in the group. They spotted cattle troughs and ran up to them, scooping the filthy feces-drenched water into their mouths. "I didn't care. I was so thirsty," Indio told me. "I would have drunk anything." He learned to hate beans and swore never to eat them again. When the group stopped during the evening, he would look up at the stars and think of his father. "I didn't think of nothing but my dad," he said. "I didn't even care about death, all I thought about was my dad, seeing my dad." When it got cold, the men in the group flanked the young boy with their bodies to keep him warm. When he finally made it to the safe house he ate plates of beans and stacks of steaming tortillas. Then he fell asleep. He slept so hard and so deeply he almost missed the van for North Carolina.

It was early in the morning when the van finally stopped in Siler City and Indio crawled out. He had traveled two thousand miles to see his father. It was as if he'd never really seen him at all, except in a dream he was have trouble remembering. Then he saw a man of less than thirty years with dark hair and a lightly shaded mustache standing in front of a red car. Between his knees was a license plate, the kind you get made at a mall, with the word MARIA, written in script, stamped on it. It was his little sister's name. Indio looked at the man and saw his brother Perico's face. He had missed his little brother so much, and now here he was, standing there, an old man; Perico and his father looked exactly alike, give or take eighteen years. Indio and his father fell into each other's arms and wept. Don Indio had been so worried. Imagine sending your son through the desert with strangers and no telephone, no way to reach him, knowing that not even children are spared the heat, the sun, the bandits, the Border Patrol, and death. Don Indio had imagined those horrors and more during the past five days. But here he was, his son. "When I saw my father I was so happy, man. I will never forget that," Indio said. "It was the happiest time in my life." Father and son spent the next year getting to know each other again.

People question migrants crossing the border without papers. But at eleven, Indio didn't know what he was doing was illegal. "It is wrong to cross the border," he told me once when we were talking about it in his room. "But it also is wrong to be separated from your father, to miss seeing him every day until it hurts. I would do it again even though it was wrong."

There is a picture I have seen of young Indio, standing on his front porch on Pelucas Avenue, just after he arrived in North Carolina, Don Indio stands beside him in a white shirt with light blue sleeves and black jeans and a tan belt. On his face there is a look of unsteady surprise. He has his left arm around Indio, who stands with boyish perkiness, his hands in his pockets, wearing a black, long-sleeved shirt with a red and white stripe across his chest and arms. Indio is happy and is smiling, which is, in itself, strange, as all his pictures from then on show him with a serious expression—as if he were posing for a daguerreotype. But it is his eyes that draw your attention. They are happy but weary. You can see the dust from the desert in them, you can tell the light fingers of the crossing have touched his face. All these kids bear that caress. It is a transformative event. For some it leaves only fading scars, but for others, that touch runs to the bone.

It didn't take long for Indio to become successful in school. Once he learned the rules and what was expected of him, he began to apply himself. Two years later he was selected Student of the Year. The family's living room is a virtual shrine to his academic and athletic achievements. Plaques, certificates, medals, and trophies hang from the wall or stand on the bookcase, attesting to his gifts.

He continued that success in high school, where he earned a 3.7 grade-point average. Math, drafting, and the sciences were his favorite subjects. He was less adept at English and the social sciences. But that was Indio. He was a real straight-ahead kid and not glib with lofty or abstract ideas. He wanted to be an architect, designing homes and buildings. He had worked in the home-construction industry like so many other Latinos and quickly realized who the *mero-mero,* the big boss, was. He wanted to be the one with the blueprints in his hands. But that was going to be a hard goal to achieve.

Like thousands of other migrant kids who had come to North Carolina and the South in the past fifteen years, Indio was not a legal resident and could not be accepted into the state's public colleges—despite having the academic qualifications. If somehow students like him managed to get accepted, they had to pay the higher out-of-state tuition, as if they had graduated from high schools outside of North Carolina. This obstacle made college a virtual impossibility for these kids.

It didn't matter how many A's they earned, and it didn't matter how many leadership awards they won, the state saw these kids as nonentities once they graduated from high school. There is very little difference between a chicken-plant manager who fires a Latino worker who cuts his hand or a construction foreman who lays off a bricklayer who breaks his foot and a state that says that a child who has been accepted and educated in its system is suddenly an outsider. When the Latino migrant becomes less useful or a nuisance, whether he is a child, a teenager, or an adult, he is disposed of, tossed away like so much scrap.

The treatment of these kids as out-of-state students was, on the face of it, ridiculous—a blatant insult. How can a student who has been educated for twelve years and graduated from the high school located down the road from a public university like the University of North Carolina–Chapel Hill, all of a sudden be considered a foreigner? It was absurd—a farce that could be added to the already heaping pile of absurdities that Latin American workers and their families dealt with in the United States. And a society that did not allow a community's best and brightest to achieve their dreams did so at its own peril. Bright, motivated kids will find a way to be successful. You can bet on that. The question confronting the states now was whether that success was going to be in something legitimate or illegitimate. Having a group of smart, educated people who are forced to live in a permanent underclass will do nothing toward fostering a healthy society.

Indio wanted to go to college. I had made him a promise to help him achieve his dream. He had the grades and he was an excellent athlete, the best player at JM. He had a chance of attracting the right coach at the right school, one who could help him get around the residency problem. It was funny how schools found a way to recruit and find visas for their foreign-student athletes when they wanted them badly enough. This was Indio's only real chance. If there was anyone on the team who could do it, he was the one. He had strength, skills, intelligence, but what I think most helped him get through life and achieve was his eternal and unfailing optimism. Indio always believed that things would turn out well.

A car horn sounded. Indio got up and looked out the window. "It's Guero," he said, pulling the curtain back. "Oh, and Bomba is with him."

We got up and left the shed. The guys had arrived to play a *cascarita* in the backyard. In a matter of minutes, we heard Daddy Yankee's "Gasolina" emanating from the old Nissan. Guero had put huge speakers in the trunk and now he opened its doors and let the *boom boom* of the bass reverberate outward. Moments later, Fish joined the boys, followed by Loco, Perico, Beto, Pepa, and Chuy. The boys divided up into teams and started to play, making hard runs, trying to dribble around one another. I got my cleats out of my car and put on a pair of shorts. As I wrapped the black laces underneath my old-school World Cup Adidas cleats, I looked up and watched them a moment.

They lived a swell life. They were all dirt-poor and some didn't have fathers at home or were separated from their families in Mexico, but they had one another. They were a tight group, *juntado*. They played soccer together, placed bets on their games, and competed for hamburgers at McDonald's. They drank their first beers together and found the courage to ask a girl to dance in one another's company. They went to school together, worked the same shifts together, fixed one another's cars, got into fights together, passed tests or flunked classes together. Once, the guys got interested in boxing. So, being young and stupid, they decided to box some of the black kids at school. They met at the field behind Indio's house, excited and eager. The black kids showed up; they were bigger and far more experienced. But the Latino boys didn't back down. The boys put on training gloves and started banging at one another. They had four fights and lost three matches before calling a draw between Indio and his opponent. When they told me all this I couldn't believe it. What were they thinking? But they just laughed and considered it another adventure. What the black kids thought of them I had no idea.

I envied them their lives, their youth, their challenges, and the ways they found to circumvent the barriers they faced. They suf-

fered terrible defeats but also enjoyed wonderful victories. My own
school experience had been isolated, unmarked, and lonely, battling
for my place and wondering who I was. The boys I coached experienced all that too, but they did it *together*. They were a merry bunch,
and when things got too hard, they laughed it off or simply said "It's
what God wants" and carried on. Their Rubicon had been the desert and they all lived to tell about it. It showed in each of their faces.
They all knew what a hard day's work was, had been tested in hardship, experienced terrible prejudice, and faced an uncertain future.
But all that faded away when they strapped their boots on and ran
onto the pitch. If there was one place they could call home, a place
where they could really *feel* at home, it was here—between two
goals on a dusty field. And I had finally found my place as well.

"*Vamos,* Cuadros!" Indio shouted at me.

I got up and did a couple of quick stretches and trotted out to the
field. The guys were harder to play with now than they'd been during the first season. All of them were at the peak of their strength
and were sleek, speedy, and talented with the ball. But I still had a
couple of moves left in me.

18

The July sun burned bright and made the outfield grass of the baseball field reflect like shimmering green water. I squinted against the glare. It was a new season and I lugged the usual equipment into the dugout. The baseball coach was there, sitting like a statue with his arms folded and eyes closed. He woke up when I approached with a bag of soccer balls. I went through my usual harangue about using the outfield for practice, but we both know the routine, and it didn't take as long. It was progress.

The boys began arriving almost as soon as I got there. They drove up in their cars with the steady beat of regaetton pounding through the windows. Gone was the old Mexican ranchero music, the *corridas,* the *norteño* sounds, and the Duranguense drums. The fierce rap of Daddy Yankee replaced them ushering in a Caribbean beat for this new generation. Soon the field was filled with brown boys kicking white soccer balls into the air and taking shots on the practice goals. It was a new season.

But what should have been our strongest team, the one with the most promise, was turning out to be the weakest. The *cholos* had all burned out and were ineligible. Lost were Pony, Servando, Chisco, Nemo, Ro-Ro, and Santos. The only one who'd made it was Guero, barely passing his classes and staying in school. This should have been our year to make a real run for the conference championship, to beat Albemarle, and take the Yadkin Valley title. Instead it looked like we would end up in third place.

The losses we'd already suffered had left me feeling depressed about the coming season. It seemed as though we could never quite get our act together to achieve something truly great. I began thinking that no matter how hard I worked with the boys, or how much I pushed them to be greater than their individual selves, it would never be enough to overcome their problems. I wanted them to be champions, to prepare them for their lives here in the United States. I knew they would be profoundly tested by this society in unforseeable ways. The humiliations, the degradation, the pride-crushing blows—all were on the horizon for them when they graduated—if they graduated.

They had a vague awareness of what awaited them after high school. For now they lived in a bubble, unexposed to the indignities of being Latino in America. They were secure, could use their real names, and didn't have to negotiate the shadowy world of the undocumented migrant. But in a couple of years, all their achievements would be swept away and they would be left with little more than the "status" of illegal immigrants. They would have to assume new identities and live in a state of perpetual fear of being found out.

I wanted them to be victors, to be champions, to have the knowledge that they were the *best* at something in their lives. I hoped that would consolidate their identities, harden their skins, and, so to speak, fuse their bones. But all my hopes seemed to fly away on the first day of practice. We would always be contenders but never champions.

The only ray of hope appeared when I learned that Loco had been allowed to play this season. It seemed that the only class he had not completed was weight lifting, in which he was setting an A before he left for Atlanta. Moody took pity on him and granted the waiver that allowed him to participate. My core midfield had come back intact.

We had eight new freshman join the team and these boys were very different from their older brothers. Most of them were Chicanos, had been born in the United States. The Latino student population in Chatham County was changing—it was becoming more native-born. Only 3 percent of the school system were newcomers now. The vast majority of Latino students were American-born. These new kids were more assimilated, spoke perfect English and Spanish, did better in school, and had higher expectations. But they were also plagued by problems associated with poverty and alienation. They didn't quite know where they fit in, or even how well they should try to do in school. They held on to everything that made them Latino, from listening to regaetton, to speaking only in Spanish, to trying sometimes to act like *cholos,* to hanging out exclusively with one another.

There was Arabe; Kawasaki, so called because he looked Japanese; Guapo, the handsome one; Cesar; a pudgy and funny kid named Cheeseburger; Frankie; and Chaquetas, an extremely talented, skinny, and light-skinned player whose name meant something quite vulgar in Mexican slang. Of the freshmen, Chaquetas was clearly the most talented and, like Tereso before him, the most troubled.

Anchoring the entire team was a stellar midfield that consisted of Edi, Guero, and Loco and was led by Indio. The defense was strong and led by three seniors: Fish in goal, Lechero, and Anthony. Lecherito and Bomba backed them up. The true question marks were the forwards. Indio's younger brother Perico had been promoted to forward, and even though he was undersize, he could outfox defenses for goals. Next to him was La Pepa, one of the freshman from the first season who had not qualified for the second season because of too many missed classes. Pepa was an unusually tall kid, about six two, who'd worked hard during his year off to get back on the team. It was his last year of eligibility and he really wanted to be a starter. With his height and size, he easily won the spot of forward.

I was down about the team not only because of the loss of the talented *cholos,* but because I was alone for the first time. Ricardo had left after the first season. Matt was still around but couldn't drive out to Siler City too often. Lenin, whom I'd hoped would one day take over the team, had moved back to Mexico. Chuy from the first season offered to help coach during the games, as did Chad Morgan from the middle school. But it would be just me and the boys for most of it.

Our first conference game of the season would be against our hated rivals at Albemarle. We would pick up where we'd left off the previous season. All the boys remembered what the Bulldogs had done to us just nine months ago and they were eager to finally beat them. We were confident: we were older now, tested on the field, and mature in our abilities and strategy. The possession game was now working brilliantly. But soccer is a game of spirit as well as skill. The players needed to be of one mind on the field in order to truly help one another.

Before the start of the game, the referee called both teams to the middle of the field to chat about sportsmanship. This particular ref, a short white man in his fifties, took one look at the Jets and said, "Where are the Americans?" All the *chavos* groaned. I told him, "They are Americans, they are Latin Americans." He laughed but understood his little joke had upset the team. He tried to apologize, but when the first words out of his mouth were "Do you all understand English?" Again the boys groaned. I thought he should just give up now. These slights were old hat. It was not uncommon for an opposing coach to walk right past me and straight to Chad, the white guy, assuming he was the coach. I had gotten used to these affronts, but for the *chavos,* it was still new. I usually let it slide because if I got into someone's face every time it happened, I'd be living in a state of perpetual madness. The guys had to learn how to handle this stuff themselves.

All summer long I had thought about the words that could motivate the players, the talks that would bind them together and help them work for one another. I had seen something a team had done during a college football game in order to inspire their players to stick together and decided to crib it. I went to my local hardware store and had the owner cut a length of heavy chain that had some twenty-five links. I then linked the chain together with a large cara-biner and brought it with me to the game in a blue bag.

"Okay, guys, bring it in," I started. I looked at each team member but concentrated on the players that had played in the last game of the second season. "Some of you I told to remember the feeling you had when we lost here nine months ago. Now here we are again. Do you remember what they did to us the last time we were here?"

I could see in their eyes that they clearly remembered. Lechero's gaze alone could have set the field on fire. "Last year we came off this field in disgrace. Disgrace. And I said I never wanted to see that type of behavior again. We will never play like that again. Win or lose, we will carry ourselves like men. We will not be punks. We will not whine, we will not foul, we will not yell at the refs, we will not take our shirts off. Those are the things we will *not* do. We *will* play hard, we will respect our opponents, we will respect the refs, we will win games, and we will lose games. That's what being a Jet is."

This team was much less angry than the previous season's had been. "It is a new season," I continued. "And I want to say only three words. These words will be who we are this year. They are simple but they mean a lot. *Fuerza y honor.* Strength and honor. What does that mean? With *fuerza* we will win games. But with honor we will *be* winners." I pulled the long, thick chain out of the bag like a heavy snake. The guys saw it for the first time and their eyes lit up. I pushed them back to keep them from grabbing it. I held it up and asked them what it was.

Beto stepped up. "It's a chain," he said, and the guys laughed.

"No!" I yelled. "This is *us*. And when we come together we come together like this chain—strong, tough, and made of iron!" I then linked the chain together and the boys pushed their way through the circle to grab a piece of it. They swayed to the left together and then back to the right, all held tightly by their hands and the chain. Edi led us in our cheer: "Who are the Jets?" he asked. The boys responded, "We are!" And then their cheer started out low, like a rumble in their bellies, and built up until they screamed, "Let's go, Jets!" And they took the field.

The game started with the Jets playing tentatively. They were unsure of themselves. The passing between the players was not precise and we lost a number of balls to Albemarle, who, despite having lost some talent, were still playing tough. Edi seemed to be the only player who remembered our possession game and our strategy of attacking along the wings. The Bulldogs were able to penetrate into our defensive third of the field and Anthony fouled one of them. The referee awarded a direct kick from outside the eighteen. But as the Jets defense discussed how to set up a wall to counteract the direct kick, the Bulldogs took the shot quickly, while the defense was still talking, catching Fish unprepared in goal.

Albemarle had scored against us in the first three minutes. It was a clever, heads-up play. It seemed as though we could never get past Albemarle. In sports, there are teams that just have your number. They know what to do to beat you—or rather, how to let you beat yourself.

We needed to beat Albemarle not only to avenge the previous season's loss and pain, but to win the conference and get the home-field games in the play-offs. I always told the guys to concentrate on the conference, to win it, in order to play at home during the play-offs, a decided advantage. But a goal in the first five minutes was terrible. The guys were not concentrating and I could hear criticism coming from the defense for not being ready. Lechero was losing it. But Fish stepped up and calmed him down, telling him that they'd just caught us off guard, and that it was time to step up the pace.

This time, instead of folding, caving into despair and self-destructiveness, the Jets responded. They were led by Indio, who took the ball on his foot and dribbled past two Albemarle defenders in the middle of the field to pass the ball up front to La Pepa, who received it, turned, and shot it. The back of the Albemarle goal exploded as the ball hit the net and tied the game. It was our first goal ever against this team, and in that moment the *chavos* found a new sense of confidence and depth. This team would not be so easily beaten, and it wouldn't beat itself.

The second goal came quickly after the first, and again it was Indio who led the way—cutting through the middle and then passing off to Loco on the right wing, who sprinted down the sideline, burning his defender and finishing with a shot that beat the keeper. The third goal came off a corner kick from Edi to Guero, who used a head shot to put the ball in. The Albemarle coaches screamed at their players to cover and to come back, but the Bulldogs were visibly stunned. Edi got his own goal soon after, on a hard run down the left wing and a powerful left-footed shot that killed the keeper. The freshman Chaquetas scored the fifth goal of the half when he picked up a loose ball in the middle and dribbled up, firing a shot past the defeated and demoralized Albemarle keeper.

By the time the final whistle blew, we had beaten the Bulldogs by a score of 8–1, a joyous rout that countered each one of the goals that they had scored on us in the past three seasons. We had fired thirty-five shots, had six corner kicks, and had had two goals disallowed. It was a team win with goals coming from five different players. But I knew that the victory was in no small part the result of one player's determination to be the best. Indio had not scored during the game, but he came away with four assists on goal—setting up his friends to deliver blow after blow to Albemarle's heart.

The boys rejoiced on the very field where they had so bitterly wept the season before. They couldn't believe that things had turned around so much. Albemarle had been a soccer power for so long—winning championship after conference championship, but all that was over. They would never be the same team again. We had broken whatever hold they had over us, forever crushing their mystique. They were now just another team.

But the high of crushing Albemarle didn't last very long. We came crashing down in the next game against our county rivals Chatham Central. Edi made a hard run down the left wing only to be tripped up by a defender. He went flying into the air and landed on his shoulder. I knew something was terribly wrong when he didn't get up. We gently turned him over and saw he had broken his left collarbone. An ambulance was summoned and took him to the hospital. Seeing a player go down is the worst feeling in the world. We couldn't beat Chatham Central enough after that, and I couldn't wait to leave the field and go see him at the hospital. Indio, Guero, and Fish showed up to check on him.

Edi had broken his collarbone in three places, and one of the pieces of bone was sticking up at an angle. He needed surgery to insert a plate and four screws to heal it. The surgery went well, and afterward, Dolores and I took him home to their little cinder-block farmhouse. We placed him on the same couch were Enrique had lain after his knee surgery. Enrique looked at Edi on the couch and told him, "Now you know what love for the game means." They shared stories about their injuries and their scars and I teased them about how they were made of glass because they broke so easily. Edi would be out for two months.

Losing Edi was a blow to the team, even though I knew he would be back in time for the second half of the season and the play-offs. But just when I thought that we could overcome this loss, we were dealt another setback when I learned that Guero had a run in with the police.

Guero was sick of school. He didn't like his classes, they were too easy for him, but he didn't feel like challenging himself by taking harder ones. He was still taking ESL classes despite being proficient enough to move out of them. But most of his friends were taking ESL classes and he didn't want to leave them. He liked goofing off in class, acting out, and hanging out with the *cholos*.

Guero had decided that school wasn't for him. He had simply made up his mind. He was going to drop out. The Friday after the Chatham Central game, he picked up his girlfriend and drove to Bray Park. They were sitting in the car making out when a police car rolled up and busted Guero for skipping school and driving without a license. The officer took pity on the couple and didn't formally arrest them or issue Guero a ticket for not having a driver's license. Moody suspended him on the spot for three days. Guero would miss the Thomasville game on Monday. I met him that Monday afternoon before the game in front of the community center. He strolled up sheepishly and we sat down on the steps to talk about what had happened.

"*Me pincharon,* Cuadros," he started, hanging his head down. "They arrested me, Cuadros." I didn't know whether to feel sorry for him or to lay into him. Getting arrested, having the handcuffs put on and sitting in the back of a squad car for the first time, was a jarring experience. But then, Guero could have been fooling me. He was clever.

I told him that this was an opportunity for him to look at his life and see where he was going. He was heading down a dark path and this was the sign of things to come if he didn't change. "What do you want to do with your life?" I asked him. He looked at me through his light brown eyes beneath the straight, honey-brown hair and shrugged. There was a reason why all the kids called him Guero—he looked white. You'd never know that Guero was a Latino kid until he opened his mouth. He was handsome, strong, a bit dangerous, and naturally all the girls were wild about him.

I pressed him and he finally said he wanted to go to college. I didn't buy it completely. It was too easy an out for him because he was undocumented. I didn't know if Guero wanted to go to college or not, but he opened the door for me to press him to finish at least a high school education. A lot of the kids felt disillusioned about school and there were some who dropped out because it all seemed a waste of time if they couldn't go on to college. They weren't stupid. But being undocumented was also an excuse to drop out, to not try, to not risk failure.

"You don't know if the laws are going to change, Guero," I said, looking at him. "But at least you will have a high school education, that's more than your parents had. But if you keep behaving like this you'll only wind up in jail and then be deported."

But his mind was made up. "I'm going to *quitiar*." He was going to quit. I couldn't let him do so now, but there seemed no way to convince him to stay in school. I finally decided to use the team as a means to keep him in—at least for the season. I knew that my words were self-serving—I needed him on the team to win—but I thought it would also help him to reconsider. His had been an impulsive decision and perhaps, if some time passed, he would change his mind. Teenagers are like that.

"How can you quit the team?" I put more emphasis in my voice. "We are a *team*. You started this and now you have to finish it. Stay with us, Guero." I had put it all on the line. He nodded and mouthed "Okay." I could see tears forming around the corners of his eyes. Guero was a hard kid, he never cried and didn't allow himself to be vulnerable to other people.

"Look, Guero, I know this is hard, but I want to see you one day graduate from this school." Now it was my turn to tear up. I put my arm around him and drew him in. "I want to see you in that auditorium receiving that diploma. I want to see that, man."

When we left each other I didn't know if he would drop out or not. I thought I had probably only bought some time. It was ultimately up to him. We lost the game to Thomasville, 3–2, in a heavy downpour and gave up our number one spot in the conference. We had been at the top of the heap for only five days.

The loss to Thomasville created a tight race for the number one spot in the conference. We had slipped to second place behind the Thomasville and East Montgomery teams—both predominantly Latino. The dominant teams in the conference had changed this year from overwhelmingly white to overwhelmingly Latino. We rebounded once Guero came back to the team after his suspension. He had decided to stay in school.

We went on a five-game tear. By the time we were set to play Thomasville again at home, we had been on a seven-game winning streak and the boys were thrilled at the prospect of beating them after the previous loss. What should have been a close game turned into a rout as the Jets quickly responded to an early Thomasville goal by scoring six unanswered ones of their own—putting us one step closer to the conference title.

The final game of the season was away, against South Davidson, the team that had been so nasty to us the previous year. I dreaded going there again. We were poised to win the conference championship, but I feared that trouble could break out against a team we were expected to beat. Our opponents had nothing to lose by provoking us into doing something stupid.

I warned the boys not to lose control of the game or of themselves. We were on the verge of victory. They needed to hold their tempers if they were insulted, shoved, pushed, pulled, or tackled from behind. This was a test of our collective character. We would have to endure their blows. Playing a less skilled team is always harder than playing against an equal opponent. It certainly wasn't necessary to humiliate the other team, but at the same time you wanted to play your game.

We crushed them, 6–0. This time, however, we didn't hear any of the chants, the nasty insults, or the racial slurs against the boys. The fans were downright polite. South Davidson even had a pair of Latino brothers on their squad now and I could hear the Southern parents shout out, "Way to go, Say-sar!" in an attempt to pronounce the name Cesar. I guess the migration was just beginning to touch Denton. Things were changing even in this corner of the South.

There was no better example of how this team and its fans had changed when, with only a minute left in the game, one of the South Davidson players, a former football player, picked up the soccer ball from the midfield and ran toward our goal. The guys watched as this big white kid scrambled down the field. Only Fish kept his head and went out to meet him, tackling him before he could fall into the goal. The boys from both teams then jumped on Fish and the other player—creating a pile of bodies scrambling for the ball. They laughed and jostled one another in good cheer. I stood on the sidelines and watched dumbfounded, but understood what the Davidson players were doing. They had been football players, and were

graduating now, and they wanted to have a little fun. What was re-
markable, I thought, was how my boys responded in equal good
humor. In the end, you couldn't tell one boy from the other in the
scrum.

When the game ended shortly thereafter, the players from both
teams shook hands with genuine warmth. The experience had been
the polar opposite from the previous year's game, and I had to admire the coach and the hard work he had done to turn things around
at his school. Soccer is an international sport played by all the peoples of the world. There was no better example of that spirit than
that last game at South Davidson.

We had won the game and we had won the conference. I stood
on the sidelines looking at my players, feeling proud and strong. It
had taken us only three seasons to become conference champs and
end the domination of Albemarle. And we had done it in our own
way, with *fuerza y honor.* That had been my main goal, the conference championship. Anything could happen in the play-offs. A
missed offside call by a ref could end it for us. There was no predict-
ing anything in the play-offs. But no matter what happened, we
would always be champions.

19

The Jets are playing down—confused, frantic even. We can't seem to find the back of the net. We are penetrating, on the wings and through the middle, but we can't finish the job. Hendersonville puts up a valiant effort, but they are no match for the Jets. Their only real play is to penetrate on the right wing and cross the ball over to the weak side of the field for their tall curly-haired top player to stick it in. But our defense is all over that plan and we stymie it from the start. Unable to penetrate with their main weapon, Hendersonville resorts to their old tricks—trying to knock us off the ball and fouling. But this is a different team from the first year. We are not a one-dimensional team with only one brilliant player to shut down. No, this time we attack with six excellent players, all capable of scoring.

But we are keeping them in the game with our sluggish play. We win a corner kick and the boys crowd inside the penalty box, shoving and pushing for position as the kick comes in. The ball comes in high and Pepa is there, he jumps and gets his head over the ball before striking it down and into the goal. On the sidelines, I am relieved. We have scored the first goal.

The boys come in and gather around. I stand in front of them. I attempt to conjure up something, anything, meaningful to say to them.

"We are getting there but we are not finishing," I started. "You need to settle down a bit and set up the plays better. I want to see more penetration from the wings. We are concentrating too much in the middle. Kick it out to the flags and let Loco and Edi run for it. They are faster than these guys."

The guys trot out back onto the field. The lights are just beginning to glow. The field begins to shine a luminescent green. The Bearcats begin the game this time and desperately try to send the ball upfield on a long kick. Lecherito sends it out over the back line. It is a corner kick. The boys take their positions and the defense covers their men. When the ball is hit it comes in low and hard and Lecherito, who has been standing near post, goes to head it out. But instead of the ball going out, it deflects back in and Fish has no chance to save it. It is an own goal against us and the game is tied again. Lecherito is beside himself. Tears well up in his eyes and he knows he may have cost his team the game. His older brother walks over to him, angry, his eyes bulging, he is going to tear into his younger brother for the mistake, but Fish intercepts him. "Hey, calm down, Lechero," he tells him, holding out his white-gloved hands. "He doesn't need any balling out. Encourage him." It would have been hard to hear those words last year, but this team has found itself. Fish and Lechero stand there for a moment, two seniors, veterans of the field, talking and settling down. Lechero nods and goes over to his brother and says in Mexican slang, *"No te aquites,"* "Don't get all teary."

The Jets unleash a furious attack on the Bearcats. They will not be denied. But while they are able to penetrate with the ball, they are unable to score. We can't buy a goal tonight. The game ends the way it began, with two Jets shots hitting the post but not going in.

The game goes into overtime. I make no substitutions. The guys have trained hard this week, preparing for the play-off game. They are ready and none are tired. There is no taking Indio out of the game. The overtime consists of two ten-minute halves. It begins with both teams going at each other. There is shoving and pushing, guys falling down and tumbling headfirst, their cleats kicking mud in the air.

With time running out in the first overtime, Perico finally penetrates with the ball inside the penalty box. He streaks in on the left side, but before he can shoot the game-winning goal, a defender brings him down from behind. He falls forward, eating grass. The referee calls a foul. Now, finally, we will get the penalty kick that will seal the game. But the referee calls for an indirect kick inside the penalty area. No referee would make such a call when a player is attacking the goal with the ball and goes down. But the referee calls obstruction instead of the tackle. The sideline referee can't explain it either. It is a highly irregular call. The Jets take it, but the ball is deflected by the Hendersonville defenders. The first overtime ends in a tie.

"Guys, guys, okay, I want to tell you about a special phone I brought for the play-offs," I said, grabbing their attention. They were just getting into cell phones and loved playing with them. "This is a special phone. And when I pick up this phone I will be *calling on* one of you or all of you. I don't know who will answer it, but one of you has got to. I am asking right now, who will answer my call? Who will pick up the phone and say, '*Sí,* Cuadros, I am here!' Who will answer for this team? Who will step up?"

The second overtime consists of two five-minute halves. It is sudden death. The first team to score wins. With only minutes left, the stadium is out of control. The fans stamp their feet and clap their hands, blow horns and trumpets, and bang on drums. The *chavas* are on their feet chanting, "*¡Queremos gol! ¡Queremos gol!*" "We want a goal, we want a goal!" The school has turned out for the Saturday-night game—teachers, students, and staff. Even the baseball coach hangs out in a corner of the stands, watching.

We attack again and this time Indio penetrates through the middle, dribbling past two players and then passing the ball on the inside to Guero, who beats his defender and is through and inside the box. He runs at the goal, which looms larger and wider with each step. Guero can finish. But instead of firing from a distance, he continues to run at the goal. A Hendersonville defender has no choice but to bring him down from behind.

A clear foul. The referee must call for a penalty kick. But no. Again he calls for an indirect kick inside the box. The ball is placed only six yards from the goal. In a ridiculous scene, the entire Hendersonville team lines up along the goal line inside the goal from post to post.

Indio and Bomba stand in front of the ball. It is indirect, so it needs to be touched by another player before it can go in the goal to count. Indio touches the ball and Bomba steps up, extending his right leg back until the heel of his cleat touches his backside. He snaps his leg forward and makes full contact with the ball. I don't even see it fly, but it goes straight and hard. All I hear is a *plink* and then see it ricochet inside the goal. Bomba has squeezed the ball past the near post and a Hendersonville player. The bench clears and rushes out onto the field in joy, jumping up and down. I run in with them. It is a golden moment. The players are hugging and throwing themselves on the field beneath the bright lights. Everyone is piling on Bomba.

I looked out onto the field and watched as the boys laughed and cried. Finally they gathered around me. I didn't say a word. When they were silent I started. "Tonight, I said I had a special phone. I said that I was calling out the Jets to answer it. I said that someone on this team needed to pick it up. I didn't know that someone would be the quietest guy on the team. I didn't know that he would be the most silent. I didn't know it would be him. But he is a player who speaks with his acts, with his shots, and with his goals! Bomba answered the phone tonight!" The guys loved it when I was dramatic. They slapped Bomba on the back and he simply nodded. "I will see you all at practice on Monday. Do not be late!"

As the boys were leaving the field in their groups, I called out to

Bomba and Indio, who were walking together. I simply put out my hand and Bomba shook it. I thanked him.

The quarterfinal of the play-offs were against one of our conference rivals, a predominantly Latino team from North Moore High School in Robbins, hometown of former senator John Edwards. We had beaten them twice during the season and were a bit nervous for the third game because of the odds. North Moore had shocked the state in the opening round of the play-offs when they beat the number one team in the state, the defending state champs from the mountains of Polk County. Polk County had underestimated the scrappy Latino team, to their chagrin. The win opened the door for us to have all our play off games at home. It was a tremendous advantage.

The game against North Moore was relatively easy, as we found our footing and returned to our attacking and dominating style. We scored two goals in the first half that finished them off. In the second half, La Pepa scored again, this time from a nice setup on the right wing from Loco, who had learned to cross the ball in rather than just blast a shot. The game ended, 3–0, and sent us to the semifinals—to be played at home against the Surry Central Golden Eagles on Saturday. We had been on a twelve-game winning streak and nothing was going to stop us from reaching the finals now.

I was a wreck. I couldn't sleep and found myself counting the hours until the next match. We had started in July and now it was fast approaching mid-November; it felt simultaneously like we'd just started and been at it forever. The school was squarely behind the team and our run. And while that was definitely nice, it brought higher expectations. The other coaches teased me about going all the way. Moody would deadpan that my coaching position depended on winning the state championship. I became extremely superstitious. I wore the same shirt at the games, followed the same rituals, had to have the *right* whistle, clipboard, and score sheet to track the stats. You name it, I had a rite for it.

I placed an enormous amount of pressure on myself. I wanted to make the guys winners—to insulate them from the prejudice, their residency status, and allow them to overcome the barriers erected by the close-minded.

Until you walk on a sideline, you don't know how heavy the situation can be. This is something that is lacking in the club-ball soccer that is played all over the country. Those coaches don't play for their community, never have people come up to them in the drugstore and offer to shake their hand and wish them luck, never have reporters asking them how the game would go, never have the dreams of a community behind them. Their coaching is only an isolated exercise performed in front of their peers but not before the greater community. This is what makes high school ball the superior game and something I was so honored to be a part of.

The Friday before the big game, I held a lighter practice that involved shooting on goal, a light jog around the track, and a little *cascarita* because the guys had earned it. I wanted the players loose and relaxed before the game the next day. Everyone showed up for the practice except for Fish and his brother Guero. I was worried.

What I didn't know was that the night before, Fish had been working late in a local restaurant kitchen when he received a telephone call. It was his girlfriend and she was crying. She managed to tell him that his father had been shot and that he had been taken to the hospital.

Fish's father, José, had come home from the plant tired and needing to unwind. He worked long hard hours at a local auto-parts manufacturing factory. He liked to come home, eat dinner, then get together with his cousins for some beers. It was a Thursday night and he was looking forward to payday. He drove over to one of his cousins' house, where he met several friends and they all started drinking. Mexican men in Siler City drank a lot. The local newspaper's weekly crime blotter page was filled with Latino surnames and arrests for drunken driving.

On this night, José took his gun, a small snub-nosed revolver that he stuffed into his front pocket. He was sitting at the kitchen table drinking and talking when he decided to take the gun out and put it on the table. But when he reached into his pocket to pull the gun out, he accidentally pulled the trigger. The bullet tore into the flesh of his thigh and slammed against the thick bone, shattering it and emerging from the other side. He was transported to the University of North Carolina Hospital in Chapel Hill. Fish and Guero spent the night and the next day at the hospital as the doctors operated on their father.

After I found out what happened from Elisa, I tried desperately to call Fish to find out if I could help, but I couldn't reach him. I didn't know whether Fish and Guero would play on Saturday or whether they would stay at the hospital.

I stayed up all night trying to figure out what to do and how to fill the two starting positions for the game. Guero could easily be replaced by Chaquetas, the talented freshman. But replacing Fish would be the real problem. I would have to use "Univision," a bright, husky junior. I had substituted Univision during games we dominated to give him some experience and he had performed well. He was determined but he lacked command between the posts.

Fish had done well this season. He had recorded nine shutouts and had more than a hundred saves. He was a veteran of countless games and stood in the goal with a confidence few keepers in the state possessed. With him gone, our chances looked slim.

When I'd arrived at the field on Saturday afternoon, no one else was there. Usually a couple of people would be walking around the track for exercise, but today it was cool and empty. I unloaded the equipment we would need for the game: practice balls, game balls, pinnies, watercooler, water bottles, goal anchors, my bag with extra socks and first-aid kit, and the blue bag with the chain inside. I took out the corner flags from the Jets Hangar and laid them on the field. I then got out the paint striper and eight cans of paint. I wanted to paint the field well one last time for the season. The field needed to look its best for the semifinal game and my lines had to be perfect.

I started at the east corner and laid down a thick line of blue paint on the ground, tracing the back line. I thought of the season and all we had achieved. We were so close to the final. But even as I thought of our accomplishments, the thought of Fish and Guero not playing nagged at me. I shook my head at the thought of Fish's dad shooting himself in the leg. It seemed like we Latinos always found a way to shoot ourselves in the foot right at the moment when our goal was within reach. It was *la vida loca,* our disorganized way of living that always did us in and held us back. We lived in a state of drama, of turmoil, and perpetual chaos. Our lives always took the unexpected turn.

I looked down at the lines I had drawn across the field. The grass was dying now; it still had some green in it, but there were also patches of brown. The blue lines defined the field now, the white lines of the football field having faded in the Carolina sun. Within the blue lines, we could compete with the best of them and win. And even though the field had a crown, it was still the most level playing field we had ever walked on. I had spent my life searching for my own place. I grew up isolated and cut off from my own community, always on the periphery. Coaching had brought me to the center. On the field, with my boys around me, I was home. We played, fought, laughed, and cried there. And I knew that in this Southern town, on this field of green and blue, I had found a place to call my own.

The boys started arriving at five o'clock. They came in groups—friends and brothers walking in freshly washed white-and-blue uniforms. I set about getting them organized and warmed up. A few of them were already kicking the ball around and passing it to one another. Then I saw Fish, dressed in black shorts and a navy-blue short-sleeved shirt, walking onto the field. Guero was with him.

"How's your dad?"

"He's good," Fish said, cracking a smile. "He had surgery yesterday and he's going to be okay. He told us to go and play."

"I didn't know if you were going to make it," I said, grabbing him.

"I wasn't going to miss this," Fish said, and then took his place inside the goal.

The Surry Central Golden Eagles were our exact duplicates. They were an all-Latino team from northern Carolina and they had carved their way into the semifinals with a fast attacking style. I called them the Bizarro Jets—from the Superman comic books— because they were our mirror image. But as I watched them warm up, they looked more like the East Montgomery team—fast, skilled players who operated just one level above the *cascarita*. They would look for the long ball up the field for their forwards to chase down to try to score. We knew how to stop that game. We would possess the ball, work it through the middle, control it, keep them from getting the long through balls, and attack from the wings. With Fish and Guero back, I was confident we could do this.

When it was time for the game to start, the boys all came in and huddled together. There was so much to say at a moment like this. I could talk about championships, about trophies, about our community, about pride and so forth. But instead I decided to talk about our fathers.

"Tonight, I want to dedicate this game to all our fathers," I started. "Many of our fathers are here. Tonight we play for them—the men who taught us this game. When I was a boy, it was my father who taught me to kick the ball, and I know it was that way for many of you too. We love this game because our fathers love this game. And one day I know your sons will love this game." When I was done Fish came over to me and put his thick clownish white glove around my shoulder. His eyes were watery. "Shut them out tonight, Fish," was all I said.

It is a fast game and each team fights for possession of the ball. After twenty minutes the Jets are slowly managing to take control of the game. Lechero is there to head the ball away and back up the field each time the Eagles try to send their long through balls up the middle to their forwards. They cannot break through our defense.

The Jets are looking tight and nervous. Edi doesn't seem quite like himself. He's not making the streaking runs down the left wing. He looks winded and can't catch his breath. The last moments of the sun and its warmth have faded over the goalposts behind Fish and the stadium lights shine bright on the field. With only fifteen minutes left in the first half, the Jets seize control of the game. It is Indio who starts the play. He picks up a deflection from a Surry Central player and shields the player with his back from attacking it. He fakes to his left and then to his right and moves up the field on the right wing with the ball, leaving the defender in his wake. He sends a hard cross to the middle of the field and goes down on the ground. The ball bounces loose in front of Perico, who can't quite control it. But Guero is there. He takes the ball and dribbles to his right, beating a defender and pushing up the field. Three other defenders converge on Guero, but he deftly maneuvers through them. He is at the eighteen now. The keeper is close to the left post, his hands down at his thighs in classic goalkeeper position. But it is too late. Guero lets a left-footed shot fly—the ball whistles toward the right post and goes in. A Surry Central player watches the ball sail through. He puts his hands to his face and covers his eyes. He can't believe they let Guero through for the shot. It is a singular performance, one of style and speed, finished with authority. Guero has come through for his father. The crowd erupts in cheers and horns and you can hear "¡Sí, se puede! ¡Sí, se puede! ¡Sí, se puede!" from both sets of fans. I take this moment to substitute Edi out of the game. I put in the freshman Chaquetas to see what he can do. I talk to Edi and he tells me he is just nervous and can't catch his breath because of it.

Behind by only one goal, the Eagles try to come back, but the Jets defense is too strong. Fish is not challenged. The Jets continue to press on the left and right wings, moving the ball up the field and putting together one, two, three passes to different players, controlling the ball and the game.

The ball bounces high in the air and Anthony is there to send it back up the field. This time Indio receives it with his back to the goal. He turns around and goes upfield, beating one defender with the move. Another defender rushes in on him, but Indio cuts out to his right and leaves him in the dust. Indio continues to press upfield on a solo run. A third defender challenges him, but he is moving too fast and has too much control and beats him wide to the right. Loco is running with him, just to the outside, on his right, along the wing. A fourth defender steps up and again Indio dribbles around him. And then the fifth and final defender charges at him, but this time, instead of beating the defender, Indio slips the ball past him to Loco on the wing, who finds himself alone and inside the eighteen. The keeper moves to the right post to cover as Loco approaches with a shot. He has shot wildly from a distance three times this night and is cranking up for another try. There is a defender chasing Loco down from behind, and just when he catches up, the keeper comes off his line to cover a near-post shot. Loco holds up and sends a soft, low pass on the ground across the mouth of the goal. La Pepa is there. He taps the ball into the goal.

It is a spectacular goal, a classic deception to draw the defenders to the attacker while leaving the middle unguarded for the cross. You don't get much prettier goals than that and the sheer beauty of it is enough to crush the Eagles. They know the goal beats them not by force or power, but by skill and discipline. The half ends with the Jets leading, 2–0. We are forty minutes from advancing to the state finals.

The Eagles are not done, though. In the second half they come back and pressure our defense. They win a goal when the defense fails to cover the right wing. The game is now 2–1.

But the Jets respond eight minutes later. Again it is Indio who sets up the play. We win a throw in ten yards from the Eagles' eighteen. Indio races in to receive the ball in the air; he traps it and continues to penetrate on the run. But an Eagle defender brings him down from behind as he approaches the eighteen. The referee calls for an indirect kick from the spot. Indio is on the ground arguing his case, surrounded by the Surry Central defenders. They insult him and he insults them back, throwing his arms up in the air. Someone shoves him. The referee is there and breaks it up. He gives one of the Surry Central players a yellow card and the player leaves the game.

The Eagles form a wall at the top of the eighteen, five players across, with La Pepa standing at the end to block the keeper's line of sight. Indio and Bomba discuss who will take the kick. Bomba will take it. The referee makes the Eagles move five yards farther back from the ball. Indio starts the play by running over the ball and leaving it for Bomba, who steps up and sends a cracker of a shot through to the left of the wall. The ball goes through and dips down in front of the goal. The keeper loses sight of it and can't track it. It bounces in front of him and then goes up. All the keeper can do is lift his right arm to try to swat it away, but the ball is moving too fast and goes flying into the upper left corner. The horns sound again and the cheers go up for the Jets.

With less than a minute left, the Eagles manage to squeak a goal past Fish on a mixed-up play. But the game ends there and the Jets are victorious. There is a rush onto the field. We have made it to the finals.

John Phillips walked onto the field carrying two trophies. They were tall wooden plaques with gold metallic fronts and a small base. He presented the Western Division Champion runner-up trophy to the Surry Central Eagles. The boys received the trophy with no glee. They took it, nodded, and walked off the field in tears. They had played a good game, but they could not match the skill of the Jets. Their long balls and *cascarita* style had failed them.

Phillips then presented the Western Division Championship trophy to the Jets. La Pepa accepted it and liftted it above his head, and the boys all reached up into the lights to grab a piece of it. I watched them celebrate, holding the trophy in front of them, and thought how this would probably be the only championship ever won on this field. I held up three fingers as I walked over to them and the local sports reporter asked me why three.

"That's how many years it took for us to get here," I told him. The boys all wanted to pose with the trophy, including the freshmen who hadn't played a minute in the game. It was their win too. There was Lechero and his brother Lecherito. Edi and his little brother Arabe. Indio and his brother Perico, Loco and Chuy, and last, Fish and Guero. All brothers, all *carnales.* They stood with the trophy in their hands, erect and proud, the lights from the field exploding above their heads.

I felt relieved that we had won. All the stress, the nervousness, the anxious moments, not knowing if Guero and Fish were going to play, *la vida loca,* all that slipped away from me. No matter what happened in the finals, win or lose, we had achieved a great deal as a team. I didn't care about winning the state championship trophy. There was only one thing left that I wanted. And I wanted it real bad. It had been *the* thing I had wanted since starting the program, the image I kept my eye on, not even allowing myself to utter it out loud. I told no one. Through every practice and during every game for the past three years, I had thought only about this one thing.

20

The sun was setting behind the royal-blue scoreboard, taking with it the last rays of warmth. I blew my whistle and ended the practice for the day. We had only three more practices before the final game that would decide the state championship. I could count the hours that were left for the boys and me. We had played all season long with the mentality that there was always another day, another game. It was something for us to look forward to: the battles, the scores, the victories, the losses, the game went on. But there were no more games after Saturday. That was it. No one on the team wanted it to end. The boys asked if we would play against other teams in other states if we won. But the answer was no. This was it. The season would end no matter what the outcome. And even though I was exhausted emotionally and physically, I too didn't want it to end. It just didn't seem right to hang up your cleats just yet.

The practice had gone well. We worked mostly on conditioning to prepare for the big stadium at SAS Soccer Park in Cary. The field at SAS was gigantic, of professional size, and was the place the champion Carolina Courage women's team has once called home. Since the women's professional league folded, the stadium was used for collegiate and high school soccer championship tournaments.

It was a beautiful field, lush green, flat. That meant that it was 130 yards long by 75 yards wide. Most high school teams played on fields that were 120 yards long by 50 or so yards wide. With those dimensions, I knew we would be playing against two opponents on Saturday: the Devil Pups of Lejeune High School *and* the larger field. I worried about the field more than the other team.

Because most high school games were played on smaller fields, the action was usually faster, more intense; players could tackle and cover easily, not allowing a player a lot of time with the ball before being defended. But on a larger field, the boys would have a little more time to control the ball before someone was on top of them. And with so much additional width, the wings would be open, with lots of room to run down the sidelines.

We worked hard on conditioning. I made the team run four miles during the practices, gearing up for the finals. You could see the effects on the frames of the players; they were beginning to look skinny. They would come to practice with one body and leave with another. I tried to emphasize the proper diet, increasing their protein for muscle and strength and carbohydrates for fuel. I knew they would get their carbs from the countless tortillas they ate after practice, but I worried about the lack of adequate protein in their diets—it needed to be increased.

By the Wednesday before the Saturday game, I began requiring less running from them and more focus on possessing the ball over a wider space. I didn't want them to be exhausted from practice right before the game. Preparing for a championship was all about timing. You wanted to push them hard and then coast, let the momentum of your preparation take you through to the big game. The last thing you wanted was to have your players tired from a hard workout the night before.

After we'd won the semifinal against Surry Central, I researched Lejeune High School as much as I could, talking to other coaches who had played them, reading news articles I found on the Web, analyzing their record, goals, and winning percentage. I knew that Lejeune's coaches were probably doing the same in preparing for

the game against the Jets. I toyed with the idea of changing the way
we played, teaching the boys something new, coming up with a different set play, a new defensive technique or plan. But I thought it
might do nothing but confuse them. If we were going to win, we
would win with our style of game. We wouldn't change. Let Lejeune
alter their style all they wanted, let *them* come up with tricks, it
didn't matter to me. The Jets would be ready for anything.

Lejeune was ranked number one in the state. They had been to
the state finals two years before and had beaten our former conference rivals Albemarle on penalty kicks after the game ended in a tie,
a crushing loss for the Bulldogs. Lejeune was a perennial soccer
power in the Eastern Division. It was no fluke that they were making their second appearance in the finals in just two years. They
were well coached, with large players who had played in the big
club leagues around Jacksonville and along the Carolina coast. They
were known as the Devil Pups, a diminutive of the Marine soubri-
quet Devil Dogs given to the Corps by the Germans during World
War I. They were the sons of Marines stationed at Camp Lejeune
and their school was located on the base. The high school was even
funded by the Department of Defense. We would be playing against
the *Marines*.

Lejeune was a defensive team. This was their strength. They had
played most of the season with a flat-back four line of defense with
no sweeper back. This meant that their four defensive players positioned themselves in a straight line in back and looked to play the
offside trap. It also meant they trusted and relied on their goalkeeper
to be the last man on defense. This was appropriate since their goalkeeper had been the most valuable player at the state finals the year
they beat Albemarle. He was a tall athletic kid, muscular, able to
cover post to post in a flash, and had the ability to leap into the air to
deflect incoming shots. He was their star and the anchor of their
team.

They were not as strong up front but they had capable players.
Lejeune believed in the old adage that defense wins championships.
During the play-offs, they had switched their defense from the flat-

back four to one that included a sweeper back. I didn't know which defense they would bring to the finals on Saturday. But I had the forwards—Perico and La Pepa—concentrate on making diagonal runs through a flat line of players for through passes and shots on goal. We worked hard on the through runs, but I didn't believe that Lejeune would go with the flat-back four on such a large field. Because the SAS field was so wide, it allowed for more room in between players on a flat line to run through. They had played with a sweeper during the play-offs and I knew they would stick with it.

I emphasized all the things that had brought us to the final and worked on improving things I thought the team needed to do better. We worked on our possession game harder than before, preparing for the big field. I had the boys play five versus five over sixty yards by fifty-three yards, a large space for a team of five in order to teach them how it felt to possess the ball and be comfortable, over such a wide and open space. They started out awkwardly, lost in the larger space, but after about ten minutes, they began moving the ball around, sending longer passes to teammates while defenders worked on chasing the ball down. When they got the hang of it, I had them play one-touch possession. When they mastered that, I knew we were ready.

As well as possession, we focused on shooting from a distance. Because the SAS field was longer than what they were accustomed to, the boys needed to finally shed their *cascarita* ways and fire from outside the box. I had them dribble through flags set on the field in a slalom course before firing a shot at Fish.

When practice was over I jogged over to the Jets Hangar and turned on the big lights for any of the players who wanted to stay and work on technique. There was a *thunk* as the lights slowly came to life, burning a soft blue at first then bursting into brilliant white. The field was captured in light and it was impossible to see anything outside it. Once you stepped onto the field, you were in a private world, an island in the November darkness where you could play as long as the power stayed on.

Most of the boys went home to take a shower, do homework, go to work, or just hang out and play video games. But one player stayed on the field, standing tall on its crown. Indio scooped the soccer ball up on his right foot and then kicked it high into the lights before trapping it on his left foot. He did this again and again until I came over to him.

"You want to take some shots, Indio?" I asked him. He wanted to stay to practice. It didn't seem as though he paid me any attention. He kept his eyes focused on the ball and juggling it on his foot before kicking up into the lights again. He nodded. Okay, I thought, let's work on shooting from the outside.

Indio was a gifted athlete. He sliced and diced through defenses, cutting inside and outside, taking apart defenders. But there was one thing his game lacked. A devastating shot off a run. If he could finish after cutting his way through the defense, he could literally score at will. It was the missing piece in his game. He was the driver of the team. The players went where he guided them, and if he could add an outside shot to his bag of tricks, he would be the complete midfielder—one able not only to penetrate through the middle and dish out the pass on the wing, as he had done to Surry Central, but also to fire a blistering shot into the upper right V. He would be unstoppable.

I had Indio stand forty yards downfield from the goal. I took a ball and punted it high into the air toward him. He ran to the point where the ball would land, trapped it, and began running up the field. I ran toward him. He needed to shoot on goal before I reached him. He shot wide on the first six balls, but he started finding the frame on the next six.

"Okay, Indio, you need to shoot as soon as you get past me. When you shoot right after passing a defender, you screen the keeper from your shot. He doesn't know where it's coming from because the ball is already away. As soon as you pass me, shoot. No matter where you are on the field. Okay?"

"Okay, Cuadros," he said, and smiled. He was a real coachable kid. He listened and then applied what was said to him. It was the mark of a good player.

This time he sent his shot as soon as he beat me on the dribble. I didn't go in real hard on him. That was not the point. I wanted him to learn to mask his shot. Once he got the concept down, I could make it harder. After more than a dozen balls, he was finding the net. And he was finally following through on his shots, pulling his leg back, snapping it forward and through, the ball jumping up into the air as he kept his toe pointed downward and watched it land on his kicking foot.

A perfect shot is all about transference of power. A shot comes from pulling your leg back until your heel touches your butt and then snapping it forward, making contact with the ball on the laces of your shoe. The real source of the power comes from shifting your weight from your planting foot through your kicking leg as it meets the ball—transferring all that energy into the ball, and then following through and landing on your kicking foot. When the move is executed perfectly, the ball takes off with a will of its own, swaying left or right slightly as it runs straight through with no spin. A keeper can't judge where the ball was going when it lacks any spin. It's a death shot, the kind of ball that kills teams, demoralizes keepers, and makes defenders' legs tremble.

"Well, are you ready for the big game, old sport?" We had been reading *The Great Gatsby* together for his AP English class. He reminded me of Gatsby in small ways when he was on the field. His excellence, his clean game, and his talent. He was polished like Gatsby between the eighteens.

"Of course, old sport," he said, smiling. We liked to call each other that.

He walked off the field and I watched as he stepped into the diffused light around the track. He seemed to hang there for a moment, suspended in doubt—a figure out of focus—before slipping finally into the dark. I bent over to pack the balls that had been scattered on the field into their black bag and watched as Indio stepped into an unknown world. On the field he was a gifted athlete, one who inspired adoration because of his talents, and he had a promising future. But once he stepped off the field, beyond its blue lines, he became illegal—an animal to be rounded up and deported. This is the way the country saw him.

Was the soccer field any different from the tomato field? Or the chicken field? Or the construction field? Latinos were always safe when they kept to *their* fields. But when they stepped beyond them, when they moved from under the protective lights of their fields, they stepped into the darkness, the unknown world of being undocumented.

His chances of going to college were slim. He would have to rely on all his talents on the field to realize his dreams of a higher education. If he could play well enough, if he could elevate his game high enough, then perhaps a college coach would want him enough to help him overcome the burden of his status. It was his best chance. It was his only chance, really.

I was busy writing some notes on a story for *Time* magazine when a call came through. It was someone who said he was a Lejeune supporter. He called to congratulate me on reaching the finals. It was strange and a bit forward; no other fan in my three years of coaching had ever called to chat before a game. I didn't really want to talk to him, I didn't have much to say, but he persisted and asked if I had been researching Lejeune. He said he had been researching the Jets. Fine, I thought. We all know what we do before a game. What did he really want?

"Well, listen, I thought we could cut through that and just exchange information on our teams," he said, to my complete astonishment. "You tell me about your team, and I'll tell you about my team."

I was taken aback by his offer. I stalled a minute to gather myself. "I can tell you I did the same thing with Albemarle when Lejeune played them in the finals two years ago," he said.

"Why don't we just see what happens on Saturday?" I responded, thinking I would need to check with the Albemarle coaches as soon as this call was over to confirm his claim. I didn't believe it for a minute; I knew the coaches at Albemarle, and they never would have done such an odd thing before a championship game. Then he got nasty.

"You know, I was real surprised that y'all made it this far." He chuckled, digging into me. "I mean, I thought you wouldn't get past Surry Central."

If he was looking for a fight or an outburst, then he had called the wrong guy. That was never my style. I decided to play dumb in order to defuse his efforts at provoking me. It was obvious that the intention of his call was to intimidate me, get me riled up, pissed off, hoping I might reveal something he could use against my team.

"You know, we are just happy to be in the finals," I said, and did my best to sound that way.

But that didn't stop him. He asked me out to dinner the night before the game. I couldn't believe he was serious. I politely declined and told him I would see him on Saturday.

I called the Albemarle coaches right away and we all shared a laugh at the story. Sports have a way of making people behave in all kinds of different ways. In some, it brings out an ability to rise above adversity and to compete hard but honestly. In others, it raises the baser instincts—behavior that can at best be deemed unsportsman-like. If a booster wanted to exchange information about the teams, then he had succeeded. I now knew what kind of fans Lejeune had and I could infer what kind of players that kind of support produced.

Saturday morning finally arrived. I asked the boys to meet me in front of the gymnasium. I wanted them there in the school's hall of champions. They came in small groups, toting soccer bags and backpacks with their uniforms and cleats. It was early, 7 a.m., and they complained about it. "*No manches,* Cuadros" was all Indio would say. I told them I had wanted to arrive early at the stadium so that we could get used to the big field as much as possible before the game began at 10 a.m.

"There is a reason why I wanted us to meet here inside the school," I started. Some of the guys were sleepy, but most seemed alert. No doubt they hadn't slept very much the night before. "Every day you all pass by this hall on your way to class. And every day you look at these pictures." On the wall behind me was a row of giant photographs in wood frames, hung up for all to see.

There was the picture of the boys' basketball team that won the state championship in 1997. The players were black and white and they stood tall, with serious looks upon their young faces. Next to them was the cross-country team lined in a row of royal blue and white. They were all white boys with cheerful smiles on their faces. And next to them were the two neat rows of blond girls from the championship tennis team. There was one African-American girl among them. And then there were the two golf teams and their championships.

Nowhere on the wall of champions were there any students who looked like my team. For the past several years, I had wondered how it felt for these kids to walk past this wall without seeing a single person who looked like them. How were they not asking *when?* Or *why not?* I had started the team for a number of reasons—to give these kids a chance to play, to keep them in school, to give them a shot at college, but there was one motivating factor that burned in my mind more than any other: the wall. I had always thought we could be conference champions but never dared to hope that we could be state champions. The dream of getting a photograph on the wall was the kind that you never even indulge, for fear you might not ever see it come true. But since we'd won the Western Division, there was nothing else I really wanted. The photograph was the reason I wanted to win. I wanted these kids to walk down this hall and see faces that looked like them. I wanted them to know they were a part of this school, too.

"This is our picture, this brick wall," I said, touching it. "Our history has not been written here yet. Our history is still written in brick and mortar." The boys looked at me and they could see what I felt in my eyes. "But our day has finally come. Today, we are playing for our place on the wall of champions. And one day your younger brother, or sister, or even your own children will be able to come here and look on this wall and see that *you* were a champion. That *our* people can be champions. That we can be great." Fish, the senior who'd be playing his last game, understood exactly what I was getting at. This was history for us. We were making our mark in Siler City for the first time. He came up to me first and then the other boys crowded in and we huddled up for a moment in silence. We said no prayer, but sometimes prayers are spoken in humble silence. We left the hall and went to board the bus.

The bus trip from Siler City to Cary would only take about an hour. We were happy that Ms. Brickhouse was driving the bus—not only because she was a safe and dependable driver, but because she had also driven the team to all of its away games that season. The boys had come to view her as their good-luck charm. Ms. Brickhouse taught agriculture at the school. She was smart and wise and had an easy rapport with the team.

The bus passed Pittsboro and was nearing Jordan Lake, a man-made lake in Chatham County that was also home to a nuclear power plant that could be faintly seen just beyond the horizon.

I passed the time looking out the window and thinking of the past players on the team. I wished that some could be with us now. The faces of players like Pee Wee, Oso, and Dougie-style rolled across my mind's eye. Pee Wee with his kinky Puerto Rican hair and skateboarding thrasher style. Oso, towering over me with his tall treelike legs, thick and black. Doug's sly smile and baseball cap looking like a frat boy. I thought of Lenin and his round pumpkin head with his big smile, laughing on the bus with Enrique. I was wrenched out of my reverie when I heard a high loud *clank* just in front of me, up near the right front tire of the bus. I got up quickly and stood next to Ms. Brickhouse. "What was that, Brick? It sounds like we hit something, a deer perhaps?"

"I don't know," Ms. Brickhouse said, gripping the steering wheel tighter. I could see steam or white smoke emanating from the right side of the engine. We had not hit a deer. I immediately thought it might be a flat tire, but I could smell burning oil and smoke come into the front cabin of the bus. We were going to have to evacuate immediately. Ms. Brickhouse pulled over to the side of the highway and I quickly turned to the boys, "We're getting off the bus *now!*" The boys responded slowly at first, almost as if I was joking, but they knew me better and started to move. I told them they should leave their stuff aboard. We were abandoning the bus. The smoke appeared to be subsiding, but I wasn't going to take any chances. A fire could really devastate the bus.

The boys got off quickly. There was no panic and for that I was grateful. Once we were outside, I could see fluid dripping from the engine of the bus. We had blown a rod. This bus was going nowhere and neither were we.

21

"Enrique!" I said, speaking fast. I was calling everybody I knew to come and pick up the team by the side of the road. "Hey, listen, our bus broke down on 64. Can you all come earlier and pick us up?" Enrique was taking the day off from his job to see the game. His family was still getting ready to go when I finally reached him on his cell phone.

"No way!" I could see him smiling with his eyes closed. "Yeah, I'll get them ready and be over there." For the past several months, Enrique had been working as a plumber's apprentice. He loved the job and was thinking about getting his license and starting his own business.

We hung up and I went on to the next number in my phone. I had informed John Phillips of our dilemma, but he said there was no way to get a new bus to us on time. I called Leda, the reporter I'd met at the David Duke rally, and asked her to come pick up some of the boys. After the rally, Leda and I had started seeing each other and had fallen in love. She had become the team's biggest fan and I could always count on her pacing back and forth during games, screaming at the refs. I racked my brain trying to think of someone with a van or truck I could call. I put in a call to my friend Dan from the Chatham Soccer League, who I knew was coming to the game. It was only a little after 8 A.M. and we still had time to make it.

The boys had gathered on a grassy embankment by the side of the road beneath some pine trees. They were joking nervously that we were going to arrive late—as usual for Latinos. Others were genuinely upset and scared that we might have to forfeit.

"Guys, settle down. Okay, how many of you guys have crossed the border?" Immediately most of their arms went up in the air. "Let me tell you—this is easier than that." The boys burst out laughing. They knew they had been through far worse than being stranded by the side of the road. They had overcome so much in their young lives, having a bus break down was nothing. As the minutes ticked by, I was growing confident that we would get there somehow. All the skills I'd learn in my years of reporting and working the phones to track down sources I now used to find people to come and pick us up. We would caravan in like most private club teams do for tournaments. No problem. "Hey, get away from the road!" I yelled at Lechero, who was sticking out his thumb, trying hitchhike. He laughed.

Then some cars began to slow down and pull off the road behind the bus. I told the team to get dressed now in case there weren't enough cars to accommodate all our gear. Anthony's parents arrived, and so did Indio's and Leda. Then a white van pulled over. It was a working van with ladders on top and it belonged to Turner Plumbing, Enrique's employer. The owner had seen Edi and Arabe by the side of the road and recognized them as Enrique's brothers. Within moments, I had seven boys piled into the back of the van, making themselves as comfortable as they could among all the tools and equipment. We loaded four or five into the truck Enrique was driving and stuffed the equipment into one of the cars. With everyone loaded and secure, we left the big white bus behind and were off again to the stadium. In all, the incident had taken only half an hour. Leaving early had paid off. It was Loco who said, "We're leaving all our bad luck behind on the bus." I hoped so.

The Lejeune Devil Pups arrived at SAS Soccer Park in a large and imposing chartered bus with a giant picture of a Marine in dress uniform with white cap and sword emblazoned on the side. The Marines had, indeed, landed. The Devil Pups were dressed in red, black, and white. As the team was ranked number one in the state, they were expected to dominate Jordan Matthews.

We pulled up to the sidewalk entrance to the stadium in a loose collection of cars, trucks, and the Turner Plumbing van, looking more like a bunch of day laborers ready to put in a hard day's work on the construction site than a championship team. We were *mojado*—"wetback"—all the way, and I couldn't not feel the disbelieving stares we were getting from the Lejeune team and their fans as they watched the way these "Mexicans" climbed down, jumped over, and stepped off their vehicles. Dressed in their white jerseys, blue shorts, and cleats—ready to take the field—the *chavos* took one look at the Lejeune bus and said, "Oye, Cuadros, why can't we get one of those?" and "We're taking on the Marines!"

We hurried inside the stadium and stepped out onto the field. We had been designated the home team and gathered our equipment on the side of the field where the major portion of the stands and press box were. The field was beautiful. It was laid out flat, a vast green carpet of soft grass from one end to another. The morning dew had given a bright sheen to the pitch, which meant that the ball would be slippery. The day was perfect. It was cool but not cold and the sun was just beginning to warm up and burn off the wetness on the field.

The *chavos* couldn't wait to take the field and start banging balls around. I walked out onto the grass, feeling electricity shoot up my legs. The field looked big, but somehow didn't feel so big once you were on it. In my mind I had made the professional field grow to huge dimensions. As I looked at it now and passed balls around with the guys, I knew that this was a place where we could win.

Our lineup would be the same as before. Fish in goal; Lechero as sweeper; Anthony and Lecherito on the defensive wings; and Bomba as center defender or stopper. In the middle, I wanted the two fastest players on the wings, Edi on the left, and Loco on the right. Also in the middle, Guero and Indio. Up front, Perico and La Pepa. I had a short list of substitutes, but did not want to be making too much use of it during this game.

The teams had warmed up and now the fanfare began. We shook the hands of the Devil Pups, tall and large players with thick legs, and listened to the referees outline what kind of game they wanted. The announcer read the names of the players from both sides and then the national anthem was played.

We stood there in the middle of the field, our hands on our chests, and I thought back for a moment to a game from the first year. We had played on September 11, one year after the attacks on New York and Washington. The *chavos* had scored a stunning first goal and, unbeknownst to me, had worn painted white T-shirts under their jerseys that read, when they lined up together, THIS GOAL IS FOR THE USA. Afterward, the referee came over to me and said it was a violation of the rules, but he understood what the boys were saying and let it pass. I thought of that goal and that team and how the guys had wanted to express their love for their adopted country. It reminded me of the time my father sent away for a set of pens inscribed with the message I LOVE PEACE IN MY AMERICA. He rarely showed his love for this country, but for some reason he had wanted to have a box of pens with those words written on them. He asked me to proofread the incription and I didn't change a word.

On our side, the stands were filling with our fans from Siler City dressed in white and blue. They had hung colorful signs on the railings that read *¡sí, se puede!* and LET'S GO JETS! and put up numbers of their favorite players. They also brought horns, drums, and noisemakers. They were ready to sing songs, clap their hands, and cheer for their heroes. I looked out at the stands and was pleased to see that Siler City had really turned out for the big game. There were black, white, and brown students in the bleachers. Teachers came to support their kids. Latino advocates, employers, and anyone who came into contact with Latinos in town had also bought tickets. Curious fans came to see what all the hoopla was about. The media had also come out to film on the sidelines. Win or lose, I thought, we had at least gotten the town to be of one mind about one thing.

With the anthem over, we headed to our sideline and I pulled out the chain. The boys started to get pumped up. I had one last thing to say, and I intended to make it brief. As a coach, I tried to find the moment, grab it out of the air, and bring it down for my players to see and feel. I wanted the players to understand precisely what they were playing for, and to inspire them to play beyond their normal selves.

"It has been a long journey these past three years," I started softly. "Some of you were here when we started this team. Even then we had a dream: to one day be champions. That day has finally come!"

"*¡Sí, Cuadros! ¡Sí!*" They yelled.

"Today we play for all the players before us who could not be here. For those veterans who can only watch now. We play for our fathers who taught us this beautiful game. We play for ourselves and for the big picture at school. We play for all the other Latino teams that couldn't make it this far. But today, we will play in our hearts for *nuestra gente*—for *our* people. We are Mexican, Salvadoran, Guatemalan, Peruvian, and American. Today, we will play for everyone in our community. And we will all be champions!"

Edi then led us in our cheer as the boys grabbed a piece of the chain I was holding in my hand. "Who are the Jets?" He called, and the boys responded, "We are!" "Who are the Jets!" "We are!" and then everyone in unison shouted, "One, two, three, let's go, Jets!" And we took the field.

Lejeune starts with the ball and passes it back to their midfielders. But Guero is there and steals it, passing it back to Indio, who draws a defender to him and passes up to Guero, who fakes one player out and sends the ball to the left wing for Edi, who is there but is tackled. The game is tension-filled and both teams play tentatively. But the start of the game has been all JM as we have controlled the ball, possessed it, and moved it up the large field. So far Lejeune has not been able to cross the half line, continually losing the ball to our midfielders. Both teams are evenly matched for now and I realize that the game will be won in the middle of the field.

The Lejeune goalkeeper sends the ball high into the air on a goal kick over the half line, but Lechero is there to head it back into their side of the field. Perico collects the ball, spins with it like a little top, and passes to Guero, who is making a run up the middle. Guero is trying to do too much and loses the ball. The game is going back and forth in the middle. Neither team seems to be using the wings. The field is so wide that the players are playing only in the middle. I shout to them to "open up the game!"

At last, Indio gets the ball and my nerves settle a bit. Each time he touches the ball, I am confident that we can string some passes together and move it for a chance on goal. But Indio's pass to the left wing for Edi is too far and he loses it. A Lejeune player collides into Indio, kneeing him on the thigh. Indio goes down but gets back up again quickly.

Behind me the fans are shouting in unison, *"¡Sí, se puede! ¡Sí, se puede! ¡Sí, se puede!"* Lejeune gets through our middle and one of their midfielders spots a forward at the eighteen and sends him a high chip pass. But before the forward can race onto the ball and turn toward goal, Fish has seen the danger and come off his line and intercepted the ball, catching it with both hands. He launches the ball upfield in a high arcing kick. Lejeune is playing the flat-back four, lining four defenders across in their backfield. We need to find a way to penetrate through that line.

Now Anthony starts our play on the right, trapping a lofted pass upfield. He brings the ball down and charges up the field with it. As he gets pressured from a midfielder, he passes it off to Perico in the middle, who traps it with his left foot and swings around. He sees La Pepa up front on the left and sends him a chip pass. Pepa is alone and runs to the ball. The through pass has beaten the flat-back four defense of Lejeune. Pepa gets the ball and penetrates into the box. The Lejeune players sense the danger and converge on him. Pepa is now one-on-one with the keeper, who crouches down like a stalking cat. But Pepa doesn't shoot and instead calmly cuts the ball outside, leaving a pressing defender in the dust. He sees Edi, who has moved to the middle, and passes him the ball. But the ball bounces wildly at the eighteen and Edi leaves it alone because Guero is there, charging in for the shot. Guero smacks the ball with the outside of his left foot and sends a blistering shot toward the cross bar of the goal. The ball looks unbeatable, a spectacular one-touch volley. But the Lejeune keeper is one of the best in the state. He leaps high into the air and deflects the shot over the crossbar just in time. It is a stunning play by both teams and the crowd on both sides erupts in cheers.

As was the case in the last game, Edi seems unusually tired and distracted. I substitute him to calm him down. I send in the freshman Chaquetas. Edi blames his behavior on the nerves that don't allow him to catch his breath. Meanwhile, Lejeune is unable to string any passes together. We are tougher than they expected, and we have been able to put together three or more consecutive passes.

And then it happens. The play begins with the ball clearing from Lejeune to the left side of our defense. Lecherito is there to send the ball back upfield. Guero brings it down and spins, looking for a pass. He dribbles through a defender. Pepa is upfield with a defender on him. Guero spots Perico in the middle and passes the ball. Perico traps it with his back to the goal. He knows where Pepa is instinctively and spins around and sends a soft lofted pass over the heads of the defensive line into the open field at the eighteen. How many times has he performed that little move and pass in his backyard to Pepa or one of his other friends? It is the kind of sixth-sense field awareness that only comes with hours of playing together in tight spaces.

Pepa is waiting for the ball. He is through. He penetrates. It is him and the keeper now. Pepa is our main goal scorer. He can finish the play. The keeper knows the danger and comes off his line to cut the angle of the shot down. But Pepa is not worried about him. He takes his shot ten yards from the goal, a hard low one across to the far post. The keeper is off balance and desperately tries to throw himself in front of the ball, hoping to get a piece of it with his body. But it is too late. The ball goes into the goal on the left corner. The Jets score. The team rushes to Pepa, hugging him and piling on him. Siler City goes crazy. The flatback four is broken. Perico's through pass has drawn first blood, and Pepa has come through again. The kid who was ineligible the year before because of skipping school and who battled his way to the starting line this year is the hero for the moment. But with only a 1–0 lead, I cannot relax. Lejeune will not give up easily.

The goal has inspired the Jets. They mount another blistering attack on the Lejeune defense. This time Chaquetas gets through on a dazzling display of skill, cutting through two defenders and getting into the box. Indio is there to feed him the through pass. Chaquetas doesn't hesitate. The keeper comes off his line and dives to try to gather the loose through pass, but Chaquetas is there and sends in a left-footed shot beneath the keeper's body. The ball is going in when a defender appears and clears it before it crosses the line. The keeper is stunned. He can't believe that the Jets are getting through with such clear chances. He screams at his defenders to protect him better. The crowd erupts and the *chavas,* the girls, sing, *"Muy bien, muchachos, muy bien!"* "Well done, boys, well done!"

The half ends with the Jets leading 1–0.

The boys walked off the field and sat down. They were sweaty but not tired, excited but nervous. Indio didn't look like his normal self; he had suffered a thigh bruise. The trainer rubbed the injury with some ointment.

"What is the score?" I asked the team all at once.

"Zero to zero." They responded the way I had taught them; they knew anything could still happen.

"We have only forty minutes left until we are champions. Forty minutes. I want everyone to give everything they have in those forty minutes. That special phone I have to call on players when we need them? Well, I am calling on all of you—even the bench. You have to be ready. This is a tough team. Forty minutes," I said, then paused for a moment. "Life is hard. You know that. All of you *know* that. We are just beginning here. We are just starting our lives here. But wherever you go, whatever occurs, you will always know in your hearts that you were the best, you were champions, and you can do great things. And everyone—everyone in this state will know that too."

Before they took the field for one last time, I stopped Indio to ask how he was feeling. He said he was doing much better after being treated. The Lejeune players had been roughing him up. I looked at him. I needed him to step up and play to his potential. I expected more from him, he expected more. "Remember what we practiced this week," I said. He nodded. "*No te agüites,* Cuadros, we got them," he said. "Don't get all teary Cuadros."

"*No manches,* old sport."

The second half starts with Lejeune throwing everything they can at us. They know they need to equalize quickly or risk letting the game slip away. The first fifteen minutes will decide everything. And the start of the second half is all Lejeune. Our defense bends but doesn't break. Lechero is there time and again to clear through balls and bust up plays. And when the ball does get through, Fish is there, coming off his line and flying through the air to snatch away balls before Lejeune can head them in. And after fifteen minutes, I can see that the Lejeune players are getting tired. The big field is wearing them down along with our attacks.

Indio gets the ball at midfield and quickly sends a long through pass up to Perico, who lets the ball land in front of him and chases it down. He controls it and breaks inside the corner of the box with a defender behind him. He sloughs off the defender with a tricky move, but the defender, knowing he is beat, grabs him around the waist and pushes the little guy to the ground inside the box. No penalty kick is awarded. The crowd screams at the referee, who says, "Play on."

Guero looks lost on the field. He seems to be fading and not playing to his potential. I take him out and put Beto in to cover for him. Guero and I talk on the sidelines about his game. He is upset. He wants desperately to play his best, but he doesn't feel like he is doing so. I tell him to settle down and I'll put him in again. He says he doesn't want to go back in and sits down on the bench.

Now the Lejeune keeper kicks the ball upfield and Edi is there to take it from a Lejeune forward. He moves up the left wing and sends the ball to Perico, continuing to charge up the wing, penetrating into the attacking third of the field. Perico knows Edi is making his run on the sideline and sends a quick pass over the heads of the defensive line. The ball bounces out in front and into the box. Edi is sprinting down the field for it; he is alone. A Lejeune defender from the middle takes a bead on Edi and his attack. Both players meet inside the box, but Edi is too quick, he is in front with the ball at his feet. He is going to shoot, but the Lejeune defender clips his back leg and Edi goes flying into the air, his arms flaying out wildly in front of him. He crashes down on the field and his face contorts in pain. It is a clear foul from behind, necessitating a penalty kick. But the referee, who has not run to keep up with the play, signals to play on. He will not award any penalty kicks today.

I am now beginning to think we will need to win this game 1–0—a defensive struggle fraught with tension and nerves. We can't seem to finish our plays. Twice on a long kick from Bomba to the right corner, Loco has been free and gone into the box ready to shoot, but the Lejeune defense has broken up the play both times.

The Lejeune keeper will not allow any more goals. He is the strength of the Devil Pups. They let one through. No more. The keeper sends the ball up and away, but Chaquetas is there and he kicks it back up the field to Pepa. The Lejeune defenders are closely marking Pepa now and he can't turn upfield with the ball. But he sees Indio in the middle about thirty-five yards out from the goal. He sends him a bouncing pass.

Indio brings the ball down with his right foot and taps it for the left foot, which touches the ball in front of him. No one is on him yet. The Lejeune keeper is on Indio's left, covering near post. Indio is nowhere near the box, now about twenty-five yards from the goal line. It doesn't matter. We have worked on this all week. This is his time. It is his moment. He is taking it. He is taking the shot.

He takes aim and crushes the ball with his shot, hitting it with the outside of his right foot. The ball takes off in the air low and hard, climbing steadily and then dipping down toward the far right post. It is a professional shot, a killer of teams, the kind of shot that makes the highlight reels and is paused, rewound, and played over and over for its sheer energy, its boldness, its strength and fury.

The keeper is too far left and is caught off guard by Indio's cannon shot. There are some players who are born winners. Players who you know can lift an entire team and game on their shoulders, who find magic and can slip through an opponent's defenses and deliver the final blow. You want the ball at their feet in the closing seconds. They are playmakers and game breakers. And they seem to be possessed in that moment with something beyond normal human abilities. It's what makes them winners. And Indio is a winner. His shot whistles toward the goal and dips down right at the goal line and bounces into the right corner. The net plumes out like a white sail in the wind and the game is over. I know that. Lejeune knows that. The *chavos* know it too. The keeper is distraught and lies on the ground in disbelief. A Lejeune player puts his hands behind his head in the universal sign of surrender on the battlefield.

The boys leave their positions and race toward Indio. They jump on him, hug him, grab him as if to touch that magic he just produced. I see them from the sidelines as they break away. Pepa jogging in front. Edi is next to him, his arm on Lechero's chest. Lechero is next to Fish, who has Indio in a headlock. Perico trots along next to his big brother. The smiles on their faces are wide and open. There is a happiness in their eyes that seldom appears when you get beyond a certain age, but it is in us all, sleeping, waiting for a true and honest moment to emerge. That's what sport does. It awakens that buried feeling of real joy.

With only fifteen minutes left to play, Indio's goal is a death-blow. There is no way Lejeune can score three goals in fifteen minutes against a defense that has not allowed them a clear shot on goal all game. I know it is over and I put down my statistics notepad so I can simply savor and remember these final moments.

When the announcer begins counting down the final ten seconds, the game stops and the boys start celebrating. The bench clears and all the players are on the field, hugging and jumping on one another. But there is one player who stays behind. Guero doesn't feel like celebrating. All his friends, the guys he has grown up with, are happy and shouting, but he can't feel it. The only thing he feels is that he let his team and himself down. But the boys won't leave him alone and they drag him out to receive his medal.

I walked slowly onto the field to join in. As I walked, I thought of all the players who had played for me during the past three seasons. Their faces whizzed past me and I could see them running on our field back home. They were all champions now. No matter what happened in their lives, they would always know in their hearts that they could be the very best at something. When things were even they could compete and win. Tears welled up in my eyes and all that steadied me was the thought that I had done all of these things—the organizing, the fighting, the cajoling, bargaining, outwitting, playing, sitting awake for many sleepless nights ... for *my people*. I realized they were all my people, Latinos.

We had all come together on one team, Mexican, Guatemalan, El Salvadoran, Honduran, Peruvian, and American, to work together for a common goal. There are many people who think that we cannot come together for a common cause. I knew this isn't true. The team proved that. We can be *one people*. I had felt alienated and separate from everyone growing up in Ann Arbor when there were few Latinos in the Midwest or beyond the coasts. I had spent a career writing and exploring Latino communities all over the country. But as I walked to join the *chavos,* I knew I had found a home among them. They were bouncing up and down in their scrum, holding on to one another and screaming *"¡Somos campeones!"* "We are the champions!" I dived in among them.

At the center of the field, a small table was hurriedly brought out to present the medals and trophies. The Lejeune players were visibly upset at coming in second. It was hard to accept such a loss. The Jets were a different story. They couldn't stop celebrating. When each one, including Guero, had received his medal, the organizers presented the championship trophy to Fish. He looked at it a moment and then lifted it above his head. The boys stood around him in a circle, clapping. The crowd went crazy, blowing their horns and banging on their drums.

But there was one more trophy to present. The announcer named the game's most valuable player. Pepa deserved it for scoring the first goal of the game, an important score that opened up the game for us, but Indio could get it for his nail-in-the-coffin goal. "As selected by a special panel: from Jordan-Matthews High School . . . Indio." He deserved it. He'd controlled the middle of the field, set up passes, and, when he saw an opening, launched a missile of a strike that defeated the Devil Pups. Indio stepped up, all smiles, and hoisted his plaque above his head. There was no jealousy on the faces of the boys. They knew who had led this team all season.

After the presentation of the medals, the boys grabbed me from underneath and lifted me onto their shoulders. I was embarrassed but they were happy. I raised the plaque the high school athletic association had presented to me. They carried me from the field to the sidelines to the waiting crowd of folks from Siler City and beyond who had come out to support JM's first state soccer champions. A cheer went up from the crowd when I got to them. And then the boys lined up along the sidelines and started a victory lap. Fish led them, holding the state championship trophy above his head all the way. When they got back to the fans, Enrique and Dougie-style came down from the stands to congratulate them.

Somehow the school found another bus and had it waiting to take us home. On the road to Siler City, I looked in back to see how the boys were doing. The sun was shining through the windows and the day had grown unseasonably warm. I could see the freshmen in the back, happy and horsing around. They hadn't played a minute, but they seemed to revel in the victory more than the starters. Indio had changed out of his uniform into his street clothes. He was on his cell phone, smiling. Behind me, Lechero sat quietly with one of the freshmen. I could see tears slowly streaming from his eyes. This was his senior year and he was ending it a champion. Across the aisle, Edi lay with his head against the window, sleeping. He was exhausted.

When the bus pulled onto Raleigh Street in Siler City . . . we were home. We passed the steaming white stacks from the chicken plant and headed downtown. The boys leaned out the windows of the bus and waved and cheered as we passed people on the sidewalks. Along the way, cars began to honk their horns as they saw us pass. People stepped out of their homes along the main road and waved back, smiling, knowing that the team had returned triumphant. I saw white folks cheering, black folks clapping, and Latinos shouting happily. When we turned onto Second Avenue the sounds of the horns began to rise. All of Siler City now knew of the Jets soccer team winning the state championship. They were turning out of their stores, shops, and homes to stand and watch the bus pass by with the smiling brown faces of the *chavos*.

I watched as we passed by the gray stone city hall building where David Duke and his supporters had once stood and blasted the poultry workers and their families. This was a different demonstration, a joyous celebration of a team and a town that was overcoming its difficulties with the great Latino migration of the twenty-first century. Where was the town now? If accepting the migration was like going through the five stages of grief, Siler City had left its anger behind and was on its way to acceptance. All across America, local communities like Siler City were struggling with this very migration. Some were in denial, but many were angry, just as Siler City had once been. But watching the townsfolk turn out and wave, honk their horns, clap their hands, and pump their fists in the air, I knew that the team had transcended the prejudices on all sides and brought the community to root for *one* team. I knew then that these kids were no longer Latino kids in the eyes of the waving people. They were Jets. We were all on the same team.

The bus didn't stop at the school. Indio said that his family had planned a party and so I asked Ms. Brickhouse to take the bus to his house. Once there, the boys were greeted by the *chavas* and they poured into Indio's backyard, where his little field was set up. The guys quickly devoured the pizza that already had been ordered and drank as much soda as they could. They hung around swapping stories and wearing their red, white, and blue medals around their necks. The older boys sat down on the ground or on concrete blocks scattered around the yard next to the house. They were tired from the game. Fish lay clutching the game ball in one arm and his head resting on Elisa's lap. Loco sat next to him, his back against the white house, a baseball cap turned sideways on his head. Guero kissed his girlfriend and held her close. She wore his Jets jersey. The players then posed with their brothers, or cousins, or parents with the state championship trophy. The championship had been a real family affair.

When the boys had sufficiently rested they got up and started to play the *cascarita* in the yard with some of the boys who had not been eligible for the team, boys like Pony. I shouted at them, "What? You didn't get enough *fútbol* in the finals?" They responded, "*No, Cuadros, ¡queremos jugar más!*" "No, Cuadros, we want to play more!" Okay, I told them, *"No manches,"* and handed the trophy to Leda to hold. I put my cleats on and joined them for one final *cascarita*.

The next day the local newspaper appeared with a large cover photograph of the boys lifting me on their shoulders with the championship trophy. There are two covers of that paper that feature the Latino community prominently. The first is of the David Duke rally on the steps of city hall almost four years earlier. The other is of the team triumphant. Siler City had lived with the black eye of that first day for many years and the town had become notorious for the rally. But there was no doubt that the team forever wiped away this stain.

Many newspapers and television stations in the area picked up the story of the Jets. We even made the *New York Times* sports section. Siler City would be known for something else now.

A week later, I learned that Guero had dropped out of school. I went over immediately to his house to try to talk him out of it. He hadn't been back to school since we'd won the state championship. He had called it quits that Saturday. I understood now why he was so disappointed with his own play. He had decided it would be his last game at JM and he wanted it to be his best. I told him how dropping out was not the answer, but he had already made his decision and I sensed that he was intractable.

"So, what are you going to do now?"

He looked at me and told me he was already working at the chicken plant. I felt the floor fall beneath me. I didn't care if he worked anywhere else, but not the chicken plant.

"I'm working second shift," he mumbled. He seemed ashamed but he wouldn't reveal his emotions.

"You're going to learn some things now, Guero," I told him seriously. He could kiss his girlfriend good-bye. His girlfriend was no idiot. Why would she stay with a dropout working at the chicken plant? And there would be no mercy at the plant. Show up late, you were fired. Mess up on the job? You were gone. He would have to grow up now.

"Guero, it is very hard to come back to school once you leave it." He wasn't hearing it. There was no persuading him. He had played his last game as a Jet. By missing the rest of the year, he would be ineligible for the next season. I told him if he came back it would have to be in two seasons.

"Okay, Guero." I shook my head and handed him my championship ball. I had brought it because he had not signed it as the other guys had done. "If you need anything, just call."

He signed the ball and went back inside his house. I sat there for a moment. I had worked so hard to create an environment to inspire these kids to stay in school. The team was there to lift them up and keep them in the classroom. But now I felt like a failure. It was then

I realized that there was nothing I could do to save these kids. And maybe it had been hubris to think that a soccer team could do that. It was just a game after all.

I remembered what John Phillips had said to me once a long time before: "You're their coach, not their social worker." He was right. But I had coached with love and I believed in that very strongly. I couldn't abandon that belief just because Guero had dropped out. I couldn't save them. But I could be there for them. And maybe that was all anybody could do. Just be there for someone. Listen to them, help them if you can, offer advice if they want it, and just be there. They had to live their own lives. Soccer is a player's game. Once the whistle blows, it is up to the players to figure out how to play the game and work together to score and win. The coaches can do little to affect the game once it is being played. Life was like that too. There is little that people can really do for you. You have to figure out how to play at life. People can support you—parents, teachers, coaches, and friends. But ultimately you have to run down the field in order to try to fulfill your goals. I would always be there for these boys—on the field and off.

I looked down at the white ball to see what Guero had written. It said, "I promise to be back."

It took a month for the carpentry class to construct the large wooden frame for the giant photograph of the state championship soccer team. They hung the picture down the hall from the other pictures and it stands alone on a white cinder-block wall. The Jets stand and kneel proudly for the whole school to see. The guys who helped coach the team throughout the years are there—Ricardo, Matt, Chad, and Chuy, who started as a player in the first year and came back to coach in the third season. When I look at the picture everyone is there; Pepa, taller than everybody else; Edi beaming a brilliant smile; shy Bomba barely able to look at the camera; Guero hiding his face in back; Anthony off to the side; Loco standing still for a moment; Perico, the little man with the big game; and

Indio, looking so serious his eyes could burn through the paper. In the front is Fish with the game ball. Next to him is me with a proud tilt to my head. I am surrounded by my *chavos*. And every day, when the school bell rings and the kids all file out of their classrooms to go to their next class, they walk past the picture. When they do, they see more than just a photograph of boys in white-and-blue uniforms. They see themselves with the promise of a brighter future.

EPILOGUE

I was born a minority, but I will not die a minority. America is in the midst of fundamental population changes that will forever alter its national character. In the next fifty years there will be more people that will look like me, and the country's identity will be transformed. By 2050, half the population in the U.S. will be white, non-Hispanic, according to U.S. Census projections. The remaining half will be composed of people of color with Latinos representing the largest group at an estimated twenty-four percent. The discussion of race and ethnicity will forever be altered and a new language will have to be developed in dealing with America's most persistent and complex issue. The idea of a minority class of people may be discarded and a new paradigm of fellowship forged. If no one can claim a majority then no one can be in the minority and perhaps the color line that has enslaved, marginalized, and hurt so many, both the exploited through physical humiliation and the exploiter through moral degradation, can be washed away, and we can emerge together clean and at a new beginning.

America is just now waking up to the silent migration that has been quietly seeping into its towns and cities, and, like Siler City used to be six years ago, it is angry. Social conservatives, anti-immigrant organizations, and fringe white supremacist groups have seized upon the demographic change as a new cause to protect white privilege in America. This is the foul stream from which all these groups dip their cups and the source that no one will admit exists. There is a rank ugliness behind such measures as English-only laws, empowering local law enforcement officers to enforce federal immigration laws, the labeling of migrants and their children as criminals, the desire to take away U.S. citizenship from children born of unauthorized immigrants, guest-worker programs that ensure a permanent underclass status, and other punitive measures designed to punish an emerging ethnic group that will one day be the largest in America.

Under the guise of national security, these groups have unleashed their media dogs to foam at the mouth and snarl at a complex issue that requires an understanding beyond the simplistic fence building that Congress has become rabid about. Representative Peter King, R-N.Y., one of the co-sponsors of a bill that would make unauthorized immigrants felons and would allow construction of a wall on the border, has his lawn in Long Island tended by Latino immigrants—one of whom was smuggled into the country. Anyone who has stood in the Sonora desert and seen its humbling vastness and awesome beauty clearly understands that a wall will not only be ineffective in stemming migration but is in itself a sin. God sees no walls from heaven. This is why all walls that are built one day come down. America is so angry that the only proposals for dealing with this migration and the emergence of Latinos have been punitive.

Forgotten or ignored are the very forces that have spurred this latest migration. Many of its causes originate from the free-trade policies of the U.S., globalization, and the last dregs of the Cold War. And poverty. These are the push elements that compel a mother to take her children through the desert and risk their lives for a chance to feed them. Not a single proposal by the Congress or the President has even remotely looked at these forces that drive Latinos north. Until the U.S. begins to seriously address these elements, other migrations will occur. There are those who say it is not our responsibility to assist Mexico or Latin America even though neighbors do help each other. It is not our responsibility but it is now in our national interest. A strong and fair Mexico will be a buffer against further migrations. Mexico and its ruling class must now do what it has never done or cared to do—educate its people, provide meaningful jobs, and create a middle class from the poor. While the migration has been a problem for the U.S., it is a national disgrace to Mexico and its leaders.

The migration of Latinos to America in the past fifteen years has left the country angry and raw. Now America only seeks to punish—even those who are innocent of any violation of the law. Children who were brought here unauthorized by their parents should not bear the same stigma nor suffer the same consequences currently being debated. They are innocents caught up in the whirlwinds of globalization, corporate greed, and the deprivations of its aftermath. Does America now believe that the sons shall bear the inequities of the father? What will America do with this illegal generation? Is there no more room in America's heart for forgiveness, for amnesty, for children who broke no law? Is this how Pharaoh's heart hardens?

Anger is but one of the stages of dealing with this phenomenon. The country still has several more to go, just as Siler City still has to work out its white flight from its schools. Demographics is destiny. If this is true then Latino immigrants will one day be accepted. But we are far from that day.

Following the championship season, the players have moved on with their lives. They all continue to play soccer and dream of being champions again one day.

FIRST SEASON

Oso   Unable to attend college in the U.S. because of his immigration status, Oso went back to Honduras where he enrolled in the university to study civil engineering.

Pee Wee   After dropping out of high school, Pee Wee considered joining the Navy but instead hung around town working in a factory for a while and later at a restaurant. His mother moved back to Siler City and he found a home again. He went to community college, received his GED, and continues to play soccer in La Liga.

Caballo Caballo dropped out of high school in his junior year and went to work in the construction industry. He injured himself on the job when he accidentally drove a nail into his knee with a high-powered nailgun. With no health insurance, he had the nail removed and continues to recover from his injury.

Chuy Unable to attend college, Chuy instead concentrated on his job at the restaurant. He currently is the manager of his own restaurant and attends classes at a nearby community college, studying business management. He continues to help out with the team when time allows and plays on the weekends in La Liga.

Lobo Lobo graduated from high school but was unable to attend college, despite having excellent grades, due to his immigration status. He worked in the fast food industry for awhile, but has since found a job in landscaping and construction.

Fidel Fidel fell into the cholo life and dropped out of high school. He was arrested for breaking and entering and evading the police. As a legal resident, he is currently serving his time in prison and will be deported upon completion of his sentence.

SECOND SEASON

Dougie-style Doug, a U.S. citizen, is attending the University of North Carolina–Chapel Hill majoring in business administration and public policy. Doug found a true family among Los Jets and continues to come to games on his vacations. He plans on moving to Africa and helping relief organizations.

Chisco Failing to make the team after his freshman year, Chisco was able to come back and make the team in his senior year. However, due to disciplinary problems—and after being given a number of chances—he was asked to turn in his uniform and leave the team.

Nemo After missing his chance with the championship team, Nemo returned to the team in his senior year. He improved his grades and behavior and became a stalwart defender taking over for Lechero. One month before the end of the school year, he dropped out.

Pony Pony never returned to the team. Despite being talented and one of the best players at school, he continued to struggle with grades and attendance. He continues to play in La Liga on weekends.

Lenin Lenin moved back to Mexico to take care of his parents. He enrolled in a university and is studying science. He occasionally calls to find out about the team, but has not come back.

THIRD SEASON

La Pepa Pepa was ineligible to play his senior year because of his age but he continued to support the team by helping out on game days. He tried out for a team at a local college but did not make the cut. His immigration status prevented him from attending college after graduating from high school. In his senior year, he broke his leg playing soccer and I took him to Dr. Taft who performed surgery and set the break with four screws. Pepa hopes to one day open his own restaurant, and dreams of playing soccer again.

Lechero Having graduated from JM, Lechero was unable to attend college because of his immigration status. He is no longer as angry as he was during his years with Los Jets and has fallen in love with a girl from Guatemala. I last saw him marching with her holding an American flag on April 10 in Siler City advocating for a chance to become a legal resident.

Perico Perico became a goal-scoring star the following year scoring twenty-nine goals for the Jets. He helped lead the team to its second consecutive conference championship and to the state playoffs.

La Bomba La Bomba was accepted at two private universities in North Carolina, but due to the complex nature of his immigration status his admittance is in doubt. A legal resident under temporary protective status with his parents, La Bomba is learning that explaining his status is difficult and complex and many schools are unfamiliar with immigration laws. His dreams of becoming a lawyer are in doubt and has instead turned to dreaming of opening his own restaurant one day.

Loco   A high school graduate, Loco had no prospects for college because of his immigration status. He continues to work in the restaurant business and hopes to one day open his own business.

Edi   Edi was selected to play for the North Carolina State Games high school all-star team where he caught the eye of several college coaches. He was accepted to a junior college and will attend this fall, also playing for their soccer team. He hopes to one day transfer to a four-year college and play for a bigger school.

Guero   Guero dropped out of school after the championship season and went to work second shift at the chicken plant. He came back to school the following year, fulfilling his promise to me to come back, but was ineligible to play. He focused on his school work and made the AB Honor Roll in his second semester. After I spoke with Moody about Guero, he decided to give Guero his 2004 championship ring, which had been denied to him when he dropped out.

Enrique   After graduating from high school, Enrique initially struggled with a series of jobs I helped him find. He never applied to college despite his legal status and dreamed for a while of becoming a law enforcement officer. Among his jobs, he found one as a plumber's assistant that he loved. He enjoyed the hard work, the long hours, and the sense of accomplishment of installing the plumbing in a new building or house. When we drove together he would proudly point to the buildings he had put plumbing in. He plans on attending community college and getting his plumber's license and hopes one day to have his own company. He continues to live with his mother and family, raise chickens, and tend to his dogs, and loves the rural life.

Fish   Fish graduated from high school and tried out for several
college teams, but despite his talent, his immigration status prevented him from attending. He works in the construction industry and hopes to one day legalize his status to attend school and
earn his degree. He and Elisa are still together and talking marriage once he is better settled. He continues to play soccer on the
weekends and occasionally comes back to the team when I need
help coaching a new goalkeeper.

El Indio   Indio suffered a devastating knee injury in the spring
after the championship season. Following surgery by Dr. Garrett,
now at Duke University Medical Center, his recovery has been
slow and his senior year with the team was hampered by his injury. Indio struggled and considered leaving the team, but after
an emotional exchange with me, he decided to stay on and contribute what he could. He worked through the pain and stiffness,
performing spectacular plays and taking the team to the quarterfinals of the state playoffs before being beaten in double overtime.
Indio openly wept when we lost. His desire to be a champion
again could not be sated. Indio's application to the University of
North Carolina—Chapel Hill was eventually rejected. His immigration status would not have allowed him to attend at the
in-state tuition rate had he been accepted. He graduated and
plans on opening his own business with some other members of
the team. He hopes of becoming a citizen some day and fulfilling
his American dream.

On April 10, 2006, Latinos and their supporters gathered in
Siler City to march in the pro-immigrant rallies that were
occurring all over the U.S. Meeting in front of JM, I led a group of
fifty students just beyond the chicken plant to begin the march to
City Hall. We marched through the streets of Siler City, gathering
Latinos who came out of their homes to join us. White residents and
African Americans stepped out of their homes to watch, with many
in support. When we arrived at City Hall where David Duke once

spoke against the immigrant community and the "chicken pluck-ers" we were more than five thousand strong. I was allowed to step up to the podium to deliver a pep talk to the throng. Among the mass of white shirts in the crowd, I saw joyous faces as if they had stepped out into the fresh air for the first time after many dark days. They were giddy with jubilance. And then I saw them: Los Jets. Their faces were proud and in their young eyes I saw defiance. I had seen those faces before on the field many times. In their outstretched hands they clutched little American flags.

ACKNOWLEDGMENTS

In 1998 I was working for the Center for Public Integrity in Washington, D.C. writing a chapter for the center's book on Congress and campaign finance when I stumbled upon the changing labor force in the country's meatpacking and poultry-processing industry. I quickly realized that what was happening in Midwest rural areas and the Southeast was a silent migration of Latino workers spurred and facilitated by the food processing industry. From that time on I have been working on how to tell this tale of the Great Latino Migration to the interior portion of the United States and how this migration would one day change the fundamental character of the country and how we view ourselves. That day seems upon us as the mainstream media and governments, local, state, and federal have come to open their eyes to this migration that has taken a hold of the country.

I am grateful to the people at the Center who encouraged me to pursue what would be my "big story." Thank you to Chuck Lewis who helped to guide me in the process of producing a book on the Diaspora and to the journalists at the Center who encouraged me such as Bill Hogan, Bill Allison, Alan Green, Nancy Watzman, and Annys Shin and to those friends in Washington who pushed me to pursue this project including Sam Lowenberg and Sandra Mann.

This book could not have been possible without the Alicia Patterson Foundation who initially believed in the project to report and study how Latino poultry-processing workers were changing the rural South. The fellowship they offered me to move to North Carolina and Chatham County was the first step toward completion of this book.

I am eternally grateful to my friends who believed in me and put up with my questions and stories about Latinos in the South and coaching soccer. Jerome Kramer helped to guide me through important points in getting published and I appreciate his expertise. John Sullivan helped to focus me and offered encouragement when I needed it. Robert Sulewski provided me scholarly advice and an open ear over beers and games of Scrabble. And I am grateful to my friend Robert O'Neill, who acted as my personal publicist and served as my resident expert on soccer and the nuances of the game.

This book and story could not have been told without the dedication of my agent, Jeff Kleinman, who believed in this story and pushed me to get it published and guided it to its final completion. I will always be grateful to you Jeff for fulfilling a dream of mine.

To my editor Rene Alegria and the wonderful people at Rayo who became Jets themselves and understood the importance of this book from the start. Thank you for all your hard work. I know this book will serve as the first that truly documented the Great Latino Migration of the twenty-first century.

This project could not have been done without the assistance, tolerance, and cooperation of the good people of Siler City and Chatham County. They opened their doors and their hearts to me and for that I will forever be grateful. I know it is hard for some to accept outsiders but I have never been made to feel this way by these wonderful people. I hope that the country can learn from Siler City and its people in this important issue and how they behaved themselves in difficult times.

My appreciation and gratitude to Ricardo Jofré, Matt Streng, Lenin Aguilar, Mark Rogerson, Chad Morgan, and Christopher Atkins who all helped me coach the team and supported me and the *chavos*. My appreciation to the wonderful teachers, coaches, and staff of Jordan-Matthews High School. My thanks to the all the girls' soccer teams I have coached. This wasn't your story but I hope to tell yours one day. To Gale Brickhouse, who drove our bus and who is our biggest fan and to John Phillips, our athletic director, the most rational man in Siler City. And finally, my personal thanks and appreciation to David Moody for supporting the team.

A personal thanks to Gary Phillips for fighting for the creation of the team and to Ilana Dubester for advocating so tirelessly on behalf of Latinos in Chatham County. And my appreciation to Gloria Sanchez and Stephanie Scarce.

This book could not have been possible without the support and encouragement of Leda Hartman who I met at the David Duke rally and who I fell in love with from the moment I saw her with her microphone. I can't express my deep gratitude for pushing me, guiding me, and offering your opinions and edits throughout these years. You have been my biggest fan and I have always appreciated that. *Gracias mi amor.*

And finally to my family who has always put up with my dreams of being a writer. I want to thank my brothers Al, Sergio, and Willie for kicking the ball around with me and for all the times we hung out and hung on to each other even in the darkest of hours. To my mother who always supported me even when times were tough. And to my father who took me to the park to kick the ball around, went to my games, and always pushed me to write and to do something with my pen. I am the man I am today because of him. He had a poet's heart and passed away quietly in his bed during the writing of this book, but he knew that I had finally become an author and I knew he was proud. He was buried in the same church where I had grown up and where he had once cleaned. He lived an immigrant's life and was the most successful man I knew. *Gracias por todo, Papi.*

Lastly, to all the boys and girls who tried out for all the soccer teams, who sweated underneath the hot sun, who sacrificed their bodies in games, took shots, were knocked down, broke bones, and got up again to play. You have truly inspired me with your courage. I hope that one day you will read this book to your own children and they will learn how you were all once champions.

A Home on the Field

INTERVIEW WITH PAUL CUADROS

Are you still coaching soccer at Jordan Matthews? How is the team faring this year? Will North Carolina be a permanent home for you?

I am still coaching at JM and the team has done well. Immediately after the championship season we won the Yadkin Valley Conference for the second year in a row. But a series of nagging injuries to the team held us back. La Bomba suffered a back injury, Loco a groin pull, and Indio suffered a devastating knee injury. Indio had arthroscopic surgery to repair the cartilage in his knee prior to the season but it never felt 100 percent. As a result, what should have been another amazing season was cut short when we lost in double overtime in the quarterfinals of the state tournament. To answer the last question, I think that North Carolina will become a home for me. It is a beautiful state and I continue to be interested in writing about the emerging Latino community here.

In what ways has the community changed for the better since the Jets won the championship? In what ways has it gotten worse?

I think that Siler City has come together more and there is more acceptance of the newcomers. In addition, I know from the many comments from long-time residents who have read *A Home on the Field* that there is greater understanding of the experiences that typify the immigrant life in Siler City. They are also more aware of the daily obstacles immigrants face in a new country, like finding health care or getting a driver's license.

At the same time, there is definitely a limit as to what the powers that be will accept from the newcomer population in Siler City. After the April 10, 2006, immigration rally in Siler City, which drew some 7,000 peaceful demonstrators to City Hall, there was palpable uneasiness in the town in response to the sheer numbers. The Hispanic Liaison in Siler City was specifically targeted after the rally. The Liaison had been the principal organizer of the event. The local United Way decided to summarily cut the Liaison's funding for that year citing the rally as a main cause for eliminating its funds. The funding was later restored, but that hasty response to the rally was telling: Immigrants can advocate for themselves, but only to a certain point.

How did the students respond to the book? What was the response within the greater Siler City community? Was anything about it surprising?

The students and players have all responded very positively to the book. Many have even signed books for readers; they've been thrilled to have their story told. Siler City has also responded very favorably to the book. I spoke at the Siler City Rotary Club after publication and the members spoke well of the book, and remarked that it had accurately captured life in the town. I think for long-time residents, the book was an eye-opener in terms of understanding the experiences of the immigrants and their kids in town. It has allowed many people to change their minds about the newcomers.

How do you think schools should respond to the growing Latino student population, many of whom are not legal residents?

All schools in the U.S. are required by law to provide an education for all kids up until the twelfth grade. Schools have an obligation to educate any child who walks through their doors, regardless of their residency status. Many teachers come to know these kids, teach them, love them as their own, and there is little difference between the Latino students and the general population. The Latino student population in America is the largest and fastest growing group in our schools today. We all have a special responsibility to ensure this group is successful in school and continue on to institutes of higher education—not only for the benefit of the students, but for the communities that will one day come to depend on these future business and civic leaders.

The real problem when it comes to education and Latino students is access to college. Many of the Jets have been prevented from going on to college, despite having the grades to attend, because of their immigration status, whether documented or undocumented. La Bomba, for instance, has been frustrated since graduating from high school. He is a legal resident but does not qualify for federal financial aid because he has not received his green card. Because of this, he has not been able to afford to attend the two universities he has been accepted to. Instead, he has languished as a construction worker hoping and dreaming of a way to go to school. Indio has also been prevented from going to college because of his undocumented status. He continues to dream of attending school in some way.

Aside from the heartbreaking stories like La Bomba and Indio, I believe it is in the best interest of the country to allow talented and qualified students who have graduated from our high schools access to in-state tuition rates and financial aid to attend college. Communities like Siler City would benefit greatly from the additional education of its graduates if they can go to college. Like previous immigrants from the past, these kids are motivated to make their mark on the world and in our society. It is one of the ways that America is able to revitalize and renew itself.

In the book, we learn that you do not compromise the standards you set for your players, on the field or in the classroom. What are the challenges and sacrifices involved in maintaining such stringent criteria, for yourself and the players?

It is never easy being strict. I think that standards can be rigid but justice must be allowed to be flexible at times in order to be truly just. Coaching involves understanding the difference between the two. You can be tough on rules and expectations but also sympathetic to individual circumstances. It becomes a balancing game—when to be tough and when to be open. Sometimes that means cutting a player, sometimes it means expelling a player, and sometimes it means giving a player a break. You don't always get it right. That's the hardest thing for me. Did I get it right? Was I fair? As for the players, it is hard on them to maintain standards and to meet expectations. They have to make sacrifices, work hard, and stay focused, all things that can be difficult for teenagers. As coach, I also have to make sacrifices in order to achieve the same goals. That means giving up my time, lining the field, thinking about the team and our opponents, making sure the players are safe, and working hard to ensure they are having an experience they will remember.

What do you think it is about sport that has the power to change hearts and minds?

Sport has the ability to encapsulate and compress life and its passion, struggle, victory, and defeat in a finite moment of time, and can be felt by more than just the athletes. It allows us to witness life and to examine and reexamine ourselves in the process, to strive for excellence. Sport lives in the throat of the players and its fans—from there it has easy access to the heart and mind. It is theater of the moment.

Do you think there is a crisis of community in the South? How do you think the burgeoning Latino presence will affect the future of the region? How do you think communities can and should cope with the rapid change in their demographic?

According to the report by the University of North Carolina's Frank Hawkins Kenan Institute of Private Enterprise in 2006, Latinos in

North Carolina contribute $9 billion to the state's economy with expected growth of $18 billion in the next ten years. In addition, the relative youth of the Latino population in the state will have tremendous impact on the state's demographic figures in the future.

Latinos as a group are a young population, many in their prime childbearing years or about to enter them. Latinos between the ages of eighteen and forty-four in North Carolina account for 55 percent of the Latino population. Non-Latinos between those ages comprise only 37 percent of their population. In the school years, Latinos count 21 percent of their population between the ages five and seventeen, compared to 18 percent for non-Latinos in the state. The differences are even more pronounced with children under five years old. Fourteen percent of Latinos are under five, while 7 percent of non-Latinos in the state are under five. The population of Latino youth in the state's schools is expected to grow in the coming years.

Given that we can predict this growth, it is imperative that the state seize the moment to ensure that Latino children are getting a proper education in their schools. Communities in North Carolina have done a good job of anticipating the needs of these children since the beginning of the migration, but now it needs to raise expectations and demand that they are successful in school, opening the doors to college. Offering in-state tuition at the state's public universities is vital, not only for the fulfillment of the dreams of these children, but for the state to take advantage of and nurture Latino leadership, which will ensure its economic vitality.

Is there a discernible difference between the behaviors and attitudes of the community's youth and that of the adults? What are your hopes for future generations of Siler City residents?

There are significant differences between Latino youth and their parents. Latino youth are in a state of flux, not-yet-defined, and on the verge of carving out their identity, which will be different from their parents. This is particularly seen in the dating habits and expectations of roles for men and women among Latino youth. Many young Latinas want to be more independent. Their parents want them to stay at home. The conflict between the traditional family's idea of the role of Latinas and the lives they actually want to create for themselves here can lead to familial struggle. Many Latino males are well aware of the dead-end jobs their fathers are in and want something better. But too often this generation of Latinos is growing up with stifled dreams for a better life because of their residency status, low expectations, and prejudice.

I believe there is great hope for the Latino youth in Siler City and in North Carolina. Siler City is a unique community that has been through the fire on the issue of immigration. Right now, the town has done the heavy lifting in providing education to these kids but the stopping points can only be addressed by Congress and immigration reform that permits these kids to realize their dreams.

QUESTIONS FOR DISCUSSION

A Home on the Field is a thought-provoking book on how immigration is changing our communities. Many questions arise out of reading the book for readers—especially teachers and students—to discuss, including population projections, immigration issues, economic impact, globalization, the role of sports, pride and community, cultural differences between groups, and the future of our country. Here are some questions that can serve to spark discussion and debate and ideas on how to explore this trend.

1. What are some other examples of historic migrations and how did those people adjust to newcomers in their land? What is the history of the peoples of the Americas and how and from where did they migrate?

2. In comparison to the founding and flourishing of many of the countries in the world, what was unique about the formation of the United States? In what ways does the U.S. continue to be exceptional with respect to its population? How important do you think a common language is to a shared national identity?

3. Take a look at a map from Earth's orbit. What do you see? Are their any borders between landmasses? What does this say about human beings and their need to define themselves?

4. Is there a difference between migration and immigration? What is it?

5. What is the history of Latino migration to the U.S.? From where do these groups come? How is the migration or immigration of Mexicans to the U.S. different from that of Latinos from South America or the Caribbean?

6. What are the causes of migration? Can you site any recent examples where natural disasters caused a migration of people?

7. What role does big business play in migration or immigration, legal and otherwise, in the U.S.? How much responsibility should they shoulder for those who immigrate illegally to work for them?

8. According to estimates, there are 12 million undocumented immigrants in the country. What should be done with this group of people? Do you believe there should there be a penalty for entering the country illegally? Do you believe there should there be a path to citizenship? Why or why not?

9. Do you believe someone can be "illegal?" What are the implications of labeling a human being as such?

10. What are the politics behind immigration enforcement and immigration reform? What should Congress and the president do about immigration?

11. In the book, the Jets come to represent more than just a team but an entire community. What are similar examples from your own community? Are there both positive and negative aspects to these representations?

SNAPSHOTS FROM A COMMUNITY

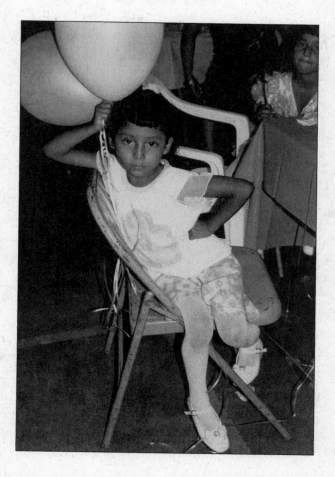

The future of Siler City and other communities in the rural South.
(© Paul Cuadros)

Snipes Trailer Park, Siler City. Many families live in poor housing conditions. (© Paul Cuadros)

A poultry worker, exhausted after two shifts at the local plant, sits outside his trailer. (© Paul Cuadros)

Palm Sunday in Siler City. Faith plays a large role in community life, as this woman shows. (© Paul Cuadros)

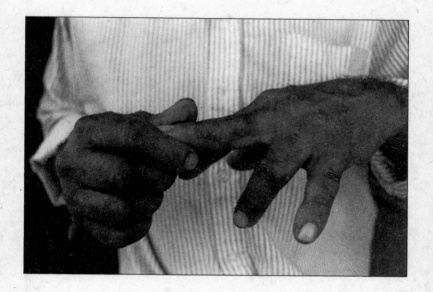

Many poultry workers suffer through pain and numbness from working long hours and doing repetitive motions with their hands. (© Paul Cuadros)

Pulgar stands with his little car in Justice Trailer Park, Siler City.
(© Paul Cuadros)